WHY
FASCISTS
FEAR
TEACHERS

WHY
FASCISTS
FEAR
TEACHERS

Public Education and the
Future of Democracy

RANDI WEINGARTEN

THESIS

Thesis
An imprint of Penguin Random House LLC
1745 Broadway, New York, NY 10019
penguinrandomhouse.com

Most Thesis books are available at a discount when purchased in quantity for sales promotions or corporate use. Special editions, which include personalized covers, excerpts, and corporate imprints, can be created when purchased in large quantities. For more information, please call (212) 572-2232 or e-mail specialmarkets@penguinrandomhouse.com. Your local bookstore can also assist with discounted bulk purchases using the Penguin Random House corporate Business-to-Business program. For assistance in locating a participating retailer, e-mail B2B@penguinrandomhouse.com.

Book design by Nicole LaRoche

LIBRARY OF CONGRESS CONTROL NUMBER: 2025012197
ISBN 9798217045419 (hardcover)
ISBN 9798217045426 (ebook)

Printed in the United States of America
1st Printing

The authorized representative in the EU for product safety and compliance is Penguin Random House Ireland, Morrison Chambers, 32 Nassau Street, Dublin D02 YH68, Ireland, https://eu-contact.penguin.ie.

*To every student I've ever taught and every member
I represent—who have taught me everything.*

And to Sharon Kleinbaum—who is my everything.

CONTENTS

WHY
FASCISTS
FEAR
TEACHERS

INTRODUCTION

In 1940, Adolf Hitler had gained power and territory across a widening swath of Europe. The leaders of Norway's government fled and a Nazi puppet was put in power. Among the first to protest the Nazi takeover of Norway were the country's teachers. And since pins and badges with the likeness of the exiled king were now illegal, teachers and students used a clever, subtle signal to show their resistance. They wore paper clips. When teachers wore them on their lapels, it signified that they "remained united—bound together like a stack of papers—against Nazi rule." The protest spread. Eventually, students took to wearing whole chains of paper clips like necklaces.

Frustrated that teachers proved so influential in undermining fascism, the Nazi government eventually created a Nazi teacher network and mandated that all teachers in the country join it. But out of an estimated fourteen thousand teachers in Norway at the time, upwards of twelve thousand refused to do so. So Nazis barged into the schools and beat teachers and students, trying to physically force them into submission. That didn't work either. So then the Nazi government closed the schools. Hundreds of thousands of parents wrote letters to the government in protest. And what did the teachers do? They kept teaching. They found places to hold classes in private and kept promoting freedom of information and freedom of thought. Increasingly incensed, the fascist government sent at least a thousand teachers to concentration camps and five hundred others to forced labor camps. But still the teachers kept teaching and students kept learning how to think for themselves. That's the power of community—and the power of education.

THE SOCIAL CONTRACT

Every single day, educators work to help every school in America be a place where parents want to send their kids, where teachers want to work, and, most important, where kids can thrive. Students need schools that are safe and welcoming as well as engaging and relevant. And that's what public school educators work so hard to create. And while there are many religious and private schools in the United States, 90 percent of schoolchildren attend public schools. That's because public schools are and have always been the key opportunity engine for America's future. In public schools, teachers teach children math and reading and writing skills, of course, and so much more, preparing them for the diverse, complicated world in front of them so that they can achieve their full potential. Public schools set children up for success, creating opportunity for all that is essential to the good of our nation. That is our north star.

Teaching is a hard job. Teaching multiplication and algebra and grammar and how to write a five-paragraph essay is challenging enough. Teachers also do everything we can to meet the needs of children who arrive at school with everything from empty stomachs to emotional distress to different learning styles and behavioral challenges. Then there's the challenges of cell phones and social media distractions and a crisis of anxiety and loneliness among youth. All of this as teachers are underpaid and public schools are underresourced.

In recent years, the job of being a public school teacher has become infinitely more challenging. Since Donald Trump was first elected in 2016, teachers have faced unprecedented attacks, and it's important to understand why. The lines of attack have been all over the place—for every percentage point shift in standardized testing, for wanting to keep kids and teachers safe during the COVID-19 pandemic, for teaching honest history, for wanting to make schools safe and welcoming for all. But the people behind those attacks and their motivations have been extraordinarily consistent. A group of anti-government, anti-pluralism, anti-opportunity fascists, oligarchs, and far-right activists are demonizing public school teachers so they can divide the American public and destroy public education as we know it. Teachers aren't being smeared and undermined because they're doing anything wrong but because they're doing something very, very right.

Teachers do four foundational things that are important to the future of our students and the well-being of our nation—but are antithetical to the fascist anti-government, anti-pluralism, anti-opportunity agenda. Teachers impart knowledge, including critical thinking skills that prepare our kids for their futures and strengthen our democracy. Teachers work to create welcoming and safe communities so we can meet the academic, social, and emotional needs of all children and their families. Teachers create opportunity for every young person to have their shot at the American dream. And teachers are anchors of a labor movement whose purpose is to champion the aspirations of working families. Together with parents, teachers work themselves to the bone every single day to do everything they possibly can to support students and help them thrive.

In contrast, the forces working to undermine our public schools say they want to help all children, but their actions prove otherwise. If we don't understand their agenda, it can seem like they have rational justifications for banning books, pushing privatization, promoting inequality, and smearing teachers as Marxist indoctrinators and more. But these extremists oppose democracy, pluralism, and the common good and will attack anyone standing in their way. It just so happens that the main job of public school teachers—the whole reason we have public education in the first place—is to create opportunity for all. We don't teach kids reading and math just for the heck of it. We teach students how to read and do math, how to think and problem solve, and how to navigate the world around them so they can become thriving adults, successful in whatever path in life they choose. That's what parents want for their children. That's what our nation needs for its future. That's our social contract with America. And that's why extremists attack teachers.

One of the first lessons I would teach my students in my civics class at Clara Barton High School in Brooklyn, New York, was about the social contract—how individual freedoms and mutual responsibility are inextricably intertwined in our democracy. This is the sacred covenant that underlies our commitment to public schools. It's the commitment to opportunity for all, in a safe environment, where every child is welcome, and where we work to engage every child so they can meet their God-given potential.

Our public schools, as well as our colleges and universities, teach the vital habits of democracy and pluralism. The foundational assertion of the Declaration of Independence—that we all share the unalienable rights of life, liberty, and the pursuit of happiness—comes from philosopher John Locke. Locke argued that the reason individuals join together to form governments is because we know that protecting the common good is essential to ensuring individual liberties. All of which Locke saw as intertwined with education. "I am sure the principal end why we are to get knowledge here, is to make use of it for the benefit of ourselves and others in this world," he wrote in *Some Thoughts Concerning Education.* "I think I may say, that of all the men we meet with, nine parts of ten are what they are, good or evil, useful or not, by their education. 'Tis that which makes the great difference in mankind." Education plants the seeds of opportunity for the good of individuals and our entire society.

Our Founding Fathers and their descendants were clear that the American experiment relied on an educated, informed public. John Adams wrote, "Liberty cannot be preserved without a general knowledge among the people." Benjamin Franklin argued, "The good Education of Youth has been esteemed by wise Men in all Ages, as the surest Foundation of the Happiness both of private Families and of Commonwealths." Thomas Jefferson was an early advocate of free, public education and wrote, "Educate and inform the whole mass of the people . . . They are the only sure reliance for the preservation of our liberty."

Democracy and public education have been linked ever since. You cannot have a country of, by, and for the people without a means for the public to prepare not just for the privileges of that democracy but the duties as well. Public schools are laboratories of civil society and, at their best, embody the multifaith, multiracial coexistence that is our nation's best future. That's why the motto of the American Federation of Teachers (AFT)—the union that I have had the honor of leading since 2008—is "Democracy in education, education for de-

mocracy." Public schools aren't a by-product of democracy but democracy's engine, constantly renewing and fueling the next generation to be informed and engaged in our unprecedented democratic
experiment.

Summarizing why he has attacked teachers and universities in
Russia, Vladimir Putin has explained, "Wars are won by teachers."
Fascists fear teachers because education is essential to democracy.
And education is essential to broad-based opportunity and empowerment. Yes, we teach reading and math. But we also teach young
people to have agency and confidence, to problem solve and be resilient. And we also teach core American values including patriotism.
We teach the fundamental building blocks for a nation unlike any in
human history—a nation founded on the radical idea that we all are
created equal, that we all deserve the opportunity to succeed, and
that power belongs to the people, and we all must have a voice. And
though those ideals have not always been realized, we have prepared
generations of young Americans to strive for that vision anew. We
don't just teach history as a relic of the past but to revitalize America's best values and ideals in our present, ensuring that future generations carry on the promise of our nation's founding.

Teachers fight for a better future *for all*—the common good. That
is the core of public education—that everyone is embraced and ac-
cepted. We meet every student where they are and try to prepare
them for college, career, civic participation, and life. Teachers and
parents and community leaders and faith leaders who fight for better public schools, stronger democracy, and greater opportunity are
fighting to make the nation better *for everyone*—including even the
people attacking us. Because we truly all do better when we all do
better.

WHY FASCISTS ATTACK TEACHERS

In 2022, a right-wing activist named Chris Rufo gave a speech at the conservative Hillsdale College in Michigan. The title of his Hillsdale speech was "Laying Siege to the Institutions." In the speech, Rufo said that "to get universal school choice you really need to operate from a premise of universal public school distrust." Rufo proposed a "siege strategy" and "narrative war" and urged supporters to be "ruthless and brutal" in advancing their goals.

For instance, by his own account Rufo took a legal construct called critical race theory (CRT) and worked to "turn it toxic" by putting "all of the various cultural insanities under that brand category." I learned about critical race theory when I was in law school in the 1980s. It is a decades-old form of legal analysis that examines the persistence of racism in U.S. legal institutions. Rufo calls critical race theory "the perfect villain." It wasn't until he repeatedly spread false claims misrepresenting what public school teachers are teaching that most teachers even knew the term or what it was. But Rufo's goal was never to tell the truth about public school teachers and curriculum. His goal, as he made clear, is "universal public school distrust."

Rufo is by no means alone, he's just the guy who said the quiet part out loud—brazenly revealing the tactics and goals of the movement of which he is a part. To be clear, fascists and autocrats and far-right extremists don't want to help all students, nor do they want to strengthen public schools. They don't want to teach students about the painful parts of American history and they don't want to level the playing field for children living in abject poverty. Because their goal is to exploit problems, not solve them. They want to divide

Americans, otherizing those who are different while attacking pluralism and diversity, inclusion, and equity as the problem. These extremists try to pit us against each other and distract us so they can
rig the system for themselves. When the far right gets enough people
to believe that diversity is a threat and opportunity is a zero-sum
game, they use the anger and resentment they foment to defund and
destabilize public education.

All of this explains why on November 21, 2022, Donald Trump's
former Secretary of State Mike Pompeo, speaking with a journalist
just days after Democrats did better than expected in midterm elections, shared his advice for Republicans running for office in 2024.
He said, "I get asked 'Who's the most dangerous person in the world?
Is it Chairman Kim, is it Xi Jinping?' The most dangerous person in
the world is Randi Weingarten. It's not a close call."

To clarify, that's the former secretary of state of the United States
of America, our nation's top diplomatic official—speaking the same
year that Vladimir Putin invaded Ukraine, the same year that "North
Korea test-launched over 70 ballistic and cruise missiles"—saying
that I am the most dangerous person in the world. It's the kind of
stuff one can't even make up.

Why would the former secretary of state, who has literally sat
across the table from demagogues and dictators, call a five-foot-tall
Jewish lesbian grandmother union leader who's married to a rabbi
the most dangerous person in the world? It makes sense when you
understand that Pompeo was utilizing a broader strategy—blame
teachers over and over and over again, truth be damned, in order to
divide the American people and defund and destabilize public education.

"If you ask, 'Who's the most likely to take this republic down?' It
would be the teacher's unions, and the filth that they're teaching our

kids, and the fact that they don't know math and reading or writing," Pompeo continued in that interview. He literally said this despite the fact that while he was serving as Donald Trump's secretary of state, an actual violent mob stormed the U.S. Capitol with the express goal of executing the vice president and overthrowing the election—a mob that a bipartisan congressional commission found then-President Donald Trump incited.

These smears aren't isolated. Back in 2004, President George W. Bush's secretary of education called our sister union, the National Education Association (NEA), a "terrorist organization." In 2019, Donald Trump's Secretary of Education Betsy DeVos attacked public school teachers as "union bullies." The efforts to blame and undermine teachers have only grown louder as this anti–public education, anti-government, anti-opportunity movement has grown more powerful. Meanwhile actual threats to our children have also grown, with the increase in school shootings, youth suicide rates, and child poverty. If the far right were genuinely interested in helping children and strengthening public education, they might try to help solve those problems.

In contrast, teachers are problem solvers. And teachers teach problem-solving skills. Likewise, I'm willing to work with anyone who wants to actually work on the problems facing our public schools. When there are serious, constructive efforts, I and my union have in the past and will continue in the future to do everything we can to help create and support education programs and other efforts that help kids—programs that will succeed and scale. Our test for decades has been, "Is it good for kids and fair to teachers?" When there are promising solutions that fit those simple criteria, we're all in—whoever proposes them. But anti–public education extremists don't just have a polite disagreement about how to improve public education in America. They want to destroy public education altogether. As we'll see, that's been consistent for decades. They attack diversity, equity, and inclusion because they want to turn Americans against each other while exacerbating inequality—using taxpayer money to pay for religious schools, homeschooling, or elite private schools for the super-rich while dismantling public education for everyone else. And yes, that disproportionately hurts poor students and students with disabilities and Black, Latino, and Indigenous students—but it also hurts everyone. Every student. Every community. Public education was founded on the idea of the social contract because public education is a public good. But fascists, autocrats, oligarchs, and far-right extremists don't believe in the social contract. They don't care about the common good.

To further their agenda of dividing us and defunding and destabilizing public education, these extremists have a one-size-fits-all strategy: Blame teachers. And they never let the truth get in their way. During the 2024 election, Donald Trump repeatedly alleged that children were getting gender confirmation surgery *at school* when every parent knows that public schools can't even give a kid Tylenol without a parent's written permission. Similarly, far-right activists who have attacked teachers for sexually "grooming" students admit, "We don't have any evidence that it's happening, either deliberately or accidentally." But the point of these attacks isn't truth or even the well-being of students. The point of the attacks is to smear teachers.

Now, before the naysayers rush in, I want to be very clear—I am not saying teachers, our union, or public schools are perfect. Of course there are things we can and must do better. And we can talk about them without demeaning and indicting every single public school teacher in America.

Should all teachers be prepared to teach and should teacher evaluation be better than it is? Yes! That's why our union is working to strengthen teacher training while also addressing teacher shortages. Should we spend more time teaching than testing? Yes! That's why we speak out against high-stakes testing schemes and other systems that turn teachers into data collectors mired in paperwork and don't actually strengthen teaching or help students. Should schools have opened sooner than they did during the COVID-19 pandemic? Of course! Which is why, in April 2020—just one month after schools shuttered—I led the AFT in developing a concrete plan to reopen schools as quickly and safely as possible. And, God forbid, if there is another pandemic, we should do what many countries in Europe did and prioritize students and schools instead of bars and restaurants. Nevertheless, the far right still tries to blame me for closing schools during the COVID pandemic—a power, I would point out, I do not have. But the irony is not lost on me that those trying to blame me for closing schools are the ones who have literally been trying to shutter public schools forever.

I've spent my life trying to make schools better. I'm not perfect either; I've made my share of mistakes. But whether it was helping to create the Chancellor's District to improve New York City's most struggling schools with more funding, research-backed curriculum, longer school days, and after-school and summer and weekend programming; to lifting up the Teacher Union Reform Network that local unions started in order to push the AFT and NEA to advance teacher-driven education reform; to pioneering new projects and initiatives like bargaining for the common good, community schools, and career and technical education that help students thrive, I have always put what is best for students, best for public schools, and best for our nation at the forefront of everything I do.

And even if I deeply disagree with tactics or ideas, it is vital that we distinguish between those trying to strengthen public schools and the forces that are trying to destroy public education as we know it.

I decided to write this book for two reasons. First, I wanted to celebrate public school educators—the teachers and paraprofessionals and bus drivers and so many more. They make a difference in children's lives and the future of our nation every single day and should be revered, not reviled. And second, I wrote this book because the coherent, well-funded strategy behind the vilification of teachers and war on knowledge needs to be exposed. If we don't understand what they're doing and why they're doing it, we can't fight back. And we need to fight back to save and strengthen public education.

For decades, extremists have been working to undermine public education under the guise of "reforming" it. And while many of us see through their lies and understand their true agenda, among parents and community members whose attention is often pulled in a million directions, the so-called reformers often get the benefit of the doubt—and somehow educators who devoted their lives to children are cast in suspicion. But, finally, here was Rufo confessing the whole plan. With that one quote—"to get universal school choice you really need to operate from a premise of universal public school distrust"—Rufo revealed that the far right smears public schools and public school teachers in order to push school privatization.

This is just the latest chapter of the long-standing effort to undermine—rather than protect and strengthen—public education. The far right and other extremists are trying to end public education as we know it—and, in doing so, destroy the ladder of opportunity on which generations of Americans have relied and still depend. They are attacking knowledge, pluralism, civic engagement, and freedom of thought—all of which our Founding Fathers knew were essential to our nation and our liberty and dependent on robust public education. If the forces attacking public education win, our children and our country will lose.

WHAT IS FASCISM?

Today, concepts like fascism and authoritarianism and oligarchy are increasingly relevant to understanding what's going on in the world in general and in the United States in particular—including the relentless attacks on public education.

In his book *How Fascism Works*, scholar Jason Stanley defines fascism as "ultranationalism of some variety (ethnic, religious, cultural), with the nation represented in the person of an authoritarian leader who speaks on its behalf." Timothy Snyder explains, "It's hard to create an academic definition of fascism because the whole point of fascism is that you reject reason in favor of will." Fascism, he says, involves people "rejecting standard forms of logic and empirical evidence in favor of a commitment to will and ability to place their belief not in what's happening in the world but in the mind of a leader."

In other words, fascism is an approach to politics that rejects independent critical thinking and instead mobilizes people around fear and rage—which makes them more receptive to strongmen leaders who then strip away collective rights and freedoms. Fascists construct an extreme story of us versus them, replacing facts and critical thinking with propaganda that romanticizes the nation's past while casting ethnic, religious, and social minorities as fundamental threats to that nation's present and future. That scapegoating whips up not only resentment but also dehumanization and violence.

Meanwhile, freedom and democracy decline. As do pluralism and a sense of community.

I am a schoolteacher, a lawyer, and a union leader. I am not an academic and this is not an academic book. This book is a warning. I want to explain why the attacks on public education are intensifying and how they connect to a concerted strategy. My views reflected herein are informed by a lifetime of work, an analysis of historical and current events, and, importantly, the perspective of teachers—who are some of the most trusted leaders in the United States but never get the support they need or the pay they deserve and are increasingly besieged by baseless smears and attacks. Why? What's going on? And for those of us who respect teachers and value public education, how can we respond?

While there are important, subtle distinctions between fascism, authoritarianism, oligarchy, anti-government extremism, and the far right, in practice at this moment in history these forces and others are conspiring to destroy our public education system and, with it, the building blocks of opportunity for all. Which exact word we use isn't as important as the warning. I will use these terms and others interchangeably because the attacks they are launching on our education system, our students, and our teachers are interchangeable and interconnected. "The task of generalizing about such phenomena is always vexing," Stanley writes. "But such generalization is necessary in the current moment." The perfect definition of fascism will be clear in the rearview mirror—but by then it may be too late for our children and our country. The more important point, whatever the wording, is that the fascist agenda is not only antithetical to public education but poses an existential threat to public schools, to young people, and to democracy.

Those hell-bent on unraveling democracy, pluralism, and opportunity have always attacked teachers and education. It's a very old playbook. In the 1930s, Hitler and Mussolini persecuted teachers and tried to control curriculum. Iran's Cultural Revolution closed universities and restricted academic freedom. From Russia to Indonesia to Hungary to Chile, fascist and authoritarian governments have sought to attack teachers and control not only what students learn but what they think.

Authoritarian attacks on teachers aren't new in the United States either. In the Reconstruction era following the end of the Civil War, the United States tried to remedy the inequalities of slavery and the ways in which that legacy continued to shape the country's economy, politics, and culture. In the South, one of the first things newly freed Black people did was build schools. As the North Carolina–based anti-slavery *Journal of Freedom* reported at the time, "The Freedmen . . . has got a disease for learning. It is a mania within him." But violence by white people "determined to hold onto the pre–Civil War racial hierarchy" was extreme. In 1866, white extremists burned down four schoolhouses in North Carolina, and others were shut down because of threats. In the fall of 1870, white mobs burned "nearly every colored church and school-house" in Tuskegee, Alabama. When a white mob attacked a white teacher from the North who was teaching at a Black school in the South, the mob said, "The [n-word] were bad enough before you came, but since you have been teaching them, they know too much and are a damn sight worse." Things got so bad that Congress passed a series of laws in 1870 and 1871 to try to force states to stop willfully ignoring the Ku Klux Klan.

"Education," said Frederick Douglass in 1894, "means emancipation. It means light and liberty. It means the uplifting of the soul of man into the glorious light of truth, the light only by which men can be free. To deny education to any people is one of the greatest crimes against human nature." But beginning in 1873, a series of Supreme Court decisions limited Reconstruction-era laws, and in 1877, Rutherford B. Hayes smoothed over congressional hurdles to his election as president by promising to withdraw federal troops from the South, paving the way for Jim Crow segregation to yet again make white supremacy the law of the land. As we'll see, fierce anti-integration movements would continue to shape education policy throughout American history, including today.

In the 1950s, there was Senator Joseph McCarthy. McCarthy used the machinery of the government to launch a relentless crusade supposedly aimed at rooting out Communists in society, but actually focused on silencing and squashing dissent about how the United States was conducting the Cold War. In fact, the *American Heritage Dictionary* now defines McCarthyism as "the political practice of publicizing accusations of disloyalty or subversion with insufficient regard to evidence." About six hundred teachers reportedly lost their jobs because of McCarthyism.

In the 1970s, we had Anita Bryant—a former Miss Oklahoma and hawker of orange juice. In 1977, Bryant was outraged when Miami, Florida, became the fortieth city in the United States to say that gay people couldn't be fired or discriminated against for being gay. To attack the idea of nondiscrimination, Bryant invented the evil specter of gay teachers using schools to recruit—incendiary accusations we hear echoed by extremists today. In fact, as we'll see, Florida's "Don't Say Gay" law and recent book bans follow the same repressive pattern as Bryant—the far right trying to control Americans' freedoms and choices by concocting myths accusing marginalized communities of being the ones seeking control.

Today, fascism is an amalgam of people who either outright oppose diversity and pluralism, want to shrink government as much as
possible, or both. Whether they're motivated by ideology or plain
greed, what fascists and oligarchs and autocrats of all sorts have in
common is that they don't want to solve problems. They want to create problems so they can exploit our anger and fear—to give themselves more power and more money, and take power and opportunity
away from ordinary citizens. That's it. That's their whole playbook.

Donald Trump was once quoted as saying that real power is fear.
Those who seek in this moment to attack and undermine public education are exploiting real pain and trying to mobilize it into fear and
resentment. For instance, good middle-class jobs have been hollowed out in the United States, and many of our public schools are
not as good as they should be. But middle-class jobs were hollowed
out in part because mega-corporations moved their manufacturing
overseas, not because more immigrants came to our country. And
when our public schools struggle, it's not because of a handful of
transgender students or curriculum issues, but because of the reality that society's problems don't end at the schoolhouse door and
decades of disinvestment creates barriers to effectively addressing
those challenges. The fascist playbook is a shell game of fear—taking
our real, understandable concerns as Americans but making us look
somewhere else, blame someone else, as the cause. Because fascists
need enemies to justify their attacks on public education and our democracy and society as a whole.

These extremists don't actually believe in the extreme threats
they mythologize, nor do they really want to do anything to solve the
underlying economic or social anxiety of their supporters. Fascist
leaders use ginned-up fear and resentment as an excuse. Their goal
is to distract and divide us to the point where we willingly—even

desperately—hand over absolute power and control to a singular cultlike leader we believe will save us.

The question of whether Donald Trump is or is not a fascist featured prominently in the last days of the 2024 presidential election. Retired General Mark A. Milley, who served as chairman of the Joint Chiefs of Staff under Trump and served our country for over forty years in the military, said that Trump is "fascist to the core." Trump's own White House chief of staff, Marine Corps General John Kelly, recounted stories of Trump talking admiringly about Hitler and saying his former boss is "an authoritarian" who "falls into the general definition of fascist." Meanwhile, as Anne Applebaum reports, Trump and his orbit have embraced Hungarian president Victor Orbán's autocratic playbook as a model. For instance, Trump's vice president, J. D. Vance, once said that Orbán—who has weakened judicial independence and undermined freedom of the press while generally increasing corruption and decreasing democracy—is someone "we could learn from in the United States." However, my point here is not to label people but to understand the behaviors, why they are doing what they're doing and what the rest of us can and must do in response. Repeated hatemongering against immigrants and transgender people. Deploying the military against peaceful protesters. Calling for the jailing of political opponents. These are all examples of fascistic behavior.

As the Russian-American dissident journalist M. Gessen noted, "Trump is now performing his idea of power as he imagines it. In his intuition, power is autocratic; it affirms the superiority of one nation and one race; it asserts total domination; and it mercilessly suppresses all opposition." Gessen concludes, "Whether or not he is capable of grasping the concept, Trump is performing fascism." Gessen wrote that amid Trump's first term, during what might be considered the dress rehearsal for the breathtakingly swift and comprehensive authoritarian production that is Trump's second term.

But while labeling someone a fascist might make for a good headline, it misses my point. The point of this book isn't to label anyone a fascist and, spoiler alert, I am not going to engage in name-calling or labeling. Plus I know that some who criticize teachers and public schools undoubtedly do so out of a genuine concern for students and a desire to strengthen our nation's education system. The point of this book is not to attack anyone but to understand the fascist agenda and its manifestations—which repeatedly, baselessly accuse public school teachers of undermining education when in fact it's the fascists, authoritarians, and far right who very clearly want to systematically end the very idea and existence of public education.

In 2023 alone, 110 bills were introduced in state legislatures attempting to curtail what teachers can and cannot do. Fascists want to end public education as we know it. And fascists are attacking teachers because we're standing in their way.

THE FIGHT TO SAVE PUBLIC EDUCATION

This book shines a light on incredible teachers all across our country who spend every waking hour trying to strengthen public education and the future of our children and our nation. The following chapters are organized around the four things teachers do that are so important to the future of our students and the future of our nation—and why those things pose such a threat to fascism.

First, teachers teach critical thinking. The Founding Fathers of our nation understood that education and democracy go hand in hand. A citizenry unable to think critically about history and policy and news and information is a public ripe for autocracy and fascism. Public schools—and public school teachers—help create thoughtful and engaged students capable of reviving and strengthening democracy in perpetuity. And fascists don't like that because fascists don't like democracy. They know that the best way for the American people to willingly hand over power to authoritarian figures is if we believe fascist fearmongering, disinformation, and propaganda. Ironically, the far right accuses teachers of indoctrination to distract from the fact that they're the ones who are actually trying to indoctrinate the next generation.

Second, teachers work to make every school safe and welcoming for every single student—so that every child can succeed. We know that different students need different things to succeed and, sadly, too many children arrive at school not able to focus on learning because they're hungry or sick or suffering from all sorts of challenges that have their origins outside of school. As teachers, we work to support every student and make sure they get what they need to learn and thrive and achieve. That's essential for fairness in a diverse, multicultural society. And it arises from the fundamental belief that children are equal. But fascists believe in hierarchy and elitism and want our nation divided into "haves" and "have-nots" so they can pit the "have-nots" against each other. Teachers build communities that are safe and welcoming for all—which undermines hierarchical elitism.

Third, teachers create opportunity for all. We see infinite possibilities in every child and know it's our job and the job of public schools to make sure every student gets access to tangible skills and tools and training to access their best possible future. That includes innovative programs that connect all students to the jobs of the future. Teachers build the ladder of opportunity that is the American dream. But fascists want to destroy opportunity for all. The billionaire class that increasingly rule not only our economy but also our nation want to aggregate power and money for themselves and only care about regular folks insofar as they need us as grunt workers. They might say they believe in meritocracy, but really they believe in entitlement—that they're better and more deserving than everyone else. These self-aggrandizing wannabe kings hate teachers because we fight for opportunity for all—and believe every child has potential and deserves a path to a successful future.

And fourth, teachers create agency for themselves and all working families through building strong unions. In the twenty-first century, teachers are the most unionized profession in the nation. Though unionization rates vary from state to state—in part because of state policies meant to undermine unions, as we'll see—nationwide, 69.4 percent of public school teachers belong to unions. But fascists hate unions because unions stand for everything fascists oppose. Billionaires and corporate executives don't want to share power—but unions give regular working folks power and a voice. Unions are democratic organizations that make our economy more just and fair, not just for union members but for everyone. And unions are at the forefront of expanding economic prosperity and strengthening democracy, throughout history and today. Plus in the case of teachers' unions, we fight for what students need—and when we fight, children, families, and communities win. Yes, we're a thorn in the side of those who want to cut funding for public education and deny students and communities the resources they need. And we're proud of it.

Throughout the book, I will not only detail the plot to destroy public education but the many, many ways in which teachers, parents, and communities are working together to fight back. Because while fascists have tried throughout history as today to blunt critical thinking, imperil opportunity, and hobble democracy by attacking teachers and undermining public education, they have been stopped before and we will stop them again. In fact, despite the extraordinary threats to public education in this moment, there are signs the extremist agenda is already cracking.

In 2021, a new far-right activist group called Moms for Liberty launched an effort to take over local school boards across the country, railing against COVID closures and critical race theory, the soup du jour of the far right's "blame teachers" strategy at the time. In one Pennsylvania county alone, extremist candidates hostile to public education won thirty-three school board races. Reporting a multimillion-dollar budget in 2022, bankrolled by a handful of the wealthiest far-right donors and institutions in the country, Moms for Liberty wasn't really a spontaneous grassroots group of parents trying to "protect" the community but a construct of the long-standing movement to defund public education. Instead of actually fixing the problems they ran for office complaining about—remember, fascists and their enablers don't want to actually fix problems—they merely amped up their culture war in our classrooms.

The Central Bucks School District, a politically purple community an hour north of Philadelphia, offers just one example. The Moms for Liberty extremists there were so aggressive in banning books and attacking LGBTQ faculty and students that the Pennsylvania ACLU filed a formal complaint and the U.S. Department of Education's Office for Civil Rights investigated. Instead of fixing the air-conditioning that causes Central Bucks schools to close when the weather is too hot, the Moms for Liberty school board faction spent $1.5 million of taxpayer money on legal fees to defend itself.

Nationwide, a recent study found that the far right's culture wars have cost our public schools more than $3 billion in the 2023–2024 school year alone—money spent on increased security at school board meetings and additional school staff to handle misinformation and the flurry of records requests. But two years after they were voted in—in some cases, by a margin of less than a hundred votes—the Moms for Liberty candidates in Central Bucks were resoundingly defeated. And in school board elections across the country, pro–public education candidates won race after race. Americans want to strengthen our public schools. They don't want culture wars that break public education.

Now, the term "culture war" is misleading. The construct of a war implies two sides, but the reality is that fascists and their far-right enablers have launched a unilateral attack on teachers. Fascists accuse teachers of indoctrination, when it's really fascists who are trying to control what Americans think and believe. They manufacture controversies about diversity, equity, and inclusion to instill resentment and hate. They accuse teachers of being an obstacle to quality education to distract from the fact that the far right is working to dismantle quality education. Fascists and their enablers repeatedly, unjustifiably point fingers at educators in order to divide the American public and justify their autocratic agenda of thought control, silencing dissent, and defunding and destroying public school as we know it. As education scholar Diane Ravitch points out, many of the advocates and parents who make hay about "indoctrination" are in fact the very ones who "want public money to pay for tuition at religious schools, whose very purpose is indoctrination." Sigmund Freud called this projection—when we attribute our own thoughts or feelings or behaviors to someone else. The fascists point fingers and shout about "indoctrination" when they're the ones who want to control what everyone thinks and does. Just as they point fingers and shout accusations of "intolerance" when they're the ones who don't believe everyone is equal and deserves equal opportunity.

That doesn't mean I think that those on the far right are the only ones ever guilty of intolerance. Cancel culture has its progenitors on both the left and the right. As a schoolteacher, you learn that a disagreement is an opportunity to hear each other out, not shut anyone down. It's not an easy muscle to build. In 2024, I taught a course at my alma mater, Cornell University's School of Industrial and Labor Relations. And in the back and forth with the students in my course, I had to at times stop myself from arguing when I disagreed with their viewpoints. It's a skill you learn as a teacher—to ask questions rather than assert your own opinion as truth.

In my close to thirty years as a union leader, I have learned to be a problem solver trying to seek solutions, not an ideologue trying to win arguments. I'm not loyal to a worldview—I'm loyal to schoolchildren, their families, their educators and best interests. Which means I'm regularly criticized by extremes—on the left and the right—because I don't hesitate to call out intolerance wherever it's coming from and I consistently champion critical thinking and dialogue over conformity and cancellation. Having a different opinion from someone else doesn't make you evil, it makes you an American.

Still, while I think some on the left are sometimes too intolerant, they're not trying to destroy public education or the very foundations of our democracy. The far right is—which is why they are the focus of this book. You'll notice I don't pull any punches in the following chapters talking about neoliberal Democrats who have intentionally or unwittingly aided the right in their agenda to destroy public schools. But I draw a profound distinction between leaders who believe in public education but I might disagree with on solutions versus leaders who want to end public education altogether. It's the difference between firefighters and arsonists. Teachers are working to build better schools. Fascists are trying to burn them down.

During the first few weeks of his second term in the White House, during which this book was written, Donald Trump made clear his desire to burn down public education as we know it—trying to abolish the Department of Education, fire federal workers, and end collective bargaining rights, among other attacks. We saw this coming. During the 2024 presidential campaign, the influential far-right Heritage Foundation think tank released the Project 2025 blueprint for a second Trump presidency proposing to end major federal programs like Title 1 that help poor students and the schools that serve them, getting rid of federal civil rights protections for LGBTQ students, and cutting federal funding for students with disabilities. And Project 2025 promised a massive expansion of taxpayer-funded private school vouchers, which, as we'll explore in the chapters that follow, comes from an ugly history in American education and is nothing more than a giveaway to wealthy families that also defunds public schools.

In the early days of his second presidency, Trump made good on Project 2025's promises. He froze a broad swath of federal funding, affecting Head Start and school lunches as well as Medicaid and other programs that help the neediest Americans, with the goal of destroying as much of our nation's government as possible. Using his misleading attacks on "diversity, equity, and inclusion" as an excuse, Trump unleashed Elon Musk—the unelected, unaccountable wealthiest man on earth—to make massive cuts to public programs that help ordinary Americans. In the Department of Education—which Trump called "a big con job" and said should be "closed immediately"—Musk and a team of "young, inexperienced engineers" unilaterally canceled contracts and gutted a research operation that tracks the progress of American students. They also took down applications for the federal student loan forgiveness program and tried to access the personal data of over forty-two million Americans with federal student loans. And that was just the beginning of their all-out war on government, opportunity, inclusion, and public education for all. On March 20, 2025, Donald Trump issued an executive order to shutter the Department of Education. And on March 27, 2025, Trump signed an executive order trying to curtail collective bargaining rights among workers across the federal government. Trump's White House has also acted to condition education funding on bowing to the administration's ideology. These and other actions will continue to be challenged by us and others in the courts, in Congress, and in the court of public opinion. For instance, arguably, Trump can't shutter a whole federal agency given that Congress created it. But no matter what, it appears Trump will continue to do everything he can to hurt America's opportunity anchors—public schools, unions, and key programs on which we all rely like Medicare, Medicaid, and Social Security.

But here's the thing to remember: In the fight between fascists and teachers, over and over again, the American public sides with teachers. Americans want our public schools to be strengthened, not discarded. Even in the 2024 election that returned Trump to the White House, every single school voucher ballot measure was defeated—even in deep red states like Kentucky and Nebraska. In fact, despite massive backing from wealthy donors and interest groups, school vouchers have been rejected by voters every time they've ever been on a ballot. Plus, in the 2024 elections, voters in

Massachusetts rejected high-stakes testing, voters in Utah changed the state constitution to increase funding for education, California voters passed a $10 billion bond to support school and community college infrastructure, Florida voters passed funding increases all over the state, and cities from Detroit, Michigan, to Toledo, Ohio, to Bozeman, Montana, also passed local school funding increases. And according to polls, 68 percent of Americans—including majorities of Republicans, Independents, and Democrats—agree that "We should increase funding to improve public schools so that they better meet the needs of students for the jobs and careers of the future." That's one other reason fascists fear teachers—because no matter what they throw at us, teachers are still respected and trusted. Why? Because teachers want what students need.

TEACHERS JUST WANT TO TEACH

Teachers just want to teach. They want to make a positive difference in the lives of their students. Every year, we get a new group of students and it's our sacred job to learn what each of them needs to be able to succeed and fulfill their dreams. Childhood is such an important time, and our teachers play such an important role introducing us not only to ideas and skills but to possibilities for our future. And while this book focuses on teachers—because the far right's ire is trained on public school teachers—paraprofessionals and bus drivers and support staff are part of the beautiful village that makes public school communities work. Every single one of these educators wakes up every day thinking about how they can help our students thrive.

One of the educators I think back on was David Swift, my eleventh-grade English teacher at Clarkstown High School North in New City, New York. Mr. Swift was also the advisor of "Cue and Curtain," the drama club. I was one of those just-in-time students in high school, doing only what was necessary to get by academically and usually only at the last minute. I didn't really become a hard worker until I got to law school. But Mr. Swift saw something in me I didn't see in myself—and during my senior year he asked me to be the production manager for the high school productions. That's when I really learned I had leadership skills to manage a team.

Now, Mr. Swift didn't care what I would do with that talent. His only agenda was for me to succeed at whatever path I chose. Just like when he had us read *Julius Caesar*. I had blown off the homework he assigned. It was obvious, and in big, bold letters on top of the pop quiz, he wrote, *"Et tu Brute?"* I never blew off an assignment again. But Mr. Swift didn't care what we thought about Shakespeare's play, he just cared that we were engaged and thinking—learning to analyze the text critically and to write essays that were well argued (and ideally mostly grammatical). I could have gone into business or worked in government or something else and Mr. Swift would have been equally proud of me for using my education and applying myself.

It just so happened that at the same time, budget cuts were taking a hammer to the school programs we loved. While the budget crisis in New York City was getting all the attention, the suburbs were not immune. The school board was threatening layoffs. So my classmates and I went to school board meetings and made a ruckus and ended up petitioning the whole community to push back on the cuts—because we wanted to save beloved teachers like Mr. Munson and Ms. Grove. We partly won; we saved some but not all of the teachers' jobs. But I learned so much about the importance of teachers and teaching—and the power of organizing and building agency and a voice, and that even when you lose, you shouldn't give up fighting. In July 2008, when I was elected president of the AFT, one of my high school teachers, Mr. Dillon, honored me with his presence. I can't tell you how proud I am to be president of the union that my own teachers who taught and nurtured and pushed me were members of.

When I was a civics teacher at Clara Barton High School, it was my turn to teach my students the skills and knowledge they need to soar. Whether the lesson was about the Constitution or movements that helped change the Constitution to create even greater justice and freedom, such as the suffrage movement that led to voting rights for women in 1919, I was equipping my students with as much information as possible to form their own ideas and opinions. To teach them how to think critically, how to problem solve, understand differences, how to engage with others as they navigate the world, and to be resilient and persistent in the face of adversity.

Ironically, there is one thing fascists and teachers agree on—that we cannot create a truly democratic, inclusive nation committed to opportunity for all without public schools. Fascists fight against public education because they want to control our minds, control our ideas, and control the future. And what do teachers do? We teach. It's that simple. Class after class, year after year, we equip the next generation to think for themselves and preserve our nation's precious bond between individual liberty, opportunity, and the common good.

The following chapters reflect my opinions about this moment in history for our nation in which our public schools, our democracy, and our values are under attack. But this book also reflects my profound optimism. I'll share example after example of teachers who teach critical thinking, create a safe and welcoming environment for all students, create opportunity for all, and make our economy and our society fairer. You'll read about teachers who come up with clever, real-world lesson plans to teach their students about the rules of voting and how to think carefully about whether information on the internet is fact or fiction. You'll meet teachers who are themselves proof of the endurance of the American dream, many who fought poverty and discrimination to become the first in their families to go to college, who now are trying to rebuild that dream for others as elementary school teachers, high school aides, and even professors themselves. You'll hear the ideas teachers have for transforming education so that every community has great public schools—schools that every parent wants to send their children to and every student wants to go to, where they're prepared for the jobs of today and the future with the skills and knowledge that responsible civic participation demands. And you'll learn about why teachers form unions, how our union works, and how we fight for what students and communities need.

Now more than ever, it is vital that we all understand what teachers do, why they're being attacked, and why we should join teachers to fight for the right to learn and the right to teach. In the history of the world, there has rarely been a movement for democracy, justice, opportunity, or fairness without teachers playing a leading role. And at the same time, in the history of our nation, I doubt there has ever been a person who has achieved some goal in their life, great or small, and not thought back with gratitude to a teacher. This is our job—to stand in the front of the classroom and to stand in the breach—for every child, for every family, for every community, for every future.

1

TEACHERS TEACH CRITICAL THINKING

In October 2022, about a year after Russia invaded Ukraine, I led a small delegation of educators and health professionals to visit the Ukrainian city of Lviv. We met with teachers and their union to find out what the international community could do to help them and their students recover.

My wife, Sharon, is a rabbi and joined me because she deeply understands ministry amid trauma, across generations and contexts. And on our way to Ukraine, entering through Poland, we made a point to stop at the Janusz Korczak Monument in Warsaw.

Henryk Goldszmit was born to a Polish Jewish family, trained as a pediatrician, but reached acclaim as a children's book author under his pen name Janusz Korczak. But Korczak wanted to do even more to help children. So he became a teacher.

In 1912, Korczak took a position as the director of an orphanage for Jewish children, which he organized as a tiny democracy. The students had a newspaper, a parliament, and even a court where they would hear and resolve grievances. Korczak thought it was important for his students to think critically and freely, especially as the space for free thinking was closing up all around them. He taught them the value of democracy, even as the world around them was sliding into autocracy. The memorial Sharon and I visited sits on the site of the former orphanage. It shows Korczak with a thoughtful gaze, his arms gently resting around a gaggle of children, one of whom stares up at him with the same look of reverence that I feel.

Nazis had already gone after Jewish children attending German schools. In 1938, Jewish students were completely banned from them. In 1940, when the Nazis created the Warsaw Ghetto in Poland, Korczak's orphanage was forced to move there and Korczak, of course, went with his children. As fascism was closing in all around him, he kept teaching his students how to free their minds. But then, in August 1942, the Nazi genocide came for Korczak's Jewish students. Nazis came to round up the 190 or so orphans under Korczak's charge. Korczak dressed the kids up and each of them carried a favorite toy or game. Korczak walked with his students to help them keep calm. And though Korczak himself was offered sanctuary, in part because of his fame, he refused. He insisted on staying with his students. Korczak walked with his young students, and together they boarded the train that would ultimately take them to concentration camps. They were never heard from again.

When Sharon and I walked along those same train tracks, we reflected on Korczak's devotion as a teacher—literally guiding his students in every way, shepherding them until the very end. And we reflected on his simple act of rebellion—daring to teach children to think for themselves and be themselves amid encroaching autocracy. The goal of education in the Third Reich and fascism in general is indoctrination of youth—trying to compel young people to embrace only certain ideas and certain people. Critical thinking is the antidote. Critical thinking means you form your own ideas and your own opinions about the world, based on your own knowledge and analysis, not blind loyalty or fear. Fascists, autocrats, and other extremists are afraid of critical thinking and they fear teachers because teachers teach critical thinking that is foundational to a free, knowledge-based society. The ability to reason through complex problems, to separate fact from fiction and information from disinformation, to apply reasoning and form one's own opinions is central to knowledge and essential to the very democracy that fascists and autocrats want to destroy. Fascist attacks on critical thinking are part of a concerted strategy. As philosopher Umberto Eco observed about the same era of fascism in Italy, "All the Nazi or Fascist schoolbooks made use of an impoverished vocabulary, and an elementary syntax, in order to limit the instruments for complex and critical reasoning."

In 1924, Korczak wrote that students "should be allowed to grow into whoever they were meant to be—the unknown person inside each of them is our hope for the future." That hope—that boundless possibility of self-actualization in every young person—is disruptive to fascism and essential to democracy. Korczak fought for that hope, that self-actualization, with every fiber of his being. That's what great teachers do—no matter what. And critical thinking has been central to public education in the United States since our nation's founding. Because our Founding Fathers understood what Korczak knew—that a free society depends on free minds.

THE FOUNDERS' CASE FOR PUBLIC EDUCATION

The founding of our nation and the creation of public education have always been intertwined. James Madison, who helped draft the

Constitution and served as the fourth president of the United States, called education "the only Guardian of true liberty." Madison once wrote, "The American people owe it to themselves, and to the cause of free Government, to prove by their establishments for the advancement and diffusion of Knowledge . . . What spectacle can be more edifying or more seasonable, than that of Liberty & Learning, each leaning on the other for their mutual & surest support?"

Indeed, there were early versions of public schools in America even before the United States became a nation. The Boston Latin School was founded in 1635, well before the Declaration of Independence in 1776. It was funded by public money, though it was only open to male students (women weren't admitted until 337 years later, in 1972). Some of Boston Latin School's early students would go on to help forge our new nation—students including John Hancock, Samuel Adams, and Benjamin Franklin.

It was Horace Mann who really expanded public education in the United States. In the mid-1800s, as secretary of the Board of Education in Massachusetts, Mann started a movement for "common schools." They were called common schools not because they were plain—though they definitely were by today's standards—but common in the sense of "common good." "Education," argued Mann, "beyond all other divides of human origin, is a great equalizer of conditions of men—the balance wheel of the social machinery."

As education professor Jack Schneider and journalist Jennifer Berkshire write, "Universal, taxpayer-supported schooling was initially a civic project. The aim was to ensure the kinds of basic competencies for all young people that had for so long been the exclusive preserve of the middle and upper classes." They note that historian David Labaree calls this the "democratic equality" objective of the common schools movement.

A century after Horace Mann, President Franklin Delano Roosevelt would add, "Democracy cannot succeed unless those who express their choice are prepared to choose wisely. The real safeguard of democracy, therefore, is education." And decades later, President John F. Kennedy would say, "Only an educated and informed people will be a free people, that the ignorance of one voter in a democracy impairs the security of all." The idea that democracy and public education are inextricably linked is a constant theme of the American experiment. As the eminent education historian Diane Ravitch points out, "Without knowledge and understanding, one tends to become a passive spectator rather than an active participant in the great decisions of our time." Critical thinking skills among the citizenry are essential to fulfilling the promise of democracy.

The idea of critical thinking as central to enlightenment and individual liberty dates back well before the founding of the United States of America. In Ancient Greece, Plutarch advanced both modern philosophy and education by arguing that true wisdom involves critical thinking and questioning common knowledge rather than just accepting it. He said, "For the mind does not require filling like a bottle, but rather, like wood it only requires kindling to create in it an impulse to think independently and an ardent desire for the truth." In his book *Politics*, Aristotle argued that in order to have an engaged citizenry, "it is manifest that education should be one and the same for all, and that it should be public."

The ideas of the Greek philosophers paved the way for John Locke and others—Enlightenment thinkers who influenced our Founding Fathers and argued that a free society was not possible without an educated citizenry. "Universal teaching must precede universal enfranchisement," wrote John Stuart Mill. Because, of

course, democracy is more than just picking one candidate or another. Democracy is being deeply, substantively engaged in the problems and solutions of our society. Which means critical thinking
and education are absolutely essential to and intertwined with the
practice of democracy. When we think critically, we have our own
ideas and opinions, but we simultaneously scrutinize them, weighing other facts and ideas to be as rational as possible. We listen to
and really wrestle with ideas and opinions that conflict with our
own. And we engage earnestly with people who may think differently from us, exchanging facts and opinions, not taunts and smears.
Strong critical thinking is the most important muscle in a strong democracy. That's why our Founding Fathers saw fit to establish public
education as a central component of our new nation.

The correlation between democracy and education is enduring
and profound. Experience and extensive research from around the
world strongly suggests that "education is a prerequisite factor that
definitely promotes democracy." A 2019 poll across Europe found
that from Italy to France to the Czech Republic to Bulgaria, citizens
who are more educated are more likely to be satisfied with democracy than those who are less educated. And in the United States,
higher levels of education are correlated with higher rates of civic
participation.

On the other hand, diminished critical thinking makes voters
ripe for the disinformation that helps undermine democracy. Consider the 2024 presidential election in the United States. Yes, many
voters in that election had valid reasons to feel angry about their
economic plight and were understandably desperate for change. For
instance, adjusting for inflation, men in the United States who've
completed high school but not college made 22 percent less in 2019

than they did in 1979, forty years earlier. This is downward mobility and it inflicts economic and psychic wounds on individuals, families, and our nation. Plus voters often vote for change in general. From 1969 to 2021, there had been only one instance in which the party that won the presidency maintained control of Congress beyond the following midterm election. In fact, in 2022, when Democrats gained a seat in the Senate two years into Biden's presidency, it defied decades of precedent.

But without a doubt, disinformation and its amplification by the unparalleled right-wing media ecosystem was a significant factor in the outcome of the election. For instance, the violent crime rate in the United States is falling. That's an undeniable fact. But Trump repeatedly said otherwise. "On Joe Biden's watch, violent crime has skyrocketed in virtually every American city," said a Trump campaign press release. Trump, in a speech, said that under the Biden-Harris administration, communities were "plagued by bloodshed, chaos and violent crime." None of this is true. Never mind that the murder rate increased by 30 percent during Trump's first term. But polling showed that voters who believe the false statement that "Violent crime rates are at or near all-time highs in most major American cities" favored Trump over Harris by a 26-point margin. Voters who knew that statement was false preferred Harris by a 65-point margin.

In an era where artificial intelligence (AI) and social media lack guardrails and nonpartisan media and media literacy are declining, it's more important than ever that voters have the tools they need to think critically and discern fact from fiction. As President Joe Biden said in his farewell address from the Oval Office, "Americans are being buried under an avalanche of misinformation and disinformation enabling the abuse of power. The free press is crumbling. Editors are disappearing. Social media is giving up on fact-checking. The truth is smothered by lies told for power and for profit."

In her book *Twilight of Democracy: The Seductive Lure of Authoritarianism*, historian Anne Applebaum writes that "people are often attracted to authoritarian ideas because they are bothered by complexity." Fascists know this. They not only distract from the truth but cultivate division and discord to present themselves as the simplistic, obvious antidote.

Critical thinking, on the other hand, embraces complexity and nuance—and democracy. Philosopher Hannah Arendt, who studied the conditions under which ordinary Germans were complicit in carrying out the Holocaust, said, "What makes it possible for a totalitarian or any other dictatorship to rule is that people are not informed." Totalitarians, Arendt argued, deprive people of their "capacity to think and to judge," and warned that "with such a people you can then do what you please." Destroying critical thinking and destroying democracy go hand in hand. The prominent developmental psychologist Jean Piaget once wrote that the principal "goal of education is to create men who are capable of doing new things, not simply of repeating what other generations have done—men who are creative, inventive, and discoverers." Piaget continued, "The second goal of education is to form minds which can be critical, can verify, and not accept everything they are offered." This could be a recipe for critical thinking in the age of propaganda-laden elections.

When he was still a student at Morehouse College, Martin Luther King Jr. wrote an essay in the student newspaper titled "The Purpose of Education." He argued that education has two main purposes: "the one is utility and the other is culture." Education helps students develop concrete skills and tools and learn how to use them to achieve their goals in life. But that second purpose King wrote about? That purpose is really democracy. "To save man from the morass of propaganda, in my opinion, is one of the chief aims of education. Education must enable one to sift and weigh evidence, to discern the true from the false, the real from the unreal, and the facts from the fiction."

"The function of education," Dr. King went on, "is to teach one to think intensively and to think critically." Critical thinking is vital to accurately understanding societal problems that need to be solved and, together with our civic peers, engaging, analyzing, and innovating as we constantly renew and reinvent our democracy. Critical thinking is the most important muscle in the exercise of democracy. No wonder fascists want to weaken it.

WHY FASCISTS HATE CRITICAL THINKING

"Democracies die more often through the ballot box than at gunpoint," writes historian Heather Cox Richardson in her book *Democracy Awakening: Notes on the State of America*. Fascist leaders may campaign for our votes, but modern democracies more often fall because of autocratic candidates who work within the system to dismantle it, rather than coups or military takeovers.

"Authoritarian regimes have become more effective at co-opting or circumventing the norms and institutions meant to support basic liberties, and at providing aid to others who wish to do the same," writes the international democracy-monitoring organization Freedom House, reporting on the trend of "democratic backsliding" worldwide. It was Trump, for instance, who fought endlessly to overturn the results of the 2020 election, still refusing to admit that he lost. And during the 2024 election, Trump said to his supporters that after this election "you're not going to have to vote." He's not the first. Far-right political strategist Paul Weyrich once famously declared, "I don't want everybody to vote. Elections are not won by a majority of people. They never have been from the beginning of our country, and they are not now. As a matter of fact our leverage in the elections quite candidly goes up as the voting populace goes down."

Prominent authoritarianism historian Ruth Ben-Ghiat explains that fascist and authoritarian leaders want to "damage or destroy democracy." Democracy is people power. But fascists want one leader or a small group of elites to have all the power. And that is what's happening in the United States right now—billionaire Trump enabling his shadow governing partner Elon Musk, the wealthiest person in the world, to act as his co-president. Meanwhile, Trump's initial second-term cabinet was on track to be the wealthiest in history, "worth at least $382 billion—higher than the GDP of 172 countries."

The problem for fascists, then, is that a public with strong critical thinking muscles is more likely to strengthen democracy and resist authoritarianism. Scholars who study democracy worldwide are incredibly clear on this point: "On the whole, higher levels of education are associated with stronger democracies—a country with an educated populace is more likely to become or remain a democracy." Looking at data from Latin American elections, researchers Amy Erica Smith and Mollie J. Cohen found, "The more education you have, the less likely you are to vote for an authoritarian." In fact, some global scholars have gone as far as to suggest that "education causes democracy."

So is the opposite true? Yes, history has shown us that. For instance, in 2017, the *Financial Times* found that among Dutch voters, having attained less education was the greatest predictor of support for the country's anti-immigrant far-right political party. And after winning a primary election during the 2016 election, Donald Trump bragged how well he did with certain demographics, saying, "We won with poorly educated. I love the poorly educated." This may or may not have been just another sloppy aside from Trump, but it does reflect a deeper truth. Donald Trump was able to rise to power, yes, because of his keen political instincts and charisma, but also because he routinely says things he thinks voters want to hear, whether he can actually do anything about them or not.

Analyzing the source of his 2024 election win, Trump said, "I started using the word—the groceries. When you buy apples, when you buy bacon, when you buy eggs, they would double and triple the price over a short period of time, and I won an election based on that. We're going to bring those prices way down." But after his win, he admitted, "It's hard to bring things down once they're up. You know, it's very hard"—and indeed many of his second-term proposals, including tariffs and mass deportations, would arguably increase the price of groceries and other consumer goods. In fact, immediately after Trump's 2025 inauguration, the price of eggs went up.

Authoritarians actively attack truth, knowledge, and critical thinking because an uninformed public is easier to control. Degrading public education and critical thinking skills may only prime more Americans to not recognize disinformation and misinformation and take authoritarian leaders like Trump at their word. Psychologist Bob Altemeyer studied personality traits that make people more receptive to authoritarian leaders. In his 2006 book *The Authoritarians*, Altemeyer documented his "Right-Wing Authoritarianism" scale, writing:

The authoritarian follower makes himself vulnerable to ma-
levolent manipulation by chucking out critical thinking and
prudence as the price for maintaining his beliefs. He's an "easy
mark," custom-built to be snookered. And the very last thing
an authoritarian leader wants is for his followers to start using their heads, to start thinking critically and independently
about things.

In other words, those inclined to support authoritarianism exhibit a
general avoidance of or allergy to critical thinking. And authoritarians like it that way.

It makes me wonder whether far-right extremists are trying to
deliberately inculcate an anti–critical thinking, pro-authoritarian
disposition by undermining public education. Research conducted
in 2004 and 2007—even before our hyperpolarized current political
climate—found that "blue states" that tend to vote for Democrats
spend more money on education than "red states" that tend to vote
for Republicans. Not incidentally, the students in red states also fare
worse on math and reading assessments. As Diane Ravitch notes, if
Trump loves the poorly educated, "His plans for his second term
guarantee that there will be more of them to love."

Certainly, Trump's first executive orders in 2025 pointed in that
direction—asserting unprecedented federal control of local school
curricula to enforce the administration's personal ideology against
diversity, equity, and inclusion, while also directing federal funds
for public schools to be used instead for private school vouchers and
homeschooling. That level of federal strong-arming is contradic-
tory, by the way, given that Trump has called for sending education
"back to the states"—although states have always controlled education and have since the beginning of the republic. As we'll see in

chapter 2, the federal government has a limited—but important—role to bolster opportunity for all, which of course Trump is also threatening. These tactics neither help students nor improve education. Trump's executive orders merely perpetuate the strategy of demeaning public school teachers and sowing division while systematically defunding public education.

It's a downward spiral. Faced with some of the lowest-performing education systems in the country, do these red states work with teachers to improve math and reading instruction or maybe incorporate innovative, skills-based learning models? Do they take action to adequately fund public education? Certainly some states have—like Mississippi, which worked with teachers to dramatically improve literacy rates statewide, a program that was so effective it inspired the AFT to work with several partners to launch a similar approach called Reading Universe. But more often than not, instead of these states working to improve public education, we see a troubling trend in the other direction—red states doubling down on far-right indoctrination. In Oklahoma, the state's extremist school superintendent required every school in the state to teach the Bible and tried to use taxpayer money to buy Trump Bible editions. Plus the Oklahoma superintendent tried to force every school in the state to show students a video of him praying for Donald Trump. This is the same Oklahoma superintendent who, after a terrorist attack in New Orleans on New Year's Day 2025, blamed teachers' unions for "teaching kids to hate their country" in classrooms that were actually "terrorist training camps." What's more disturbing than people in positions of power saying this garbage is that people actually believe them. During the 2024 election, when Donald Trump and others falsely accused immigrants in Springfield, Ohio, of "eating pets," those outrageous, flagrant lies led to dozens of bomb threats against local schools and other public agencies. Again, the goal wasn't knowledge and truth but lies and indoctrination.

And what do fascists do when they're worried that students might learn about the truth on their own? They ban books. Book bans are a very old and deeply disturbing tactic that, frankly, I never thought we'd see with such horrifying scope and scale in our country. But here we are. According to the ACLU, in 2023, "more than 3,000 books have been banned in schools across America. These books disproportionately feature stories about LGBTQ+ communities, people of color, and others who have been marginalized." Even though gun violence is the leading cause of death among children and teens today, the far right goes to extraordinary lengths to block any restrictions whatsoever on access to assault weapons or high-capacity rounds of ammunition. But they'll use every means at their disposal to make sure high school students can't check a book about gay identity out of the restricted section of the school library.

This has profoundly disturbing precedents. In March 1933, an election consolidated Hitler's power. Two months later, Nazis ransacked the Institute for Sexual Science, a pioneering medical center that studied gender and sexuality. The institute advocated for queer rights. Nazis removed all of the books from the institute—twenty thousand books in total—for the first book burning in the Nazi regime. Book burning is part of a broader fascist pattern of attacking knowledge, freedom of information, and critical thinking. The Nazi government also closed down or took over newspapers, controlled radio broadcasts, and even made it treasonous to tell a joke about Hitler. And the attack on gay and trans books wasn't just symbolic. The Nazi government eventually rounded up and jailed gay and trans Germans and thousands were sent to concentration camps—which presaged slaughtering six million Jews as well as people with disabilities and others. Dehumanizing groups of people isn't just rhetorical; it paves the path for violence.

The point of diverse books isn't to promote one identity or another—it's to make sure all students have access to age-appropriate reading to inform their lives and choices. Factual, trustworthy, honest information isn't propaganda—it's power. Over the past several decades, one of the most banned books in America has been *It's Perfectly Normal* by Robie Harris. At quick glance, it's sort of easy to understand why. It's a book about sex, all different kinds of sex, written in an age-appropriate way for a middle school audience, with illustrations. Ideally, every child would be learning about safer sex and healthy relationships at home, but many aren't. Plus the far right has systematically attacked and undermined sex education for decades.

Age-appropriate books and curriculum about health and safety provide vital information to all students and can even be lifesaving for some. One story about *It's Perfectly Normal* stopped me in my tracks. A ten-year-old girl at the library with her mother checked out a copy of the book. Eventually, the girl showed her mom the chapter on sexual abuse and said, "This is me." The girl was being sexually abused by her father and the book gave her a way to tell her mom what was happening. Eventually, when the father was convicted, the judge in the case said, "There were heroes in this case. One was the child, and the other was the book." Robie Harris, in retelling the story, said the girl's mother was also a hero for listening to her daughter. And the librarian who ordered the book was a hero, too. Over the decades, Harris was smeared as a pornographer, a child abuser, and worse simply because she believed "kids have a right to have the accurate information that can keep them healthy and safe." Banned books save lives. When we ban books, we take away power from parents to decide what information they do or don't want their children to have access to. Banning books is anti-democratic and anti-American. That's why the majority of Americans oppose the government legislating what can or cannot be in schoolbooks. And a majority of Americans "oppose efforts to have books removed from their local public libraries because some people find them offensive or inappropriate and do not think young people should be exposed to them."

Books give students the power of knowledge and critical thinking. That's why, in contrast to those banning books, the AFT *gives out books*. In schools and at book fairs, during school days and on weekends, we've given away more than ten million free books to children and their families over the course of our decade-long initiative. In just the last two years alone, we organized four hundred book giveaway events in twenty-five states as well as the District of Columbia, Puerto Rico, and the Virgin Islands. Our agenda is literacy. For students and their families, literacy is the key to knowledge. And loving reading is the key to literacy. We give away books that are geared to interest and excite young people and foster the love of reading.

I remember a grandmother of Haitian descent at one of our free book fairs in New York City. With pride in her eyes, she thanked me for the wide variety of books we were giving away while she clasped a copy of *Freedom Soup*, a book about the traditional New Year's Day dish that celebrates Haitian independence. She was excited to read it to her grandchildren so they could learn about their heritage.

At another book fair in McDowell County, West Virginia, a little boy had a book clutched so tightly to his chest that I couldn't even read the cover. He exclaimed to me, excitedly, "I'm going straight home to put this in my library!" I asked him what other books were in his library and, without missing a beat, he gushed, "This is the first one!" While fascists want to control what children read and how children think, teachers spread knowledge—and literally give away books.

We partner with the organization First Book and we use member dues to help buy books in bulk. Our members agree that buying books to give away is an expression of our values. In 2024 alone, we gave out over 575,000 books in 144 events across the country. The year before that, we put over one million books in the hands of children, parents, and teachers from Portland, Oregon, to St. Petersburg, Florida, and everywhere in between. Our members love this work. They know access to books and information is key. We just want kids to read and learn and think for themselves. We want to help them learn how to think, not what to think. Because that's fundamental to their development and to a healthy democracy.

In the introduction I talked about the extremist Moms for Liberty activists, bankrolled by billionaires and the far right, who took over school boards and launched a culture war by banning books and pride flags. In the Central Bucks School District outside Philadelphia, the Moms for Liberty–controlled school board banned several LGBTQ-themed books under a policy secretly written with the help of a far-right Christian "think tank." In the case of one of the books they banned, there was only one copy in the whole district. But extremists were apparently so concerned it was "dangerous" that *they mailed images from the book to seventeen thousand households in the community.* Try to wrap your head around that. It just goes to show that Moms for Liberty's real goal is to spread anti-LGBTQ hate and fearmongering to divide the community and distract from the fact that they are trying to systematically defund public education. But remember, it didn't work. In 2023, in that district and nationwide, Moms for Liberty school board members were roundly voted out of office—by Democrats, Republicans, and Independents horrified that fascist factions were creating problems in our schools instead of solving the actual problems local districts are facing. Americans don't want far-right culture wars. They want teachers, school nurses, better science labs, decent ventilation and air-conditioning—and they want their kids to be adept at critical thinking.

THE ASSAULT ON CRITICAL THINKING—AND THE TEACHERS WHO ARE FIGHTING BACK

Still, despite the setbacks for far-right organizations like Moms for Liberty, democracy remains under attack in America. In its 2022 report on the state of democracy worldwide, the International Institute for Democracy and Electoral Assistance found not only that between 2016 to 2021 "the number of countries moving toward authoritarianism is more than double the number moving toward democracy" but that among those nations experiencing "democratic backsliding" was the United States. Looking at the period from 2000 to 2018, political science professor Jacob Grumbach documented that, measured by fifty-one indicators from gerrymandering to the availability of post-election vote verification audits, states dominated by far-right Republicans have become "substantially less democratic." And of course, in 2020, Donald Trump became the first modern presidential candidate in U.S. history to refuse to concede the results of what was a free and fair election. In the weeks after the 2020 election, Trump spread lies about the election results and egged on election denialism, and was still denying the results well into 2024. Meanwhile, a bipartisan congressional inquiry found that on January 6, 2021, President Trump "lit that fire" of an attempted insurrection during which his supporters stormed the U.S. Capitol attempting to overthrow the results of our nation's free and fair election. But Trump has tried to reframe that violent attack on our democracy as "a day of love," and on his first day back in office in 2025 he pardoned every January 6 insurrectionist—including those convicted of assaulting police.

As of May 2023, almost one-third of Americans still believed that the election of President Joe Biden was fraudulent. Trump's supporters spread false accusations of voter fraud again throughout the 2024 election—until President Trump won and they stopped. But American democracy clearly remains under threat.

The far right has convinced many Americans that our democracy is broken because they *actually want to break our democracy.* And it might be working. Even before Trump and his supporters tried to overthrow our democracy, a 2017 poll found that almost a quarter of Americans said they would prefer a system of government in which a "strong leader" could make decisions without interference from other branches of government. A 2024 poll was even more ominous. Over 60 percent of respondents agreed with the phrase "What our country really needs is a strong, determined leader who will crush evil, and take us back to our true path." One in four respondents strongly agreed. Most respondents also agreed our nation has to "smash the perversions eating away at our moral fiber and traditional beliefs" and "silence the troublemakers spreading bad ideas." These are authoritarian-primed perspectives.

In 2024, our nation elected a candidate who campaigned on similar narratives and worse, threatening to use the military to seek vengeance on his political enemies while also promising to abolish the federal Department of Education. As we've already discussed, at the start of his second term in the White House, Trump has swiftly made good on those threats, enacting his anti-education, anti-pluralism, anti-government agenda while arguably sidestepping Congress and undermining the Constitution—major threats to the American system. Elon Musk hacking away at the federal government is case in point. Suffice it to say, the richest man in the world presumably has little understanding of the ways in which federal funding for school lunches, Veterans Affairs hospitals, and Social Security helps average Americans. But even more disturbing is that, at the time of this writing, Republicans in Congress proposed massive cuts to Medicaid, food assistance, and student loans in order to pay for tax cuts for the super-rich. Meanwhile, Musk—whose companies made $8 million per day in 2023 from contracts with the federal government—started dismantling federal agencies that oversee his businesses.

Trump's attacks on government go hand in hand with his attacks on education and democracy. Just as attacking teachers primes Americans to be willing to dismantle public education, convincing people that our nation's government is nothing but waste and fraud makes them less likely to mind when their power to shape that government is taken away. "Trump has been conditioning Americans throughout this campaign to see American democracy as a failed experiment," argues Ruth Ben-Ghiat, speaking about the 2024 election. "He has used his campaign to prepare Americans for autocracy."

Democracy is an idea. It only continues to exist if we believe in it and understand it. Foreign policy leader Richard Haass observes, "One major reason that American identity is fracturing is that we are failing to teach one another what it means to be American. We are not tied together by a single religion, race, or ethnicity. Instead,

America is organized around a set of ideas that needs to be articulated again and again to survive. It is thus essential that every American gets a grounding in civics—the country's political structures and traditions, along with what is owed to and expected of its citizens—starting in elementary school." In other words, what makes us Americans isn't a singular identity or a singular ideology but a shared belief in democracy and the freedom and liberty for all that democracy creates. That belief is our shared creed. Remember, the first official motto of the United States—still emblazoned on our nation's seal and most of our currency—is *e pluribus unum.* Out of many, one.

Fascists and oligarchs want to divide us—attacking those who are different and turning us against each other so they can destroy America's democracy and hand disproportionate power to a few of their chosen elites. But I know that we, the people, believe in the promise of our nation—that *all of us* are created equal—and that working together while thinking for ourselves is the essence of American liberty. And who helps each and every one of us learn how to work together and think critically? Public school teachers. Public school teachers strengthen democracy.

Ryan Richman is a high school history teacher at Timberlane Regional High School in Plaistow, New Hampshire. He tries to engage his students by showing how historical events relate to and inform the present, often by bringing current events into his classroom. So he gives his students a weekly assignment—to find something in the news and bring it to class, prepared to talk about how that current news event relates to history. According to Ryan, most of the stories his students bring in are about oppression. Those are the current events that catch their attention. "They're about the Rohingya genocide, they're about the Uyghur genocide, which are going on right this second," says Ryan. "They're about Black Lives Matter." He's responding to his students' interest and helping them make connections with national and world events of yesteryear.

Before his second presidency, during which Trump unleashed an all-out attack on "diversity, equity, and inclusion" as a misinformation-fueled smear to destabilize public education writ large, in September 2020, during his first presidency, Trump signed an executive order banning what he called "divisive concepts" in diversity training within federal agencies. With that cue, Republican legislators in at least twenty states introduced "divisive concepts" laws to restrict how teachers discuss inequality and injustice.

New Hampshire passed one such law in 2021. The law itself was convoluted and vague, mandating among other things that students not be "taught, instructed, inculcated, or compelled" to believe "that one's age, sex, gender identity, sexual orientation, race, creed, color, marital status, familial status, mental or physical disability, religion or national origin is inherently superior to people of another" or that any person might be "inherently racist, sexist, or oppressive, whether consciously or unconsciously." So would talking about the Rohingya genocide and tying it to other ethnic cleansing campaigns in history violate the law or not? It wasn't remotely clear. In fact, the vagueness of the law was the point—to sow confusion about what could or could not be taught and thus create a broad chilling effect. When the New Hampshire law was passed, the state education commissioner created a website encouraging the public to file complaints accusing teachers of violating the statute. And the far-right organization Moms for Liberty literally pledged a $500 bounty "for the person that first successfully catches a public school teacher breaking this law."

As the *New Hampshire Bulletin* noted, "The new teaching law comes as social studies classes have embraced new teaching methods. Gone is the strategy of rote memorization of dates and battle names. In its place is a model by which students lead discussion of thorny historical issues, and use research to arrive at their own conclusions." This "inquiry method" is meant to emphasize critical thinking. But laws like the one in New Hampshire inhibit teachers from encouraging students to debate and discuss and think for themselves.

Would the New Hampshire law mean that Ryan's students couldn't discuss a topic like affirmative action and the recent Supreme Court decision, which was not only in the news but affecting them as soon-to-be college applicants? What if they were debating the topic? If a teacher shared research data showing the benefits of affirmative action, would that violate the law? What if the teacher was overseeing a class discussion where a student criticized affirmative action and the goal of racial justice? Would that break the law? In 2021, Ryan and two other New Hampshire public school teachers joined with two parents to sue the state, arguing that the law was unconstitutionally vague and would make it impossible to comply with New Hampshire state education laws that require all schools teach about "intolerance, bigotry, antisemitism and national, ethnic, racial or religious hatred and discrimination [that] have evolved in the past, and can evolve, into genocide and mass violence." The brief filed in their lawsuit went on to state:

> New Hampshire law thus requires students to examine—and it follows that teachers shall provide the instruction for students to learn—controversial events from multiple perspectives and

ideologies and learn to defend and challenge differing views on a wide variety of topics. In short, New Hampshire state law promises to develop students into well-rounded, well-educated young adults who are prepared to embrace all the challenges, complexities, privileges and responsibilities of American citizenship, who are prepared to live in an increasingly diverse world, and who can compete successfully in the New Hampshire, national and global economies.

In other words, historically, New Hampshire's education laws not only encouraged but mandated that students be equipped with critical thinking skills. But the politically motivated "divisive concepts" law wanted to censor teachers and control not just what students learn but what they think. The vagueness of the law was the point—so teachers never knew what was and wasn't permissible.

In May 2024, a federal judge ruled that the anti–critical thinking law was unconstitutional. U.S. District Judge Paul J. Barbadoro wrote that the law amounted to "viewpoint-based restrictions" that were so vague they would open the door to "arbitrary and discriminatory enforcement."

As a final exam question, Ryan often shares a passage from writer and Holocaust survivor Elie Wiesel. It was Wiesel who said, when receiving the Nobel Prize, "I swore never to be silent whenever and wherever human beings endure suffering and humiliation. We must always take sides." In their final essays, Ryan asks his students to reflect on Wiesel's insights on bystanderism in the context of present-day events. And Ryan says that his students—the liberal ones, the conservative ones, and all the students in between—often draw connections to racial oppression in the United States. They're thinking critically about the present and the past and making those links.

Which, frankly, we want them to do, right? We don't want the leaders of tomorrow to forget about the mistakes of the past—lest they repeat them. We history teachers have a saying—that "past is prologue." We have to talk about—and think critically about—all aspects of history, honestly, fully, with all perspectives reflected and debated, so that we create well-rounded, informed, thoughtful citizens armed with the skills of critical thinking. That's the point. That's what teachers do.

Ryan Richman adds, "I won't be badgered into whitewashing the experience that my students deserve." I stand with Ryan and every other teacher in America committed to the dispassionate teaching of honest history and developing the muscle of critical thinking among our nation's young people.

To be clear, K–12 teachers have never been able to just teach whatever they wanted. There have always been guardrails and requirements in place. Every state has curriculum frameworks—state laws that lay out what students are expected to learn, and often limit what students can be taught. Teachers know this when committing to teach. We not only work within these frameworks, we support them—because they're based on commonsense pedagogical theory and learning goals with age-appropriate concepts and benchmarks. We don't have carte blanche to teach whatever we want, and teachers take that code of conduct seriously. As I have long said, we teach students how to think, not what to think.

So imagine my surprise when Republican Glenn Youngkin, during his 2021 campaign for governor of Virginia, piggybacked on that idea, saying, "We must *start* teaching our children how to think, not what to think" (emphasis mine)—as if teaching critical thinking was something teachers were not already doing. Often, the far right's accusations against us are in fact confessions about their own actions. They are the ones who want to control what students are taught, learn, and even think. The campaign Youngkin ran for governor was described as "tapping into culture war fights over schools," and when he won, his first act in office was to ban teachers from teaching "divisive concepts."

Teachers work so hard to equip students with critical thinking skills—so they can see all sides of an issue and figure out the truth for themselves. Teachers must have latitude to teach core curricula and facts in ways they believe will be interesting and motivating for their students. That's why the AFT has committed to defending teachers who get in trouble for teaching honest history and basic truth.

Truth isn't an agenda. Truth is how we build common understanding from a starting place of fact and reality. Students need exposure to all ideas and perspectives—including those they disagree with—so they can form their own. And reckoning honestly with the past is essential to understanding our present. But deliberately and misleadingly romanticizing the past by whitewashing history and trying to control what we know and what we think are common fascist tactics. In his aptly titled book *Erasing History*, Jason Stanley explains that authoritarians are routinely guilty of "erasing perspectives and events that are unflattering to the dominant group, and replacing them with a unitary, simplified account that supports [their] ideological ends." This is, for the record, what Donald Trump is trying to do in misrepresenting the January 6, 2021, insurrection as "a day of love"—not only pardoning all those convicted of seditious conspiracy and violence but going so far as to delete the Department of Justice's case records. He is literally erasing history.

Republican Governor Ron DeSantis tried to do the same thing with statewide curriculum reforms in Florida. In 2023, DeSantis's administration put into place a new curriculum for Florida public schools in which teachers instruct students about the positive benefits of slavery—"how slaves developed skills which, in some instances, could be applied for their personal benefit." Defending this misrepresentation that tries to recast slavery and white enslavers in a more flattering light, DeSantis heaped praise on the curriculum and said, "They're probably going to show that some of the folks that eventually parlayed, you know, being a blacksmith into doing things later in life."

As Vice President Kamala Harris fired back in response, slavery "involved rape. It involved torture. It involved taking a baby from their mother. It involved some of the worst examples of depriving people of humanity in our world. How is it that anyone could suggest that in the midst of these atrocities, that there was any benefit to being subjected to this level of dehumanization?"

It's one thing to expose students to differing viewpoints. It's something else entirely for far-right politicians to deliberately skew perspectives on history in order to constrain or control what students think. Critical thinking means looking clearly at and scrutinizing all facts and perspectives, including as they pertain to our nation's history. Fascist indoctrination intentionally strips criticism from the nationalist portrait. In 2023, DeSantis also banned public schools in Florida from teaching AP African American Studies. The course, which covers basic history such as the origins of the African diaspora and the Harlem Renaissance, was referred to by DeSantis's Department of Education as "woke indoctrination" that "lacks educational value." Bear in mind, AP classes are important for students pursuing college, but in Florida, white students participate in the AP system at much higher rates than Black students—even before the AP African American Studies course was removed.

But while DeSantis's Florida has been "among the most aggressive

states in limiting what educators can teach," in 2023 alone, according to the National Conference of State Legislators, "lawmakers in
30 states have proposed new restrictions during the past year on
what schools can teach about the nation's racial history." Despite
Donald Trump pledging during the early days of his second term to
"bring school back to the states," the fact is that states and local
school boards control virtually all aspects of education policy and
decision-making. It's always been that way. In fact, federal law limits the role of the federal government when it comes to deciding what
schools teach and how they are run. So while much of our attention
may be focused on national rhetoric and cuts to funding that are
meant to help students with disabilities and schools in low-income
communities, the fact is that state-level efforts to curb what teachers can teach and undermine public education are far more consequential and thus worrying. Meanwhile, President "bring school
back to the states" Trump keeps trying to interfere with the auton-
omy of states and local communities in deciding how they run their
schools. For instance, in an April 3, 2025, memorandum, Trump's
Education Department threatened to withhold federal funding
from public schools unless state education officials can verify that
they've ended all "diversity, equity and inclusion" initiatives. Make
no mistake, this is not the federal government leaving education to
states and local communities, but the Trump administration very
much trying to control what public schools teach—while also fomenting outrage and division to undermine public education.

These crackdowns are, on their surface, based on lies and fearmongering that teachers are spreading some radical "woke" agenda.
But what do teachers actually teach? In 2022, the American Historical Association (AHA) launched a comprehensive study of what is
being taught by U.S. history teachers in over three thousand middle

schools and high schools nationwide. What did they find? "A majority of history educators embrace an approach to the past that is grounded in helping students recognize the importance of respectful attention to multiple perspectives, even those with which they may vigorously disagree." The AHA research also shows that most teachers are using a variety of materials from a variety of sources. In other words, they're just doing their jobs—helping students learn and form their own complex opinions about our nation's complex history. Isn't that a good thing? Don't we want students to learn both our nation's achievements that make us proud and the failings that make us strive to do better? Shouldn't teachers be free to answer students' questions? Isn't that our job? Research shows that inclusive curricula lead to higher academic engagement and higher graduation rates. Students should have the freedom to learn. And teachers should have the freedom to teach—without the fear that good teaching will get them fired.

But, the AHA study also reported, politically motivated laws that restrict what teachers can teach have been "extremely corrosive of teacher morale and detrimental to the integrity of good history teaching." Research by RAND found that this torrent of enacted and proposed legislation targeting even the mention of "controversial" topics—sweeping and open-ended restrictions on what can be taught—has teachers teaching on eggshells. Arguably, that's the point—fascists want to create a climate where teachers are constantly harassed and feel under suspicion. A 2023 survey by RAND found that two-thirds of teachers in the United States say they have limited discussions of political and social issues in their classrooms. Many said they self-censored because they feared losing their teaching licenses or because they did not trust that administrators would defend them from parent complaints.

The push for high-stakes standardized testing, under the 2001 federal No Child Left Behind law and beyond, has only made this worse. As *Washington Post* education reporter Valerie Strauss notes, research has consistently shown that "standardized test scores are most strongly correlated to a student's life circumstances." Not to mention that our goal as a society shouldn't be to produce young people who are skilled at test prep and knowing which bubbles to fill in on a form. We need young people who can understand the world around them, empathize with and live in a nation with others, and work together to solve problems. Americans agree. Even a majority of Trump voters believe that it is important to increase education funding focused on "preparing children to work well in a diverse environment as adults." That's the important learning that public school nurtures. But teachers don't have time to teach critical thinking and incorporate project-based learning on civics if they're constantly forced to teach test prep.

If we really want to safeguard democracy, not only should we stop undermining critical thinking in education, but we should start expanding civics education to grow real civic understanding and engagement. In the United States, while reading and math scores have been going up for decades, civics knowledge has been in decline. As of 2024, more than one-third of Americans can't name all three branches of government. Over one in ten can't even name one. About one in five Americans cannot name a single freedom guaranteed by the First Amendment. Meanwhile, worldwide, as civics scores have dropped, autocracy has risen. This is not a coincidence. In 2024, Republican strategist Sarah Longwell noted, "You go into a focus group and you say, do you think Donald Trump's an authoritarian? The number one thing that people say back to you is, what's an authoritarian?" Americans can't prevent fascism if they don't understand it—or understand what's at stake in our democracy.

As of January 2023, "Only eight states and the District of Columbia require a full year of high-school civics education. One state (Hawaii) requires a year and a half, 31 require half a year, and 10 require little or none." We have the chance to change this and dramatically increase investments in civics education nationwide. Which is exactly what Raphael Bonhomme is doing in his classroom.

Bonhomme is an elementary school teacher at School-Within-School at Goding Elementary School in Washington, D.C. His passion about his students and helping them be engaged citizens in the world is infectious.

In one of Raphael's lessons, his third-grade students look at the inner workings of Advisory Neighborhood Commissions in D.C., which are nonpartisan neighborhood groups elected to inform city policymaking. The third graders come up with their own policy proposals, imagining themselves as members of an Advisory Neighborhood Commission. And then Raphael even has a real-life D.C. city council member come to class to listen and respond to the students' policy ideas.

Raphael focuses on hands-on learning to make civic concepts tangible and help students reflect and share their learning in real time with each other. "This kind of learning works because it taps into more than one type of intelligence," he explains. "Students feel empowered and connected to their own work." And, of course, they're learning about civics while building critical thinking skills.

Through AFT's Share My Lesson, Raphael shares his curricula ideas with teachers around the country. And he is now a member of AFT's civics design team, a national group of teachers creating curricula and professional development for elementary, middle, and high school educators. Teachers are designing new curricula for civics education and defending democracy. And that's what the fascists are so afraid of.

TEACHING DEMOCRACY

In my office in Washington, D.C., I have a picture of a group of my history and government students from when I taught at Clara Barton High School in the 1990s. Now, that was an underfunded high school filled with kids who were too often underestimated. And the most heartbreaking thing was that they often underestimated themselves. We often competed in the We the People civics competition, a nationwide contest for high school students that not only tests their knowledge of the Constitution and the Bill of Rights but also their skills in applying civic knowledge to real-world issues and policy debates. And in 1995, after we won the city competition, we raised money to get ourselves to the New York State competition, and when we won first place, we raised money to get ourselves to Washington, D.C., for the finals. They were excited, they worked so hard, and they were so disappointed when they came in fourth. They worked for hours and hours. They stretched themselves and relied on each other. And there were times when they were really mad at me and my co-teacher Dr. Leo Casey because we pushed them so hard.

But I was so proud of my students. I watched them weave their lived experiences into legal arguments that were as sophisticated as I had heard experienced lawyers make in courtrooms and boardrooms. And they placed fourth out of the entire country! My AP kids at a non-elite technical-skills-focused public school in New York City! I still beam with pride thinking about what they did. And you know who was even more proud? Their parents. These students learned what they were capable of and showed how smart and talented they were. And they learned how to take a loss and still hold their heads up high. I had the deep honor of being a part of that as their teacher. When I spoke at the Democratic National Convention in August 2024 and talked about the valuable lessons I learned from my students, this is what I meant. My students taught me how, with hard work and support, they could do anything. And I knew that by learning civics and critical thinking, they were preparing to be the informed citizens and leaders of the future that our nation needs.

Al Shanker, my mentor and arguably one of the greatest union leaders and civic leaders of the twentieth century, said that the essential job of our public schools is "to teach children what it means to be an American."

"One is not born into something that makes you an American. It is not by virtue of birth, but by accepting a common set of values and beliefs that you become an American," Shanker wrote. And the point of schools is to inculcate and safeguard the very important foundational principle and practice in the United States that is democracy. "If we want democracy we have to demand it," writes historian Timothy Snyder, "and we have to be able to educate children who will make and remake it."

In 2003, the AFT published a statement signed by over a hundred American leaders, from Congressman John Lewis to businessman Eli Broad, reaffirming the role of education in democracy. It reads, "democracy is the worthiest form of human governance ever conceived" and continues:

We cannot take its survival or its spread—or its perfection in practice—for granted. We must transmit to each new generation the political vision of liberty and equality that unites us as Americans, and a deep loyalty to the political institutions put together to fulfill that vision.

"The process of education has naturally enough been the basis of hope for the perdurance of our democracy," wrote Justice Felix Frankfurter in a 1952 Supreme Court case striking down loyalty oaths for teachers and other public employees. "To regard teachers—in our entire educational system, from the primary grades to the university—as the priests of our democracy is therefore not to indulge in hyperbole. It is the special task of teachers to foster those habits of open-mindedness and critical inquiry which alone make for responsible citizens, who, in turn, make possible an enlightened and effective public opinion."

To the extent that teachers ever proselytize, it is in the sense that Justice Frankfurter evokes—as "priests of our democracy." Congresswoman Barbara Jordan noted in 1995 that the term "Americanization" had "earned a bad reputation" as racist and xenophobic. But she redefined and reclaimed it. "Americanization means becoming a part of the polity—becoming one of us," Jordan said. "The United States has united immigrants and their descendants around a commitment to democratic ideals and constitutional principles. People from an extraordinary range of ethnic and religious backgrounds have embraced these ideas." That is what teachers do. We knit together shared belonging, understanding, and purpose—the foundations of American democracy. And in that regard, teachers are preaching. We're preaching democracy. As we should be. It's been the point of public education all along.

Critical thinking is the heart of democracy, the muscle at the core that keeps democracy healthy and strong. We don't tell our students who to vote for, we don't tell our students what to believe. We teach them how to think for themselves, why democracy is important, and how they're an important part of making it work and making it better. But rather than help teachers build a stronger America based on knowledge and truth and freedom of thought, fascists use fear, bullying, and culture wars to try to shut down teaching and democracy.

2

TEACHERS FOSTER SAFE AND WELCOMING COMMUNITIES

When Lyndon Johnson was in college, long before he was the thirty-sixth president of the United States, he needed to take time off from school to earn money to pay his tuition. So he went to work as a teacher in Cotulla, Texas. He taught fifth, sixth, and seventh grades at a segregated school of Mexican American students along the Texas border. And though Johnson himself had grown up poor, he was still shocked by the extreme deprivation of his students, whom he witnessed diving into garbage cans to find food to eat. "I shall never forget the faces of the boys and the girls in that little Welhausen Mexican School," Johnson would say years later.

Remember that Johnson took that teaching job in the first place because he needed money for tuition. Nevertheless, just like the 90 percent of teachers today who spend their own money on school supplies for their classrooms, Johnson took money out of his own paycheck to pay for extracurricular activities at the school. (During the 2023–2024 school year, it's estimated that teachers spent on average at least $800 of their own money on school supplies for their class-rooms, even though they are still paid 26 percent less than their peers with the same levels of education.) Johnson also organized student debates, spelling bees, and sports teams. He embraced what teachers call "project-based instruction," making skill more rele-vant and fun. His interventions were so transformative that the su-perintendent of the district took notice and named LBJ, then just twenty years old, as principal of the entire school.

By all accounts, Johnson's experience of working in an extremely poor school district and witnessing discrimination against his Mex-ican American students accounts for why he later fought so hard for civil rights and made the War on Poverty the centerpiece of his pres-idency. As President Johnson himself explained, "You never forget what poverty and hatred can do when you see its scars on the hope-ful face of a young child. I never thought then [that] I might have the chance to help the sons and daughters of those students and to help people like them all over this country. But now I do have that chance—and I'll let you in on a secret—I mean to use it."

In June 1965, a year after he signed the Civil Rights Act, and just months before he would sign the Voting Rights Act, President John-son gave a commencement address at Howard University. Johnson declared, "Freedom is the right to share—share fully and equally—in American society . . . to be treated in every part of our national life as a person equal in dignity and promise to all others." But, he fa-mously continued, "freedom is not enough." Recognizing that peo-ple are equal is necessary but not sufficient to achieving our nation's promise. "You do not take a person who, for years, has been hobbled by chains and liberate him, bring him up to the starting line of a race and then say, 'you are free to compete with all the others,'" Johnson said. "It is not enough just to open the gates of opportunity. All our citizens must have the ability to walk through those gates."

Johnson was echoing what he learned in Cotulla and what all teachers know—that we can never achieve equal opportunity if we don't first believe that all children and all people are equal and then support them in every way possible to level the playing field. Writer and activist adrienne maree brown says that each and every human being—simply by virtue of existing—deserves safety, dignity, and belonging. Safety, dignity, and belonging are prerequisites to life, liberty, and the pursuit of happiness. It's that sense that you fit in the world, that your dreams are valid, that your needs deserve to be met. Teachers actively create safe and welcoming school communities, because otherwise, learning takes a backseat. Learning competes with all the other life challenges.

When we talk about public education, we're not just talking about reading, writing, and math—which are, of course, vitally important. We're talking about leveling the playing field so kids have what they need first to survive so that they can then succeed. It would be ideal if every child arrived at school with the financial, physical, and emotional resources they need to be able to buckle down and learn. But for a multitude of reasons, too many children don't have their basic needs met. Too many children don't have enough to eat. Too many children are ostracized because of where they're from or the disabilities they face. We don't just need public schools to work for well-adjusted, well-off children who arrive at school ready, willing, and able to learn. The promise of public education is that it will also help the children struggling through their parents' divorces, the children with undiagnosed learning challenges, the children who can't sleep at night because of gunshots in their neighborhoods, the children who arrive to class with their bellies grumbling, the children who are being sexually assaulted or abused or orphaned. In my case, I relied on extra support from my teachers to get through my father losing his job and the shame he felt from being laid off. Schools need to be a safe harbor welcoming every single student and giving them the support they need—ensuring each and every child has what they need to walk through those gates of opportunity.

That's the story of America. When my grandparents and great-grandparents came to the United States from Eastern Europe at the turn of the last century, it was in public schools where they learned English and embraced American culture and built the skills they needed to climb the ladder of opportunity. They loved America and they loved being Americans. The story of my Jewish Eastern European immigrant ancestors is the same as that of many others—Italians and Irish and Filipinos and Mexicans and so many more. It's also the story of education post–*Brown v. Board of Education*—of how the federal government and courts, after being pushed and prodded by the civil rights movement, made public schools more inclusive and more just. The story of how expanding quality educational access for Black and brown Americans has generally been a consistent priority since the 1960s, supported morally and legally by leaders of both major political parties until, frankly, the rise of Donald Trump and the MAGA right.

Public schools are the public square in which our unique nation is stitched together. Public schools are the public square through which our nation constantly evolves. And from immigrant education to desegregation, public schools have always been where America fights for its future. No matter where they come from, no matter who they are, no matter how much their parents earn, every child deserves to feel safe and welcome in their classrooms so they can learn the skills and tools they need to blaze their own path to the American dream.

But fascists don't believe in the equal worth and dignity of all children or in leveling the playing field to give every child a fair chance at the American dream. Instead, fascists want to demonize some groups of children and Americans so they can sow fear, hatred, and division—literally the opposite of an environment that is safe and welcoming. Far-right extremists are constantly otherizing and fearmongering whatever and whoever is different—whether anti-LGBTQ, anti-Black, anti-immigrant, anti-Semitic, anti-Muslim, anti-disability—basically, anti-everyone who is not white, straight, Christian, and generally well off or even rich. This reflects a belief that certain groups of people are inherently superior—that is by definition what it means to have a "supremacist" worldview. "The true engine of supremacy isn't belief—it's power," explains Eric K. Ward of the organization Race Forward. "Whether racial or religious authoritarians genuinely see certain groups as superior or simply wield that claim to justify white dominance, misogyny, and anti-LGBTQ policies is beside the point. Supremacy isn't about conviction; it's about enforcing hierarchy by any means necessary."

When fascists repeatedly demean and dehumanize certain communities and groups of students, that's not just based on political tactics but is their fundamental worldview. They attack inclusion because they believe in exclusion and hierarchy.

FASCISTS OPPOSE PLURALISM

Far-right extremists attack LGBTQ students, Black students, immigrants, and others not because of "political disagreement" but because the far right fundamentally believes those communities don't belong in America's future. What unites far-right ideologues, oligarchs, and autocrats throughout history and today is the idea that certain groups of people are inherently inferior to others. Whipping up resentment serves an autocratic and polarizing agenda, no doubt, but it also fuels actual hate and violence directed toward communities that fascists would rather not exist. Fascists don't want to create safe and welcoming schools because they don't want those communities to feel safe or welcomed at all—anywhere. They're often explicit about this.

Most of us would like to believe that the idea that certain groups of human beings are inherently inferior is a relic of a distant, forgotten past. But sadly, the ideology of superiority and hierarchy are alive and well among the modern American fascists. *American Renaissance* is a magazine, website, and "bursting at the seams" annual conference for "Klansmen, neo-Nazis and other white supremacists." Jared Taylor, who runs *American Renaissance*, said in 2005, "Blacks and whites are different. When blacks are left entirely to their own devices, Western civilization—any kind of civilization—disappears." Taylor is just one of many white supremacists who have rallied behind Donald Trump and praised him for "acting in the interests of whites." Laura Loomer—who traveled with Donald Trump during his 2024 presidential campaign—spoke at an *American Renaissance* conference, calling herself a "white advocate."

Fascists attack books in school libraries that criticize white privilege because *fascists embrace white privilege.* They don't want it criticized. They want it strengthened. Let's be clear, this isn't remotely true of all white people—thankfully not even most. And when we learn the honest history about racism, we don't feel bad about ourselves but learn about the mistakes of our forebears that we don't want to repeat. One can argue that the real reason fascists don't want young people to learn about the mistakes of the past is because fascists don't want to avoid those actions, they want to repeat them.

Fascists see pluralism as a threat and argue that white people need to be "protected" from multiracial democracy. This is the essence of the "great replacement" theory—a racist conspiracy theory that the increasing diversity of the United States is intended to diminish the power and influence of white Americans. This is what Trump evokes when he says undocumented immigrants are "not human" and are "poisoning the blood of our country," or that "a lot of these illegal immigrants coming in, they're trying to get them to vote." It's the same offensive conspiracy theory former Republican Speaker of the House Newt Gingrich evoked when he accused the left of supporting immigration in order to "drown traditional, classic Americans." But the "great replacement" conspiracy ultimately isn't just about immigration but the larger question of who belongs in America—including who belongs in America's schools. It's a fight about whether all children—regardless of race, ethnicity, or income— get a fair shot at the American dream.

The subtext of this hatemongering is that the far right believes it's bad for America to become more diverse because the far right believes people of color are inherently inferior to white people. During the 2017 "Unite the Right" rally in Charlottesville, Virginia, white supremacists marched down the streets holding torches, giving Nazi salutes, and chanting, "Jews will not replace us." White supremacists believe that white people are superior and racial and ethnic diversity is a threat to them and the nation. It's the same supremacist worldview and tactics the far right employs when they allege that trying to make America's universities and businesses more diverse and inclusive is an "attack" on America.

Just as they've done throughout history, autocrats and would-be autocrats exploit the supremacist worldview to pit their supporters against some dangerous, undeserving "other." Far-right leaders foment resentment and hate against "others" in order to convince "us" that those leaders are on our side, whipping us up into a desperate frenzy so we'll vote for anything or anyone we're told might help. For instance, that's why in February 2024, Trump—who was then running for president—helped tank a bipartisan proposal in Congress that would have secured the border while also creating some new pathways for immigrants. Trump didn't want to actually solve migration in a way that would make the country better. "The border is a very important issue for Donald Trump," explained then–Republican Senator Mitt Romney. "And the fact that he would communicate to Republican senators and Congress people that he doesn't want us to solve the border problem—because he wants to blame [then-President] Biden for it—is really appalling." Solving problems means addressing them instead of inflaming them. Solving problems is the opposite of exploiting them.

Fascists and their enablers aren't always explicit that they see people of color and women and other marginalized groups as inherently inferior and undeserving. But in 2024, a batch of leaked emails revealed the truth. "The core of what we oppose is 'anti-discrimination,'" wrote Scott Yenor, a professor leading anti-diversity activism for a far-right think tank. "Our sexual culture will not be healed until we once again agree that homosexuality belongs in the closet and that a healthy society requires patriarchy."

How does this supremacist worldview shape the far right's vision for schools and education policy? To pick just one example, the Keystone Christian Education Association is an organization of conservative Christian schools and churches with a mission to "protect and promote historical and biblical Christian education." A report the organization issued said the problem with public schools is that they indoctrinate students in "pluralism, world peace, and a United Nations agenda." Just so we're clear, they're saying that pluralism, world peace, and the United Nations *are bad.* Further lambasting public schools, the organization wrote that "today's system brings students from diverse and unknown families into a united school environment" where they "are expected to be part of the common community wherein all are equal and all are respected." The report goes on to say that diversity and equality are taking over "the nicest" communities.

The Keystone Christian Education Association is not unique. For example, as of 2023, the Network for Public Education identified 273 charter schools "designed to appeal to conservative white families"—incidentally, more than a quarter of which are operated by for-profit companies. Another example of one of these charter schools undermining pluralism and basic equal treatment? The Roger Bacon Academy charter school network in North Carolina requires girls to wear skirts because they are supposed to be treated "more gently" and "regarded as a fragile vessel that men are supposed to take care of and honor."

This fundamentalist ethos about the inherent superiority of some groups of students is not only wrong in principle but creates real threats to the well-being of children. Take the example of right-wing TikTok influencer Chaya Raichik. Raichik has routinely spread false rumors alleging "wokeness" in public schools, such as one about schools installing litterboxes for students who identify as cats, and she has called for teachers who come out as gay to their students to be "fired on the spot."

In August 2023, Raichik reposted a video in which a Tulsa, Oklahoma, school librarian said her agenda is "teaching kids to love books and be kind." Raichik recaptioned the post, accusing the librarian of pushing a "woke agenda." After Raichik's post, the district "received bomb threats for six consecutive days." (Oklahoma's far-right school superintendent not only retweeted Raichik's post but then rewarded Raichik—who is not an Oklahoma resident—by appointing her to a statewide educational advisory committee.)

And yes, kids have been harmed; at least one student's death can be tied to this hate. Amid the extremist anti-LGBTQ climate that Raichik and others have deliberately stoked, Oklahoma Governor Kevin Stitt signed a law in 2022 preventing trans students from using the bathroom that matches their gender identity. A few months later, a sixteen-year-old nonbinary student named Nex Benedict started being bullied at school. In February 2024, Nex was knocked to the ground during a fight with three older girls in the girls' bathroom. The next day, Nex died. Among other outcries for action, parents and advocates in the state pointed fingers at Raichik and others for stoking a climate of violence. But Raichik herself has proudly embraced the label of a "stochastic terrorist"—"someone who inspires supporters to commit violence by demonizing a person or group." Meanwhile, Raichik's influence has only risen; in February 2025, *The New York Times* documented how tweets from Raichik were directly influencing Trump's education policies and Musk's efforts to gut the Department of Education. Meanwhile, *Vice* reports that schools in Minnesota, Wisconsin, Oregon, California, Colorado and elsewhere also received bomb threats after Libs of TikTok posts about them.

It should be obvious that the opposite of dehumanizing and demeaning groups of students isn't promoting one identity or another. That's ridiculous. As a teacher, my job is to make sure students feel safe and welcome no matter who they are or what they believe. That's our job. So if that self-proclaimed "stochastic terrorist" had children in my classroom, my job would be to make them feel as welcome and included as every other student and make sure they had the same access to the same quality education. My job isn't to teach you to agree with me. My job is to teach you how to think. My job is to teach you to have self-confidence. My job is to teach you resilience and kindness and compassion and critical thinking skills and problem solving. My job is to engage you. My job is to prepare you for life, for college, for your career, and for civic engagement. What students do with that knowledge and those tools—whatever path they choose—is entirely up to them.

Fascists are the ones who want to impose their ideas and intentionally make some groups of students feel inferior while protecting the supremacy of other students by, say, not teaching painful subjects like slavery because it might make white students feel bad. Teachers just want to teach the truth while meeting kids where they're at and supporting every kid to be themselves, whoever they are.

The majority of Americans side with teachers. Even amid the deeply divisive 2024 election, with fascist race-based fearmongering reaching a fever pitch, a majority of Americans still agreed that "the fact that the U.S. population is made up of people of many different races, ethnicities and religions strengthens American society." Americans like pluralism and most believe that all of God's children deserve dignity and respect and should be treated equally. During the 2024 election, economic fear about inflation and the cost of living were the dominant issues. But Trump did everything he could to pin America's fears on immigrants, trans kids, and the boogieman of diversity, equity, and inclusion—trying to turn people against the simple idea that everyone deserves compassion and opportunity. And since becoming president again, Trump has doubled down by trying to end diversity, equity, and inclusion in the government and beyond.

Yet in spite of that, and in spite of what extremists will try to tell you, the majority of Americans support LGBTQ rights and believe in racial equality and agree we can do more as a nation to advance women's equality. And while we don't always agree about how to achieve equality or whether trans kids should be playing sports, almost two-thirds of the country agrees that "overcoming racism requires changes in laws and institutions as well as in individual attitudes." When it comes to schools, 71 percent of Americans favor helping school districts to "have more racially and economically diverse student bodies" and "providing more resources to the school districts that serve students who need the most help." And Americans overwhelmingly agree that our schools should be "safe and welcoming for every child, no matter how they learn, what language they speak at home, or whether they are transgender or not."

Americans are a good people who want to do good by each other and help those in need. And no matter how much the fascists shake their fists, teachers create welcoming schools where every student feels included, regardless of the barriers that history or life circumstances have put in their way. School staff level the playing field by ensuring students' basic needs are met, so they can focus on learning and achieving. And teachers work to create a supportive community where children won't be bullied or harassed because of their identities or beliefs. Like I said, fascists want to exacerbate problems and divisions so they can exploit them politically. Teachers solve problems—for students, families, and communities. That begins, even before a single textbook is cracked, with fostering a sense of safety, dignity, and belonging for every child. Perhaps nowhere in America is this clearer than in McDowell County, West Virginia.

THE CASE FOR SUPPORTING ALL STUDENTS

McDowell County is one of the poorest places in America. Once the thriving epicenter of coal production fueling our nation's industrial boom, in the last half century or so the county lost about three-quarters of its population. Jobs left the county, too. As of 2013, almost half of the students in McDowell lived with someone other than a biological parent. Between 2006 and 2012, West Virginia had the highest rates of opioid addiction in the United States. In 2015, McDowell had the highest opioid death rate in the nation—more than forty-five times the national average. In 2022, the median household income in McDowell was $28,235—dramatically less than the national median of $74,580 the same year. In 2022, one-third of the county lived in poverty, almost three times the national average. In 2022, the suicide rate in McDowell, the highest in the state, was almost twice the national average.

Of course, McDowell's public schools have suffered as the community has struggled and the tax base has declined. But even if McDowell had the greatest schools in the nation, it's impossible to imagine children in those circumstances doing as well in class as children in rich communities in Connecticut or California. That's because children in McDowell—just like poor kids in cities and rural communities across the country—often arrive at school without their basic needs met. They need extra help to be ready to learn. You can have the best teachers in the world—but, as *The Washington Post* noted, children in places like McDowell County who arrive at school every morning "carry burdens that hang over them like haze from the nearby coal mines." State takeover of the schools didn't move the needle. A new superintendent who started the job "armed with a turnaround strategy" threw out his plans on the first day of his job. Like so many other dynamics in the region, the education system seemed permanently broken.

McDowell had tried every reform strategy under the sun, with little impact. When Gayle Manchin was First Lady of West Virginia (her husband, Joe, would later become a U.S. senator) and she was also on the West Virginia Board of Education, she knew all too well the challenges the schools were facing—and failing to fix. So she reached out to me and AFT to help. We partnered with Democrats and Republicans as well as local and national businesses and really anyone else who would agree to work together to create meaningful support and opportunity for every student in McDowell. For instance, at the time there were no dentists in McDowell County. That meant that even if parents could afford dental care for their children, they'd have to drive hours to the dentist, which meant the parents missing work and kids missing school. And of course, many parents simply couldn't afford that visit to the dentist. The result was a lot of children with significant dental issues, literally trying to focus on a math test while their little heads were throbbing with toothaches. So we created a mobile dental clinic that travels around the schools in McDowell, doing teeth cleanings for kids and taking x-rays when needed.

The program is part of the community schools model—where schools create a welcoming and safe environment for all students by providing wraparound services students, families, and communities need to thrive. Recognizing that schools are an essential hub of communities—and in many places, like McDowell, the only source of community support—this model makes schools a one-stop shop for services that students need to be ready to focus and participate in the classroom.

In McDowell, that means things like a closet where children can get shoes or winter coats. Early intervention programs that provide books and reading instruction to children before they reach school age. Investments in career and technical education that expand job skills and entrepreneurship. Mentorship programs. New after-school programs in science, technology, and math. A juvenile drug court to divert young nonviolent offenders to treatment instead of jail. Expanded mental health counseling in schools. And so much more. In McDowell, we even built housing for teachers—the first new multistory construction downtown in the county seat of Welch in fifty years—because we knew it would help this great community attract and retain great teachers. Community schools are a major strategy to systematically meet the needs of the kids and families we serve, from adult literacy to student learning to industrial policy.

McDowell reminded me why unions need to be involved not just in economic fairness but economic growth. This isn't just a rural issue. Schools in cities, suburbs, and small towns across the country could thrive with this same investment. That's why I've worked to spearhead other projects in rural, suburban, and urban communities to kick-start economic renewal and growth—including, as I'll discuss more in the next chapter, career and workforce development education tied to specific economic investments and job growth. We can't create opportunity without jobs—good, secure American manufacturing, health care, service, finance, and technology jobs that will help our students build their futures and build our nation's future. Care and career go hand in hand. If kids don't have the basic supports and resources they need to be able to sit in class and learn, they can't possibly achieve. If they feel powerless or without agency in the present, it's hard to engage them to see a possible better future. And if there aren't any available jobs, then many wonder what's the point. Just like we need wraparound solutions for the whole child, we need wraparound solutions for whole communities. That's just another way of talking about community revitalization and economic development. This is what healthy communities do. It's what churches and Kiwanis clubs did in the past and schools are called on to do today—where in our increasingly atomized society, schools remain one of the most enduring hubs of community. With the right resources, schools can do even more good for students as well as families and communities.

As the first part of that equation, the community schools approach works. In McDowell, we cut the dropout rate by more than half, high school graduation rates rose, and scores on academic testing started to get closer to national averages. More broadly, research shows the community schools approach is effective in supporting students and improving educational outcomes. A comprehensive analysis synthesizing findings from 143 research studies on community schools found that "well-implemented community schools lead to improvement in student and school outcomes and contribute to meeting the educational needs of low-achieving students in high-poverty schools." The researchers concluded that community schools strategies help "children succeed academically and prepare for full and productive lives."

The community schools model also works to support families and communities in ways that help students outside of the classroom. From legal clinics for immigrant families in Kansas City, Missouri, to financial literacy classes for parents in Cincinnati, to food pantries for families in Washington, D.C., and White Plains, New York, community schools help families get what they need so kids can arrive at school ready to learn. Because while all kids have God-given potential, not all kids are given the resources they need to thrive. They need extra support to be able to achieve their dreams. These supports are so important to teachers and so integral to how we care for every single student that in 2019 the AFT local in Los Angeles—United Teachers Los Angeles—went on strike to expand community schools instead of charter schools in the city. The union won. Thanks to the teachers' union, Los Angeles pledged to create thirty new community schools programs in high-need areas and invest $400,000 in each program over two years. That means more support and opportunity for tens of thousands of students.

We know that children don't just carry backpacks to school, they carry baggage—and if we want them to learn, we need to support them in every sense possible to be ready to learn. That's why teachers also work on policy solutions to poverty and addiction and health care and homelessness—because we care about children and families and every facet of their well-being. That's what healthy, compassionate, fair societies do. It's not about helping just one group of students, but all kids and all communities. When students from West Virginia to Washington State and everywhere in between get what they need to learn and thrive, those whole communities and our whole nation thrives.

But fascists and oligarchs and extremists simply don't care. They don't think kids and families who are struggling should get extra support because they don't believe those kids and families are deserving. Frankly I don't know what's in the hearts and minds of these extremists. Some of them are undoubtedly supremacists who believe that only certain people or races or religions are meant to succeed. Some of them are just greedy elitists who don't want their taxpayer money going to help people they think are less deserving. Either way, the result is that they undermine the common good— and then discard and abandon programs that nurture the common good by helping communities thrive.

Community schools help all kids and families access opportunity. Fascists and oligarchs just want to hoard opportunity and power for themselves and the billionaire class they represent. They cut programs and blame teachers when education stumbles. Plain and simple. Fascists pretend that inclusion pits one group against another, when the reality is fascists want to pit children and communities against each other—and don't care if some children and communities suffer. The far right sees life through the lens of competition, and if some kids can't run the race, it's the fault of their families or their genetics—and, either way, not something for society as a whole to worry about. As teachers, we know better. That's why teachers fight for an America that is inclusive, that understands diversity is a strength not a weakness, and that supports the opportunity of all schoolchildren to learn and thrive.

I wish every parent and every politician would work with us to make sure every child has a warm coat and a notebook and hot meals and whatever else they need to thrive. But at the very least, I wish all our political leaders would support teachers as we fight for children to be physically and emotionally safe in school—in school, and in general. Which brings me to two societal threats and their profound impact on our children—gun violence and social media.

GUNS IN SCHOOLS

On December 14, 2012, the children in Abbey Clements's classroom settled down quickly. They were really quiet because they were going to make paper snowflakes before math for a PTA holiday luncheon. Then, suddenly, during their "Morning Meeting," they heard a loud noise in the hallway. At first Abbey thought it was a bunch of metal folding chairs getting knocked over. Then she realized it was bullets. Abbey rushed her class of second graders at Sandy Hook Elementary School in Newtown, Connecticut, into the coats hanging in the classroom, away from the view from the outside door. She had to open that classroom door to lock it from the outside and pulled two kids who were in the hallway into her class. Abbey quietly sang Christmas songs and read to them to try to distract the seven-year-olds from the sounds of gunshots coming over the school loudspeaker. Many of the children were crying. Over and over, they would say things like, "I want my mommy, I've got to get out of here!" Abbey was terrified, too, even when the police came to get them out. How could she be sure it was really the police and not the gunman?

That day at Sandy Hook, a man armed with an AR-15-style assault weapon fired 154 rounds in less than five minutes. He killed twenty-six people. Six were teachers and staff. And he killed twenty students, little children who were just six and seven years old.

As of 2022, gun violence was the leading cause of death for children in the United States between the ages of one and seventeen. We have more victims of gun violence, many times over, than any other nation in the free world. And many of those victims are children killed by mass shootings in our nation's schools. Since my election as president of the AFT in 2008, there have been literally too many mass school shootings to count. Marjory Stoneman Douglas High School in Parkland, Florida: fourteen students and three staff shot and killed, February 2018. Santa Fe High School in Santa Fe, Texas: ten students and faculty shot and killed, May 2018. Oxford High School in Oxford Township, Michigan: four students shot and killed, November 2021. Robb Elementary School in Uvalde, Texas: nineteen children and two teachers shot and killed, May 2022. And too, too many more.

Between January 1, 2022, and May 24, 2022—the day of the Robb Elementary School shooting in Uvalde—there were twenty-seven school shootings in the United States. That's twenty-seven shootings in just 144 days, less than half a year, amounting to roughly one shooting per week. In the supposedly greatest nation on earth—or in any nation—that's unconscionable. Especially when we know there are straightforward measures we can take to decrease school shootings, such as expanding safe storage and background checks for gun sales and restricting military-grade assault weapons and high-capacity magazines.

In the aftermath of Sandy Hook, I led my union in speaking out to demand commonsense gun violence prevention, and then pressed other union leaders to do the same. I took a lot of flak for being the head of a teachers' union speaking out about sensible gun violence prevention laws. There are a lot of hunters and other gun owners in the labor movement and they'd been convinced by years of NRA messaging that talking about "commonsense gun safety" somehow meant I was trying to take away all their guns. Indeed the NRA went after me and the AFT for speaking up to protect schoolchildren. In one video they made, the NRA—the singularly powerful corporate gun lobby most responsible for blocking commonsense safety reforms and continuing the unfettered spread of weapons of war most commonly used in school shootings—had the audacity to say, "Randi Weingarten and the AFT are one of the greatest threats to our children." That's just galling. Teachers are literally sacrificing their lives blocking their students' bodies from bullets. Because it's our job to protect our students. And a strong majority of Americans—including a majority of gun owners—support commonsense gun violence prevention. But the NRA perpetually, callously blocks any change.

I remember when I first got the call about the Sandy Hook Elementary school shooting. It felt like someone ripped my heart from my chest. I don't usually cry easily, but in a split second I, like so many others, sobbed for days. To think of these children, these tiny little children, being slaughtered in the place they should associate with nothing but possibility and joy. And then to think of teachers— AFT members like Anne Marie Murphy, a fifty-two-year-old special education teacher who was killed by the Sandy Hook gunman as she literally shielded her students with her own body. Why aren't our political leaders throwing themselves between the gun lobby and our children? Why was this not the single most important issue in the last election and every election?

Parents should be able to send their kids to school in the morning and not have to worry if they'll come back alive at the end of the day. Children should feel safe—*and be safe*. And teachers should be able to focus on teaching, instead of using their bodies—and giving their lives—as human shields. If as a nation we continue to refuse to take even the most basic steps to prevent school shootings, we are failing our children.

We must find ways to confront our excessive gun culture in America. But instead of banning assault rifles, fascists and the far right want to ban books? Books aren't killing children, assault weapons are. But Donald Trump and other extremists have called to roll back even the bipartisan gun safety measures enacted after the Uvalde massacre. After a school shooting in Iowa during the 2024 election, Donald Trump told America to "get over it." Later, he attacked commonsense gun control and said Americans need their guns "for entertainment and for sport." While the Project 2025 extremist playbook for Trump's second presidency has extensive plans for book bans and restrictions on freedom of thought, it would also expand unfettered access to guns nationwide. They clearly think their extremist interpretation of the Second Amendment is more precious than the life of a second grader. And they are more interested in fomenting divisions than making our children actually safe.

I am so grateful to Abbey Clements and her fellow educators Sari Beth Rosenberg and Sarah Lerner, who, instead of giving up, created Teachers Unify to End Gun Violence. This teacher-led advocacy organization continues to press for commonsense reforms that could save the lives of more students. If only our politicians would listen to teachers, families, and students instead of the gun lobby.

ADDRESSING SOCIAL MEDIA, TECHNOLOGY, AND LONELINESS

In our politics today, the NRA and gun manufacturers have more clout than defenseless schoolchildren, their families, and their educators. That's why America, unlike other nations, doesn't have the commonsense gun safety laws we clearly need. Likewise, today, technology companies and their billionaire owners and investors have more clout than the young people whose attention and well-being they're exploiting for profit. That's why our nation has failed to address how social media and technology addiction are causing an anxiety and loneliness crisis among our youth.

Today, young Americans are experiencing higher rates of anxiety, depression, and suicide. In the 2024 World Happiness Report, out of 143 countries studied, American adults ages sixty and older were the tenth happiest—but young Americans under the age of thirty ranked sixty-second. Economist Carol Graham attributes the mental health crisis among youth to growing uncertainty about the world, including cost of living, the future of jobs, and climate change. But without a doubt, Graham points a finger squarely at social media.

Research shows that teens who spend more than three hours a day on social media are at twice the risk of experiencing symptoms of depression and anxiety. Excessive time spent on social media is also correlated with increasing eating disorders, suicidal thoughts, and anxiety and decreasing self-esteem. Nearly half of teens in the United States say they've been bullied or harassed online, and we know that the more time spent online, the higher the rates of exposure to bullying. In polling conducted in the United States in 2022, almost a third of thirteen-to-seventeen-year-olds said they had been called offensive names online. More than one in four teen girls said they'd had false rumors about them spread online, and almost one in five said they'd been sent explicit images they didn't ask for. Meanwhile, research shows the more time young people spend online and the higher they score on metrics of social media addiction, the more likely they are to engage in cyberbullying. It's a vicious cycle—one that COVID only made worse by increasing the amount of time kids spent online while decreasing in-person social interactions.

In 2023, the surgeon general of the United States, Vivek Murthy, declared loneliness to be a nationwide epidemic. In fact, it's a global crisis. Survey data of fifteen- and sixteen-year-olds shows that while before 2012, the rate at which teens reported loneliness was rather static, between 2012 and 2018 levels of reported loneliness doubled. What happened in 2012? That's the year that smartphone ownership in the United States and in other countries studied passed 50 percent. In the years that followed, in the United States as well as Canada and the United Kingdom, rates of loneliness, depression, and self-harm among teens sharply increased. Murthy himself blames cell phones and teen social media use for the epidemic of loneliness. The surgeon general's 2023 advisory on "Social Media and Youth Mental Health" notes:

> Up to 95% of youth ages 13–17 report using a social media platform, with more than a third saying they use social media "almost constantly." Although age 13 is commonly the required minimum age used by social media platforms in the U.S., nearly 40% of children ages 8–12 use social media.

In a finding that will surprise no parent or grandparent of school-aged children, 72 percent of high school teachers in the United States say that cell phone distraction is a major problem in classrooms. And in a finding that will be no surprise to teachers, 59 percent of parents feel their teenagers are addicted to their phones.

But here's what might surprise everyone—50 percent of teenagers self-report that they're addicted to their phones and almost two in five say they spend too much time on their phones. And one in four teens say they think they spend too much time on social media. Perhaps even more significantly, almost three-quarters of teens report they "feel happy or peaceful" when they don't have their phones, and almost half say they feel less anxious. Isn't it our job as adults to protect our children from things that even they know are hurting them?

And yet parents and teachers are left to deal with these challenges all on their own. Plus schools have to grapple with disruptive and even dangerous behavior linked to "viral challenges" on social media—like challenges to destroy school property, or slap a teacher, or report hoax school shootings. While cell phones distract students, the fallout from social media clearly distracts teachers and administrators. The burden shouldn't be on parents and teachers alone to parse and police every new, highly addictive technology while simultaneously dealing with the trail of emotional and physical consequences they can leave in their wake.

Meta's own internal research about Instagram showed how the algorithms they created are harming young people—especially adolescent girls. But did the company do anything about it? No—they just tried to bury the research. The giant tech corporations prioritize preying on children instead of protecting them. And it goes without saying that, with President Trump literally giving tech billionaires the best seats at his inauguration and handing over leadership of the government to tech billionaire Elon Musk, instead of hoping for more strict government oversight of the tech industry, it looks likely we can count on the opposite. Which means it's our job as teachers, parents, and the larger community to fight back.

That's why the AFT, working with partners like the American Psychological Association and ParentsTogether, has called for clear and necessary safeguards on social media—and is pushing to get them enacted. This includes making sure that social media platforms set the strongest safety features as defaults, protect the privacy of young users, shield them from risky algorithms, and identify and implement changes that deter overuse and addictive behavior.

Honestly, this is really the bare minimum of what we should be demanding of these multibillion-dollar omnipresent corporations.

And we're not just crossing our fingers and hoping tech companies do the right thing. We are pushing for change. In 2024, thanks to the advocacy of teachers, parents, and children's rights organizations, the U.S. Senate passed the Kids Online Safety Act (KOSA) and the Children and Teens' Online Privacy Protection Act (COPPA). With overwhelming bipartisan support (only three out of the hundred senators voted against the measures), these laws would "give parents new tools to protect their kids online, hold social media companies accountable for harm, require consent before data can be collected and ban targeted advertising to kids under 17." But Meta, the trillion-dollar technology behemoth behind Instagram and Facebook, succeeded in stopping the measures from coming up for a vote in the Republican-controlled House of Representatives at the end of 2024. As of this writing, neither bill has come up for a vote again. And with Elon Musk, who owns the social media platform X, as Trump's right-hand partner, it's unlikely serious regulation of social media and technology will be revived anytime soon.

But thankfully, Democrats in California and New York enacted state laws requiring technology companies to take steps to curb the addictive qualities and negative effects of social media. New York, led by the New York State United Teachers and parents, banned cell phones during class time. And several hundred school districts across the country have filed or joined lawsuits against the companies behind TikTok, Instagram, Snapchat, and YouTube—taking on how the platforms recommended harmful content to children and not only aren't doing anything to stop it, but in fact design the platforms to incentivize addiction—including among young users.

But when our nation prioritizes the profits of tech companies over the well-being of people, especially children, trying to find so-lutions can feel like playing Whac-A-Mole. Along comes AI and parents and teachers have to figure out how to make sure students are still doing their own original work, rather than having advanced computing systems do it for them. The sad reality is that parents, educators, and communities will continue to struggle to support children and teens around the harms of technology until the tech companies and our government leaders actually prioritize protect-ing the safety and well-being of our youth.

BUILDING THE GREAT SOCIETY

Confronted with these and other societal challenges, teachers never give up. In fact, we step up, over and over again, doing whatever we can to support our students.

Lillian Keys grew up in McDowell County, West Virginia. And she didn't know that where she grew up was anything other than perfect until she went somewhere else. That happened when Lillian went off to college at Concord University in Athens, West Virginia—just over an hour's drive from where she came from but apparently, to some, a world away. During her English class in her first year, when Lillian mentioned that she was from McDowell County, another student audibly gasped and said, "Oh my gosh, I'm so sorry. I'm so glad you made it." That student probably wasn't trying to be cruel, they were just reflecting the expectations for kids from one of the poorest communities in the nation.

Lillian remembers being in middle school and one of her teachers making an extra effort to engage her in class. "We were reading a book about the ballet and . . . I did ballet at the time." So Lillian's teacher said, "Why don't you bring your pointe shoes and then show everybody, because nobody around here knows what those look like." As Lillian recounts, "It was not that big of a deal to her, I'm sure. But it was a big deal to me." That single moment, from all those years ago, made Lillian feel special. It made her feel seen and filled with potential. And it helped change the trajectory of her life.

Now, you might think this story ends with Lillian going on to become a professional ballerina. But that's not the inspiration she took from that moment. Instead, she went on to be a teacher—and decided to be a teacher right back home in McDowell, a community desperately in need of hope and opportunity and the same sort of inspiration that Lillian knew made such a difference in her life.

Sitting in her classroom at Mount View High School in McDowell County, Lillian points to her seating chart and tells the story of every child in her tenth-grade English class. Lillian knows this student's mama. She lives across the street from this other student's grandma. This one lives down the road. That one Lillian taught ballet.

I can tell you stories like this from all across the country, amazing teachers working so hard, bringing so much innovation, passion, and moxie to help their students learn, grow, and thrive. There's Michael Shunney in West Warwick, Rhode Island, an industrial design teacher who uses the latest in 3-D rendering and printing technology to excite his students about careers in science and engineering. There are educational support personnel leaders Wretha Rawls Thomas and Denetris Jones, who, with a grant from our union, run community events where families and students from Houston can get groceries, hot meals, mental health consultations, blood pressure checks, and free books—to help all families thrive so more students are ready to learn. There's Clare Berke, an English teacher in

Washington, D.C., who runs a journalism class in career and technical education where students go out in the real world and report on national stories. And there are thousands and thousands of others, all across our nation.

Teachers have a hard job even in the best of circumstances, but these teachers bring passion and purpose to students, families, and communities that too many have written off. Teachers don't just care about kids, they care about families and entire communities—and create opportunity for all.

When Lillian Keys was a student in McDowell, she didn't quite realize how many of her peers were homeless or how many had family members struggling with addiction. These are still challenges today—in McDowell and across the United States, where 1.2 million school-aged students experienced homelessness during the 2021–2022 school year alone. Over the past decade, overdose death rates have tripled nationwide. So what does Lillian Keys do in the face of these and other challenges confronting her community and her students? "It comes to a certain point where, it's like: Okay, you have to give them even more opportunities." That's why one morning I found Lillian Keys doing what no one might expect at a high school on the grounds of an old strip mine in a community with some of the highest rates of poverty and overdose in the nation. She was teaching them *Othello*.

That sends a powerful message to her students. Kids who go to Harvard read Shakespeare. Kids who go on to become doctors and lawyers read Shakespeare. Kids who live in New York and Paris read Shakespeare. And so should kids who live in McDowell County, West Virginia—kids who might go to college, who might stay in McDowell or move elsewhere, who might become doctors or lawyers or electricians or mechanics. Or teachers. Those kids deserve the same opportunities, the same knowledge, the same ability to dream and create whatever future they want as every other child in America.

Teachers like Lillian Keys show up every single day, often to teach students who bring innumerable challenges from home and life into the classroom. But they believe. They believe their students can learn. They believe their students can grow. They believe their students are filled with potential and hopes and dreams and goals—and that their job as teachers is to spark and support that potential. Teachers believe in all students. Our nation needs to believe in all students, too. And then we need to work in meaningful ways to create opportunity for every child in school and after school.

Yes, we're asking schools to do more by not only teaching students but supporting many of their basic needs. But that's only because fascists and their anti-government enablers among corporations and the super-rich have been gutting public services for decades, leaving schools to pick up the pieces. During the 2022–2023 school year, over half of public school students—over twenty-five million children—were so poor that they qualified for free or reduced lunch at school. Children can't learn math or reading when their stomachs are grumbling; that's child psychology 101.

If conservatives weren't constantly trying to cut funding for food stamps, there wouldn't be hungry children who rely on school breakfast and lunch as their only square meals of the day. And yet those on the far right still attack the government for funding free lunch for children and shame children who need help. During his first presidency, Donald Trump tried to kick almost a million children off the free lunch program and also fought to make school lunches *less* healthy. Meanwhile, many Republican governors have turned down federal funding that would allow them to expand school lunch programs to feed hungry children during the summer. As Republicans further restrict which children qualify for free lunches, many other children simply can't afford to pay. School lunch debt is soaring nationwide. The response? In one instance in Salt Lake City, forty elementary school students with unpaid lunch debt had their meals literally taken out of their hands and thrown in the trash. That's cruel and inhumane. These are hungry children, for God's sake. And yet in March 2025, Donald Trump issued an executive order to close the federal Department of Education—jeopardizing funding that in part goes to support high-poverty schools as well as support services for students with disabilities. Both the Project 2025 blueprint for Trump's second term and congressional Republicans' 2025 budget proposals pledge to cut school lunches. And one Republican congressman, Rich McCormick of Georgia, said that children who get subsidized lunches "sponge off of the government" instead of "actually getting a job and doing something that makes them have value." That's just abominable on so many levels. Meanwhile, as of this writing, our union is fighting alongside parents and communities to do everything possible to stop Trump from gutting programs and spending that Congress approved to help our nation's children.

In a perfect world, we wouldn't need schools to be the center of all social services. All children would arrive at school each morning fed and clothed and healthy and ready to learn. But that's not the world we live in and it's certainly not the world authoritarians want to create. Almost ten million school-aged children—more than one in ten young people nationwide—live in poverty. More than half of students in poverty say they come to school hungry in the morning, which we know diminishes their ability to focus in class. Almost half of students living below the poverty line have not had a recent vision screening. These are just some of the challenges that

low-income students bring to school each day that drastically reduce their readiness to learn compared to their better-off peers.

"Our schools cannot be improved if we ignore the disadvantages
associated with poverty that affect children's ability to learn,"
writes education scholar Diane Ravitch. "Children who have grown
up in poverty need extra resources, including preschool and medical care."

Teachers step into this void, providing the support students need
and creating equal opportunity in a world where both equality and
opportunity are constantly under siege from the right. Sure, it's de-
moralizing that we're being asked to do more than ever at the exact
same moment that teachers are being attacked and school funding
is being slashed. It would just be so much easier if we didn't have to
keep fighting off high-stakes testing, privatization, education funding cuts, attacks on our latitude to teach, and cuts to all other services that students and families need. Teaching is hard even in the
easiest of circumstances, in well-funded schools in well-resourced
communities. Teaching in low-income communities in disinvested
schools while teachers are constantly under political attack is challenging, to say the least. But that's the job. And teachers are honored
to do it.

And when we support all children, and include all children in the
full promise of public education, all children benefit—as does our
nation as a whole. According to the School Superintendents Association, "Study after study has shown that students in integrated
schools have higher test scores, are more likely to graduate, show
stronger critical thinking skills and have reduced racial biases."
There's a reason the first public schools in America were called
"common schools." Every child—of every religion, every ethnicity,
every belief—is promised a seat in public education, where they in-

teract with all kinds of other children and discover what they have in common. That's essential because when we understand what we have in common, we believe in the common good—including constantly rededicating ourselves to the idea that *every* child should be included in education and *every* public school should be excellent. Whether you live in Manhattan or Mobile, Alabama, rural Idaho or suburban Illinois, your kids are supposed to get a great quality education at great public schools. Every child and every classroom is a building block for America's future. When we turn away from inclusive education, we abandon the essential ideals of our nation—of liberty and justice for all.

Lyndon Johnson once said that "education is the only valid passport from poverty." Three years after President Johnson signed the Civil Rights Act, and two years after the Voting Rights Act became law, the Reverend Dr. Martin Luther King Jr. wrote a book that asks a question as relevant then as it is today: *Where Do We Go from Here: Chaos or Community?* And King proposed an answer, that racism and injustice could never be solved "unless the whole of American society takes a new turn toward greater economic justice." "In a multiracial society," King explained, "no group can make it alone."

President Johnson shared a similar vision, which he called the "Great Society." "The Great Society," Johnson said, "rests on abundance and liberty for all. It demands an end to poverty and racial injustice, to which we are totally committed in our time. But that is just the beginning. The Great Society is a place where every child can find knowledge to enrich his mind and to enlarge his talents." Teachers are building that great society one classroom at a time. But we need help, and our students need help, yet fascist and authoritarian behaviors are making things even worse.

3

TEACHERS CREATE OPPORTUNITY

Since the civil rights movement, there has largely been a consensus—at least among mainstream leaders in both parties and the majority of Americans in general—that inclusive education and opportunity for all are inextricably linked. That means that in order to challenge racial and economic inequality and the effects of historical discrimination, we have to ensure that children of all races, all classes, all backgrounds have access to quality public schools so they can achieve the American dream. But sadly, far from challenging inequality, fascists and their far-right allies condone or even champion inequality. In this regard, American history is repeating itself, and not for the best. Today's attacks on public education are rooted in our nation's history of segregation.

Robert Russa Moton was a high school for Black students in Prince Edward County, Virginia, during the Jim Crow era of segregation in the United States. The law at the time said public education had to be provided to students of all races but at "separate but equal" schools. Of course, the "equal" part was just on paper. The main building of Robert Russa Moton High School was so overcrowded that the district built tar-paper shacks—basically, glorified chicken coops. Originally designed to hold 180 students, the school was bursting at the seams with over 470. The cooplike shacks "had no plumbing" and were heated with woodstoves. As one student at the school described it:

> These structures were cold and drafty and heated with pot-bellied stoves. The students who sat closer to the stove were too hot and the other students were too cold. During the winter, we often sat in class wearing our coats and boots to keep warm. When it rained, we helped our teachers place pails around the room to catch the water and, at times, opened our umbrellas. We moved our desks around so that water would not drip on our notebooks. We were not comfortable in our classrooms. This was not fair.

There was also "no dedicated gymnasium, no cafeteria, no science laboratories, and no athletic field."

In 1951, Barbara Johns was a sixteen-year-old student at Robert Russa Moton. And she had had enough of the unequal, unfair facilities. She knew she and her peers deserved better—deserved just as good an education, in good buildings, as the white students down the road. So several years before the Montgomery bus boycott and the Greensboro lunch counter sit-ins and the Selma voting rights march, in April 1951, Barbara led her fellow students in a walkout. But Barbara and her classmates weren't just fighting for a new school—they were taking on an entire system designed to deny them opportunity.

Barbara called the attorney for the Virginia NAACP, who said he would take the case if Barbara and other students agreed to sue not just for equal facilities but complete desegregation. Barbara's lawsuit was eventually folded in with several others to become the land-mark *Brown v. Board of Education* case in which the Supreme Court ruled, in 1954, that racial segregation in public schools was uncon-stitutional. But as we'll see, Barbara's story and the fight over school integration would continue.

Just so we're clear, in 1954, the Supreme Court—the highest court in the land—ordered schools nationwide to end racial segregation. But in reality, Prince Edward County actively resisted school inte-gration well into the early 1970s. Then, just like now, the far right has tried to defund and destroy public education because they don't believe in equality or opportunity for all.

OPPORTUNITY STARTS WITH PUBLIC SCHOOLS

Public school teachers know what Americans know—that for our economy to really work for everyone, we need to provide access to the skills, information, and education everyone needs to be able to fairly compete. And to enable fair competition, we need to ensure that schools level the playing field and foster opportunity for all. Yes, all parents want their children to learn how to get along with others and be good citizens, but what every parent hopes is that an educa-tion will help their children prepare for and succeed in their lives as adults. That's what public schools do. Our goal as public school teachers and support staff is to equip every single child with the skills and knowledge they need to thrive in our nation's economy and achieve their dreams.

Education democratizes opportunity. That is the main through-line of this book—that public education, democracy, and opportunity for all are inextricably intertwined and absolutely essential in the

United States of America. Public schools are the foundation of the American dream. Quality public education is the only way the kids of janitors have a shot at competing with the kids of CEOs. Fascists and oligarchs know this—which is why they are so keen on attacking teachers and destroying public schools.

Economist John N. Friedman has shown that twenty-five students having a great classroom teacher for just one year will increase their collective lifetime earnings by $1.25 million. But even in an economy that's often rigged for the rich, the effect of education is profound. For instance, the United Nations Educational, Scientific and Cultural Organization (UNESCO) has found that, worldwide, if students in low-income countries were simply equipped with basic reading skills, 171 million people could escape extreme poverty. With education, children from relatively poor families not only earn more than their own parents but earn more than "many of their peers with more advantaged family backgrounds who did not obtain equivalent education," finds Ron Haskins of the Brookings Institution. Still, Haskins notes, schools can and must do more to help poor and working-class students access opportunity. Friedman writes, "With the right level of investment, education can not only provide more pathways out of poverty for individuals, but also restore the equality of opportunity that is supposed to lie at America's core."

In 2011, President Barack Obama said, "A world-class education is the single most important factor in determining not just whether our kids can compete for the best jobs but whether America can outcompete countries around the world. America's business leaders understand that when it comes to education, we need to up our game. That's why we're working together to put an outstanding education within reach for every child." Competition works in the economy, but it doesn't work when we're talking about children. Our job is to prepare all kids to succeed. You see, the thing is, if I have twenty kids in my class and in the first grading period, ten of them get As and Bs but ten get Cs and Ds, as a teacher I still have an obligation to *all of them*. I have an obligation to help them all succeed. Capitalism produces winners and losers, but in public schools our job is to help every child win.

That's why it's important not just to understand education as a common good but a *public good*—available equally, to everyone, and financed by the public. "Access to education does not belong in the marketplace," writes Diane Ravitch. "Like police and fire protection, public parks, public highways, and clean air and water, public schools are public goods, funded by and belonging to the public." Inequality doesn't fix itself. In fact, if we don't prioritize equal opportunity through education and other public policies, inequality will just compound and worsen.

Just as the children of the super-rich shouldn't be the only ones who get clean air and clean water, they shouldn't be the only ones with access to a high-quality education. In fact, arguably it's even more important for poor and working-class and middle-class kids to get a great education, so that they have a shot at climbing the ladder of opportunity when their rich peers already start at the top rung.

And yet today, too many Americans—and a majority of young Americans—say that the American dream is out of reach. Without a level playing field, the American dream is an illusion—or, worse, a lie. Strengthening public education is one of the only vehicles we have to ensure that all children have the opportunity to thrive and achieve in America. A majority of voters and parents say that one of the most important goals for our public schools is to ensure that "all children, regardless of background, have opportunity to succeed." George Washington Carver was born enslaved and went on to become a professor and one of the most important scientists of the early twentieth century. He once wrote, "Education is the key to unlock the golden door of freedom." From college prep to apprenticeships to other career and technical pathways, public schools give every single American that key of opportunity.

But oligarchs and extremists do not believe in education for all. In fact, as we show below, many fight against the fundamental idea of education for all by privatizing public resources while questioning whether we should even have public schools. This is the agenda behind school vouchers—which take taxpayer funds away from public schools and give them to private schools.

FASCISTS OPPOSE BROAD-BASED OPPORTUNITY

The history of vouchers begins in the wake of the *Brown v. Board of Education* decision, right back in Prince Edward County. As historian Nancy MacLean writes, "In 1955 and 1956, conservative White leaders in Virginia devised a regionwide strategy of 'massive resistance' to the high court's desegregation mandate." And the centerpiece of that "massive resistance" strategy was giving taxpayer money to white families to subsidize the cost of segregated private schools—the birth of what are now called school vouchers.

In 1954, Gallup found that the majority of Americans—55 percent—supported the desegregation goals of the *Brown v. Board of Education* decision. This was the early days of the civil rights movement. The far right feared that support for integration would only grow. And so they decided to strategically exacerbate racial resentment, using America's public schools. Instead of embracing public schools as places where children go to learn together and build a shared future, the far right cast integration as a threat to white children and white well-being. "The mixing of races in the schools will mark the beginning of the end of civilization as we know it," South Carolina Governor James Byrnes declared in 1954. North Carolina judge I. Beverly Lake said, "If we must choose between a generation of inferior education and the amalgamation of our races into a mix-blooded whole, let us choose inferior education since that is an evil which another generation can correct, while miscegenation is a tragedy which can never be undone."

And so that's what the far right chose. When Prince Edward County, Virginia, was finally forced to integrate its schools in 1959— five years after the *Brown* ruling—the local government decided to shut down all of the county's schools instead of integrating. Local officials voted to cancel school taxes for the year and, instead, created a whites-only private school, similar to others popping up around the country, known as "segregation academies." At the same time, Virginia created a voucher program, giving taxpayer money to white students so they could attend the private segregation academies. Things went on like this in Prince Edward County until 1964, when yet another Supreme Court case forced the county to reopen its public schools. Even then, the county only allocated $189,000 to funding integrated public schools while it spent $375,000 on private school vouchers. This is the legacy of school vouchers. And the politicians and activists pushing for vouchers today are using the same playbook that segregationists did in the 1950s and 1960s—starve public schools and funnel public dollars into private hands.

From the very beginning, vouchers have been promoted by extremists who don't want the government to play any role in creating equal opportunity and just want to hoard their tax money. It was the prominent conservative economist Milton Friedman who, in

1955—the year after *Brown v. Board of Education* was decided—wrote a manifesto proposing school vouchers as a strategy for privatizing education. He saw the backlash to integration as an opening to push an extreme anti-government, anti–public school agenda. "In my ideal world," Friedman said in 2004, "government would not be responsible for providing education any more than it is for providing food and clothing." In 2006, Friedman would be even more explicit, advocating to "abolish the public school system and eliminate all the taxes that pay for it."

Friedman, notably, went on to confirm his fascist bona fides when he advised Chile's authoritarian military dictator Augusto Pinochet. He helped Pinochet institute universal school vouchers in Chile, which research shows was "largely found to have exacerbated inequality, reduced public school enrollment and [had] minimal to no impact on student achievement." Nevertheless, when Friedman died in 2006, the right-wing Heritage Foundation praised him as the "Father of Economic Freedom." The Heritage Foundation is also the institution that produced the Project 2025 playbook for Trump's second presidency, which calls for enacting universal school vouchers nationwide. To be clear, the privatization schemes Friedman pushed under Pinochet are the same ones Trump's allies want to impose on America today.

Today, those supporting school vouchers come from several camps. Some are without a doubt still avowed segregationists. They don't like the idea of their children "mixing" with diverse others, whether because of race or sexuality or who knows what. Then there are those who are simply wealthy elites who don't care about other people's children and just want to cut their own tax bills and shrink government in any way they can—who see vouchers as a shortcut to defunding public education or ending public schools altogether. The billionaire Koch family, for instance, have been among the leading proponents—and financial backers—of school vouchers in the United States. In 1980, David Koch ran for vice president on the Libertarian Party ticket by agreeing to bankroll the party. The Libertarian Party platform that year read:

> We advocate the complete separation of education and State. Government schools lead to the indoctrination of children and interfere with the free choice of individuals. Government ownership, operation, regulation and subsidy of schools and colleges should be ended.
>
> As an interim measure to encourage the growth of private schools and variety in education, we support tax-credits for tuition and other expenditures related to an individual's education.

The Koch/Libertarian Party platform spells it out loud and clear. Vouchers are a means to an end—the end of public education as we know it.

Then there are those motivated by religion, who don't want their children to attend secular schools that teach evolution instead of creationism or other biblical teachings. Many of these proponents are billionaires—showing how the motivations are all tangled up together—but education policy scholar Josh Cowen notes that these religious extremists believe deeply that "religious education is fundamental to their religious practice." For instance, billionaire Betsy DeVos is one of the nation's leading advocates and funders of the voucher movement and served as secretary of education in Donald Trump's first administration. In 2001, DeVos told a gathering of ultra-wealthy Christian conservatives, "Our desire is to ... confront the culture in which we all live today in ways that will continue to help advance God's kingdom." Her husband added that they have bankrolled the voucher movement because "the church—which ought to be in our view far more central to the life of the community—has been displaced by the public school." Instead, they bankroll the voucher movement so more children can attend religious schools so "more and more churches will get more and more active and engaged in education," leading to "greater Kingdom gain."

Amid these disparate motivations, the thing that unites the most vociferous backers of school vouchers is extreme wealth. The vast majority of families who receive taxpayer-subsidized vouchers were not enrolled in public school, but were rather homeschooled or already attending private school. In other words, despite the clever branding, vouchers don't give most families a "choice" but rather reimburse them for decisions they were already making—and affording—previously. And the majority of the families taking advantage of voucher tax credits earn over $200,000 per year, placing them among the top 10 percent of the wealthiest Americans. Which means that, in reality, vouchers don't give all families choices but merely reimburse wealthier parents for their preexisting decision to provide their children with a private education. In Texas, after legislators from rural and urban areas, both Democrats and Republicans, repeatedly defeated Republican Governor Greg Abbott's campaign for vouchers, billionaire donors backed Abbott's successful push to oust Republicans in the state legislature who rightfully said vouchers would harm their rural communities.

Vouchers are not a broad-based program. "This is, at the end of the day, about subsidizing private schools," says Cowen. Vouchers take money from shared, public schools and funnel them to wealthy, private interests. Alec MacGillis sums up:

The risks of universal vouchers are quickly coming to light. An initiative that was promoted for years as a civil-rights cause—helping poor kids in troubled schools—is threatening to become a nationwide money grab. Many private schools are raising tuition rates to take advantage of the new funding, and new schools are being founded to capitalize on it.

But also, writes MacGillis, the strategy to start with marketing to needy kids and then expand benefits to wealthy elites is part of a "decades-long effort by a network of politicians, church officials, and activists, all united by a conviction that the separation of church and state is illegitimate." Thus, billions in taxpayer dollars have been redirected from public schools mainly to private, religious education.

In order to funnel public money to private, religious schools, the far right has resorted to undermining and attacking the Constitution's separation of church and state, one of the most important freedoms in American society. For instance, Republican Congresswoman Lauren Boebert of Colorado once declared, "The church is supposed to direct the government. The government is not supposed to direct the church. That is not how our Founding Fathers intended it and I'm tired of this separation of church and state junk. That's not in the Constitution." She's wrong.

The very first section of the First Amendment to the Constitution reads, "Congress shall make no law respecting an establishment of religion, or prohibiting the free exercise thereof." Thomas Jefferson wrote that that clause amounted to an important "wall of separation between Church and State." That's because Jefferson and our other Founding Fathers wanted to prevent the government from inserting itself into religion and believed faith would thrive by being individually chosen rather than collectively enforced. They were right. Research has found that nations which officially establish and preferentially fund a dominant religion have substantially lower rates of engagement in that dominant religion compared to states without religious favoritism. Arguably, America has more churches than any other nation in the world not in spite of separation of church and state but because of it. As my wife, Rabbi Sharon Kleinbaum, and I wrote in an op-ed in 2024, "America has had a strong wall separating church and state for nearly 250 years. This wall has strengthened religion and the ability of public schools to help all children thrive."

Still, whatever the singular or mixed motives of voucher proponents, the end effect of vouchers is always the same—to funnel our shared taxpayer money toward elites and bankrupt public education. But voucher advocates have always understood they can't sell the idea of ending public school as we know it by handing over taxpayer money to private schools and elites. Thus voucher proponents pretend they want to "fix" public education by giving families a "choice." So, state by state, the first voucher programs they try are limited—*just* for poor kids or *just* for students with special needs. They cleverly frame vouchers as an equity tool for children and families who, to be sure, are most often being left behind by underfunded public schools. This is an Orwellian playbook the far right loves, like when they restrict voting rights and purge voting rolls claiming that they're "protecting democracy." You can almost count on the oligarchs and extremists to be doing the exact opposite of what they're claiming. Because once those narrow voucher programs get passed, voucher advocates then push to make them "universal"—so the taxpayer vouchers become open and available to all families. But the term "universal school vouchers" is really a misnomer. They only benefit a few wealthy families, while hurting everyone else and all public schools in general.

This is painfully clear from the example of Arizona. In 2006, the state passed a voucher program limited only to students with disabilities and students in foster care. These are among the kids who often struggle to get adequate support services when public schools are underfunded or lack specialty staff, so the appeal to families and the public in general seemed both compassionate and compelling. Plus voucher advocates could point to that narrow, initial version of the program to argue that vouchers didn't really hurt public school budgets. But then, year after year, Arizona expanded the program— to kids with military parents, kids attending schools classified as "failing." Finally, in 2017, having inoculated the public to the idea of vouchers, Arizona legislators made them "universal." Overnight, instead of a couple thousand students being eligible, 1.6 million Arizona students could get vouchers. In 2018, 65 percent of Arizonans voted in a ballot measure to repeal the universal voucher legislation. Nevertheless, Republicans ignored the will of the people and kept trying to expand vouchers over and over, finally instituting a universal voucher program statewide in 2022.

But what we know now is that Arizona's "universal voucher program" does not benefit all Arizona students. Three out of four students who receive taxpayer-funded school vouchers were already attending private school before they got their vouchers. In other words, those students' families could already afford private school without taking taxpayer money away from public education. Not surprisingly, the majority of voucher money goes to the wealthiest zip codes in the state. Meanwhile, in 2024, Arizona faced a massive budget "meltdown"—a $1.4 billion budget shortfall that nonpartisan researchers attributed mostly to voucher spending. When the far right says they want "school choice," what they really mean is "no choice but bankruptcy." Meanwhile most parents don't really get to choose; it's the private schools that ultimately get to pick and choose which kids they accept.

Vouchers are not a strategy to fix public education. "Voucher programs have been in place for more than three decades," reports Diane Ravitch, "and they have not produced academic gains for students who use public money to transfer from public to private schools; recent studies of vouchers in Louisiana, Washington D.C., Indiana, and Ohio consistently show that, if anything, such students often lose ground academically." Vouchers are a strategy to end public education.

"This is the goal of the privatizers," writes Ravitch: "Starve public schools." The agenda is simple, Ravitch continues: "Everyone gets a voucher and public schools go away." Nationwide, while state funding over the last decade increased by just 1 percent per year after adjusting for inflation, state spending on tax breaks and subsidies for private schools increased by 408 percent, or $7 billion. The wealthy don't want to share opportunity—they want to hoard opportunity by funneling money into private education that benefits their own children and no one else.

And yet, despite the constant drumbeat from the right and massive backing from wealthy donors, school vouchers have been rejected by voters every time they've ever been on a ballot. In 2024, even with President Trump winning a resounding victory, voucher measures on the ballot failed in Kentucky, Nebraska, and Colorado—by wide margins. Even the reddest county in Nebraska—which voted 95 percent for Donald Trump—voted against vouchers. Because red, blue, and in between, the American people know what teachers know—that when we strengthen public schools, we strengthen opportunity for all.

THE BATTLE TO CREATE OPPORTUNITY FOR ALL

For some students, the path of opportunity runs through college—and great public schools prepare their students to get into college and succeed once they're there. But for many students, creating opportunity means building the skills they need to join the workforce right after high school, whether as licensed health care workers, mechanics, graphic designers, or entrepreneurs. That's why my union has pushed and prodded public schools across the country to invest in career and technical education, apprenticeships, stackable credentials, and other job readiness training for high school students. The hands-on learning of career and technical education builds critical thinking skills in an applied, safe, goal-oriented environment. Because, yes, kids need to learn John Locke and Shakespeare, but they also need practical career-oriented skills for the future. While billionaires push privatization, teachers are building real pathways to economic mobility through career and technical education.

And parents want more non-college pathways for their students, particularly since about two out of five high school graduates don't go on to college. Families with children in career and technical education programs are even more satisfied than other families with the education system. Plus students who participate in career and technical education programs have higher rates of graduation and earn higher wages in adulthood. Investor and economic analyst Steve Rattner notes, "The number of Americans earning more than their parents has been steadily decreasing over the past 80 years." Which makes it even more important to follow the research showing that students who don't go on to college can have great professional careers—with strong wages—if they have the right technical training and job experience early on. And in the digital and AI era, it turns out that career and technical education can help lead to long-term, secure jobs. That's why the overwhelming majority of Americans—82 percent of voters—agree that the government should increase funding for skills training in our nation.

Yet in 2022, the federal, state, and local governments spent 775 times more supporting colleges and universities than career and technical education apprenticeship programs. Our nation desperately needs to expand domestic manufacturing to compete with the rest of the world. The Biden administration's CHIPS and Science Act put $280 billion in funding for new domestic manufacturing of semiconductors in the United States, and we need the science, technology, engineering, and mathematics (STEM) workforce that will drive the industry. That's where career and technical education comes in.

Just one example of innovation in career and technical education can be found in Peoria, Illinois—a struggling city that has historically represented so much of the Midwestern Rust Belt's economic promise and peril. For over a hundred years, the construction equipment manufacturer Caterpillar has been manufacturing tractors in Peoria, and still makes its large track-type tractors there today. In recent years, the city has worked hard to diversify its economy and bring in tech start-ups and other new industries. But people kept leaving Peoria, moving elsewhere for opportunity. The city's career and technical schools would complain that there weren't jobs for their students when they graduated. But at the same time, businesses in Peoria complained they couldn't find enough qualified workers to fill jobs. How was that possible?

Jeff Adkins-Dutro, the president of the AFT local union in Peoria, realized the problem was that schools and businesses weren't communicating and coordinating their needs. So Jeff brought together business leaders and school leaders, along with other community figures in Peoria, to create an integrated "Pathways to Prosperity" plan to make sure that the career and technical education offerings in the school district would more directly support the skills and labor needs of businesses in the community. For instance, Jeff collaborated with business leaders and the local government to align career pathway courses and create a robust internship program for students to get hands-on experience. In the 2016–2017 school year alone, the Pathways to Prosperity project created over four hundred internships and job placement opportunities in fields ranging from manufacturing to health services to city government. Our union nationally gave financial assistance to the project through our AFT Innovation Fund, which made it possible for Pathways to Prosperity to hire a staff person to coordinate the program and keep it going.

Peoria student Kianna Pittman was worried about finding a job when she graduated. But a career and technical education class her senior year changed everything:

One day we visited Alcast Company, which manufactures aluminum castings. The plant's five buildings include a computer numerical control machine shop and a foundry, where metal is melted into giant hot pools and molded into castings for parts supplied to customers like Caterpillar and Amazon. There's also a core building, where workers make the sand cores that fit inside the metal molds, and a finishing building, where the parts are sanded or grinded down until they're perfect and ready for shipping. And then there's the maintenance department, with technicians who are trained to maintain and repair all the plant's machines. Everything I saw was so cool. I knew immediately that I needed to work there.

Not only did Kianna get a job at the Alcast plant, but the company paid for her associate's degree in industrial applied sciences. That's a lot of work, plus school—often leading to eleven- or even fourteen-hour days. But Kianna loves what she's doing. Kianna is such a great example of the Pathways to Prosperity program's success that she was recently asked to speak at the year-end dinner for the Woodruff Career and Technical Center that she attended. Kianna talked about how career and technical education "shows you what's possible and gives you the skills to create a great future for yourself."

In central New York State, Micron is building a 2.4-million-square-foot semiconductor manufacturing plant that will bring fifty thousand jobs to the region. With the state government and our affiliates in New York State and New York City, AFT and Micron have created a pilot program in ten school districts that will prepare middle school and high school students for these high-tech jobs. The program includes hands-on learning as well as an emphasis in critical thinking and problem-solving skills, which are as important for technology as they are for democracy. And in Syracuse, New York, Micron and the Governor Kathy Hochul combined $74 million in joint funding to build a brand-new science, technology, engineering, arts, and math (STEAM) high school—the first county-wide STEAM high school in the state.

In the Cleveland Metropolitan School District, the Lincoln-West School of Science and Health is based within the MetroHealth hospital, creating incredibly unique hands-on learning for students studying for careers in health care. In addition to their more traditional high school courses, students learn advanced health care protocols like CPR and defibrillator use and eventually complete an internship working in the hospital. Students are assigned mentors and attend presentations by different hospital network professionals to learn more about all of the career possibilities in health care. And juniors and seniors can enroll in an accelerated credential program to be certified as state-tested nursing assistants while still in high school. As Lincoln-West principal Juliet King puts it, "We are building a school-to-workforce pipeline." Other nations are ahead of the curve in building technical training programs through public-private partnerships. In Switzerland, for instance, nearly two out of three young Swiss students between the ages of sixteen and eighteen participate in combined vocational and educational training. Swiss employers invest heavily in apprenticeship curriculum development to make sure that the training programs match workplace needs. And it pays off. According to the Urban Institute, "Most Swiss employers recoup their investments *during* the apprenticeship." This overall investment in a strong vocational and technical education program may help explain why Switzerland has one of the highest per capita GDPs in Europe as well as one of the lowest rates of unemployment.

Here in the United States, more than eight out of ten voters across the political spectrum support increasing government funding for skills training. And it was encouraging that Trump's current Education Secretary in his second term, Linda McMahon, said during her confirmation hearings that vocational and technical education should be "front and center"—that our country needs "more post-secondary pathways, career-aligned programs, apprenticeships and on-the-job learning." I agree. And this could have been a great opportunity to work together. But, as Mark Lieberman and Brooke Schultz of *Education Week* explain, some of the Trump administration's cuts to the U.S. Department of Education "have contradicted the Trump administration's stated priorities, such as the slashed research funding for studies on career and technical education, which presumptive Education Secretary Linda McMahon has emphasized. DOGE axed the first congressionally mandated national survey of CTE programs in a decade." In fact, the Association for Career and Technical Education (ACTE), a membership group of CTE educators, said that the Trump education funding cuts "run counter to" the goal of creating "access to high-quality CTE programs and related opportunities."

While fascists want to break public education, break our economy, and break the American dream, teachers want to work with parents, communities, and businesses to build the future. In school districts across the country, teachers are engaging students who might otherwise check out of classes or school altogether through providing real-world, applied learning opportunities and training. And teachers are working with CEOs, chambers of commerce, Republican and Democratic mayors, parents, and whole communities to strengthen pathways of opportunity for all. Because opportunity for all is possible when every child has access to a high-quality public school.

MONEY MATTERS

Imagine the difference it would make for America's children if we did everything we do in our best schools in every school nationwide. That requires not only best practices but something our country has never done—summoning the will to adequately fund all schools. And that's made extra challenging by the fact that public schools in our country receive a significant share of their funding—more than four out of every ten dollars on average—from local taxes. Local funding for public education means that wealth and income inequalities between communities shape inequalities in schools.

For instance, Panther Valley School District in Pennsylvania spends $10,313 per pupil per year, while New Hope-Solebury—less than two hours' drive away—spends $28,437. That's because the average income in Panther Valley is $42,433 while the average income in New Hope-Solebury is $154,229. Those kids in Panther Valley are undoubtedly super hardworking and bright and have passionate teachers who really believe in them—but how are they supposed to have the same access to opportunity as the kids in New Hope-Solebury at schools with more than twice the resources? Especially when the kids from New Hope-Solebury are mostly starting off a few rungs up the ladder of opportunity with wealthy, connected families who can afford tutors and extracurricular activities and all other sorts of added advantages.

Nationwide, we see how schools are disproportionately impacted by the differences between funding streams. Black students are three and a half times more likely to live in school districts that are "chronically underfunded." Rural schools are also often underfunded and have lower average teacher pay, both of which contribute to achievement gaps. This is one big reason why federal government funding appropriated by Congress and distributed by the Department of Education is so critical—because these funds go to help address funding gaps and thus level the playing field for these students. A child's potential in life should not be bound by demography or geography. And to be clear, these disparities don't just reflect a wealth gap— they reflect a policy choice. We could fund every school equitably and adequately tomorrow if politicians wanted to. And if the far right and oligarchs weren't doing everything they could to stop it.

I often think of a story education scholar and writer Jonathan Kozol tells. He'll be talking about education reform at a fancy dinner party in New York City and the people around the table will invariably ask if more money is really the way to fix public schools. Dripping with sarcasm, Kozol then points out that the very same people asking that question are often paying gobs of money to send their own children to private schools because, presumably, they do in fact think that more spending means better education.

The fact is, money matters. One study found that when a district increases per-pupil spending by 10 percent, high school graduation rates rise by 7 percent and average wages for students once they enter the workforce also go up 7 percent. And a study of ten thousand school districts found that when schools pay teachers more, they attract more experienced teachers and have better retention and better morale—and student achievement goes up, too. In fact, economist Eric Hanushek spent decades arguing that spending more money on schools wouldn't make them better until, after a comprehensive review of dozens of studies, he realized he was wrong and changed his tune.

And yet the average starting salary for teachers in the United

States was $44,530 during the 2022–2023 school year—which is *below* the annual mean wage for all workers in the United States in 2023, including for jobs that don't require college degrees and years of training and certification. That pay gap has been worsening. According to the Center for Economic and Policy Research and the Economic Policy Institute, in 1996, teachers earned on average 6 percent less than comparable workers when adjusting for education, experience, and demography. As of 2023, that pay gap had mushroomed to 26 percent. Now imagine how much worse it would be if teachers didn't have a union. If our nation wants great schools, it needs to pay a salary that attracts and retains great teachers.

But attacks on teacher integrity on top of low pay and poor conditions have led to more and more teachers leaving the profession—or not joining the profession to begin with. Once upon a time, 75 percent of parents said they would want their children to become teachers. Today, it's only 37 percent—mainly citing poor pay and benefits, the stresses and demands of the job, and lack of respect or being undervalued. Between the 2010–2011 school year and 2020–2021, enrollment in teacher training programs has declined by 45 percent, leading to three hundred thousand fewer trained teachers annually than before. Teacher vacancies in the country have reached crisis-level proportions. In response, districts are hiring more uncertified teachers, which harms student outcomes.

An AFT task force I convened to study and respond to teacher vacancies found record low job satisfaction ratings for many school personnel and almost 80 percent of teachers dissatisfied with their current working conditions. Meanwhile, because of the shortages, school districts have filled posts with an estimated 270,000 underqualified teachers nationwide. We'll learn in the next chapter why teachers form unions to fight for better wages and better working conditions, but these are the sorts of challenges we're up against every single day when anti-government extremists and oligarchs continually push to cut government programs on which ordinary Americans rely.

Yet the fact remains that our nation has some incredible public schools. More often than not, they're in incredibly wealthy communities. My friend Lily Eskelsen García, former president of the National Education Association, often said we should use those excellent, well-funded public schools as "living models." Instead of pilot project after pilot project and accountability metric after accountability metric trying things to "fix" poor schools that no wealthy community would ever stand for, Lily threw down the gauntlet. "No more experimenting on our most disadvantaged kids," she said. "What works with our most advantaged kids is exactly what will work with every kid: Equal access. Equal opportunity. Equal respect."

"Public education is not broken," writes Diane Ravitch. "It is not failing or declining. The diagnosis is wrong, and the solutions of the corporate reformers are wrong. Our urban schools are in trouble because of concentrated poverty and racial segregation. But public education as such is not 'broken.'" Yet there are certainly people trying to break it.

Senator Bernie Sanders is correct when he says, "Over the past decade, there has been a coordinated effort on the part of right-wing billionaires to undermine, dismantle and sabotage our nation's public schools and to privatize our education system." And they're not shy about it. Billionaire Vivek Ramaswamy, an ally and once-appointee of Donald Trump has said, "I favor school choice on steroids. . . . Starve the bureaucracy in those broken public schools."

What happens to the children whose families can't afford private schools even with vouchers, or who don't have private schools in their communities, or who need special education services that private schools refuse to provide? The billionaires don't really seem to care.

Billionaires pushing privatization don't care about the well-being of children; they care about their wealth and the workforce needs of their profit engines and little more. In their book *A Wolf at the Schoolhouse Door: The Dismantling of Public Education and the Future of School*, Jack Schneider and Jennifer Berkshire elaborate: "What good is it to Walmart or Amazon if their employees read poetry in their spare time or understand American history? What use is it for the affluent class if lower- and middle-income earners can paint or play an instrument?" The point, they explain, is, "Give the public whatever minimal education is necessary, but no more." Billionaires want lower school taxes—as if they need more money—and they want the masses to be just educated enough to work for them, but not so educated that they feel empowered to demand change.

Extremists pushing vouchers don't care about your kids, your schools, or your communities. In stark contrast, teachers believe in all children and want to build a ladder of opportunity for everyone. Public school teachers fight every single day to help every child—and fight for the funding schools need so all students can get ahead. And the good news is if we stop funneling resources to private school vouchers and instead focus on funding all public schools adequately, we can make opportunity more equitable, too. When we invest in public education and support public school teachers, we strengthen opportunity for all.

WHERE CHARTER SCHOOLS FACTOR IN

As we've seen, the history of school vouchers is inextricably tied to efforts to undermine integrated, equitable, quality public schools for all. The history of charter schools, on the other hand, is more complex.

Charter schools are quasi-public schools that operate with taxpayer money and are tuition-free for students, but operate outside of the traditional administration and oversight systems of public schools. At their best, charter schools are a way for local governments and nonprofits to experiment—like laboratories of innovation that try out new models and methods that might eventually be applied to and improve public schools more broadly. But at their worst, charter schools are rife with corruption, push a privatization mindset, and don't actually produce better educational outcomes.

The push for charter schools is a hallmark of neoliberalism—which argues the free market is better at doing everything, including running public services like education. The argument is that if schools are run like businesses, they'll supposedly introduce "competition" into the "marketplace" of public education while mandating "efficiencies" like circumventing teachers' unions and standards to which public schools are held. Charter schools have all the privileges of public schools—namely, the taxpayer funding—but few laws require any accountability. Many charter schools are free to pick whichever students they want, teach whatever they want to teach, and hire and fire teachers as they see fit, ignoring requirements about teacher qualifications and training. In theory, a free market approach might seem alluring. But the model can be—and often is—abused. Research shows that charter schools continue to under-enroll special needs students, for instance—which isn't surprising when you realize that "efficiency" means refusing students whose learning needs are harder and more expensive.

Now, like Al Shanker, I thought we should not simply reject charter schools—that they could be an important vehicle for innovation. In fact, in 2008, when I was the president of the United Federation of Teachers in New York City, I cofounded a charter school in the Bronx to see if we could use the laboratory of education model in partnership with unionized teachers, as opposed to opposition. It remains among one of the most effective charter schools in the Bronx. So I don't remotely think the idea of charter schools is inherently bad. But what I do believe is that the private market model is not inherently better when it comes to education. We've known for years that when you control for differences in socioeconomic status, private schools aren't any better at educating children than public schools. And a 2016 internal audit by the federal Department of Education at the end of the Obama administration—which aggressively pushed an expansion of charter schools in the neoliberal model—found that the lack of accountability posed a serious "risk of waste, fraud, and abuse."

For instance, in Pennsylvania, "cyber charter schools" have taken about $1 billion per year from local public schools. The state's push toward charter schools has exacerbated a dynamic where public schools statewide are severely underfunded by $6.2 billion but charter schools in Pennsylvania are often running a surplus, which is tantamount to profit. In the case of cyber charter schools— virtual-only "schools" that you'd think we all learned are bad ideas during the pandemic—in some cases, their budgets have grown by 92,000 percent. And what do they spend it on? Well, according to one investigative report, Pennsylvania's cyber charter schools spent

$21 million in one school year alone on advertising and gift cards. One cyber schools company accumulated $88 million in real estate—purchased with taxpayer money—including several parking lots and an old Macy's that don't seem remotely related to the business of trying to teach children online. Of course, if a public school mismanaged money like this, the privatization crowd would immediately demand its closure. But when charters do it, they call it "innovation."

But students must have learned more at these "innovative" schools, right? Wrong. At one of these schools, PA Cyber, only 31 percent of students scored proficient or better in English language arts assessments, compared with 55 percent of students statewide. And only 13 percent of PA Cyber students were proficient in math, compared to 38 percent statewide.

Why? When you make schools like businesses, you make profit the goal—not education. Those cyber charter schools are spending millions on gift cards to lure parents to enroll their kids not because it's good for their kids but because the charter schools get more taxpayer money the more students enroll. And they could spend that money on making their educational experience better but they don't because that's not their goal. Their goal is profit.

Plus, unlike public schools that serve all students, charter schools get to pick and choose. In the wake of Hurricane Katrina, corporate opportunists turned New Orleans's entire education system into charter schools and were quickly sued by parents and the Southern Poverty Law Center for not admitting and providing services for students with special needs. The lawsuit led to an independent oversight monitor being put in place. Meanwhile, 54 percent of New Orleans schools earned D or F ratings in 2022. Schools that "failed" were routinely closed—meant to punish teachers and administrators, but it's really the upended students who suffer. When a school isn't working, you don't close it, you fix it—because those children and communities rely on it working. Recognizing this, in 2024, New Orleans began slowly restoring its public school system. In the fall of 2024, a brand-new pre-K-through-eighth-grade public school opened, welcoming three hundred bright and excited students into a building vacated by a charter school that closed.

Let's be clear—the model of pure hypercompetitive capitalism isn't just a problem for schools but for communities as a whole. In New Orleans and across the United States, thirty-nine million Americans—more than one out of every ten people—live in "food deserts" where they are at least a mile from a grocery store, because private companies have determined those communities aren't worth serving. Unfortunately, we also have opportunity deserts in our country, whole neighborhoods and communities that private industry, private housing developers, and private schools have written off. Capitalism produces great wealth but also staggering poverty. According to U.S. Census data, the percent of children living in poverty more than doubled from 5.2 percent in 2021 to 12.4 percent in 2022. More than one in ten Americans currently lives in poverty. And the share of Americans in the middle class has shrunk over the last ten decades. We can't put millionaires and billionaires in charge of designing an education system that works for all. They'll only keep systems that work for themselves—and then, as soon as they can, replace us all with as much artificial intelligence as they can get away with.

The answer isn't to make public education more like capitalism—making children compete in an extreme, cutthroat, winners-versus-losers framework. Nor is the answer to privatize public schools and cut education spending, which only helps billionaires and tech entrepreneurs who want to operate with no regulations or guardrails and want their taxes slashed. The answer is to work to make sure all children have a fair shot at success. Privatization builds consumers. Public schools build citizens. That is, of course, why oligarchs and fascists want to destroy them—and precisely why it is essential that we have *public* schools.

OPPORTUNITY FOR ALL

Despite the aggressive expansion of vouchers and charter schools, American families remain overwhelmingly committed to their local public schools. An overwhelming majority of American parents report they're happy with their children's public schools. And in states like Ohio which was early in the push for vouchers, as of 2021, only 2 percent of the state's 1.7 million students use vouchers and 6 percent are enrolled in charter schools, "most of which are rated D or F by the state," reports Diane Ravitch. Public education remains America's opportunity engine, and America's families continue to believe in—and support—public schools.

Two decades after *Brown v. Board of Education*, the Supreme Court was asked to address inequality and segregation in schools that resulted not from explicit policies but because communities remained unequal and divided. The court ruled in *Milliken v. Bradley* that districts weren't required to address this more insidious, widespread de facto discrimination.

Justice Thurgood Marshall, the first African American judge appointed to the Supreme Court, wrote a stinging dissent to the *Milliken* case, stating that "the very evil that *Brown I* was aimed at will not be cured but will be perpetuated." Marshall, who had been one of the NAACP attorneys who litigated the *Brown* case, added a stark warning: "Our nation, I fear, will be ill-served by the Court's refusal to remedy separate and unequal education, for unless our children begin to learn together, there is little hope that our people will ever learn to live together." Teachers know there cannot be equal opportunity for all without equal access to quality, public education. Just like there cannot be democracy without integration. The American dream isn't a private commodity. It should never be apportioned based on skin color or wealth or religious faith. In the United States of America, we remain committed to the universal ideal that everyone deserves access to education because everyone deserves access to opportunity.

I'm proud that our union has always stood on the side of equal opportunity for all. In 1951, we became the first union to stop giving membership to segregated locals. And in 1957, we expelled locals that refused to desegregate. And when Prince Edward County's segregationists shuttered the public schools, gave private school vouchers to white students, and left Black students without schools, our union also stepped up. In the summer of 1963, local Black community leaders in Prince Edward County worked with the AFT to bring educators from the North down to Virginia to run free schools for the county's Black students. In fact, these schools were one of the inspirations for the freedom schools that were part of the civil rights movement's Freedom Summer in Mississippi a year later in 1964. Many of the same AFT members went on to teach in those freedom schools, too. And today, AFT members continue to work tirelessly, day in and day out, to improve our public schools as engines of opportunity for all.

Barbara Johns—the student who started the protests at Robert Russa Moton High School—never got to study at an integrated school in Prince Edward County. Following the *Brown v. Board of Education* lawsuit, she received so many death threats—including the Ku Klux Klan burning a cross in her yard—that her parents sent her to live with relatives in Alabama. And after college, Barbara settled down in Philadelphia. And do you know what profession she chose? She became a teacher, working as a librarian in the city's public schools.

4

TEACHERS BUILD
STRONG UNIONS

Karen Lewis was born into a family of teachers on Chicago's South Side. Early on she understood the promise of education, but also the challenges. She went to Dartmouth College the year it finally admitted women, becoming one of the last Ivy League schools to do so, and she was the only Black woman in the class of 1974. Karen loved chemistry and went to medical school, planning to become a doctor. But when she realized she "hated medical school," she went into teaching instead "and fell madly, passionately in love with it."

But it wasn't until she served on a local school council that Karen got involved in labor organizing. During her time on the school council, she witnessed a principal use his power to enrich his friends. Karen said, "That got me involved with the union, which I saw as the only protection against unfairness." She understood that it isn't one leader who makes a movement, it takes all of us working together. Teachers, families, and communities make a movement.

In 2010, Karen was elected to lead the Chicago Teachers Union

(CTU), representing tens of thousands of teachers in one of the country's most complicated school districts in one of our nation's most complicated cities. In the 1960s, as the city's Black community grew, the Chicago school superintendent made waves when he erected portable buildings to address overcrowding in segregated Black schools rather than enroll those students in white schools nearby. In 1979, mismanagement led to multiple missed paydays when the district literally ran out of money. In 1995, the Republican state legislature voted for mayoral control of the city's schools, unleashing "an era of school reform focused on accountability, high stakes testing, austere budgets, and zero tolerance policies." The act also severely limited the collective bargaining rights of the city's teachers.

Jan Resseger, former chair of the National Council of Churches Committee on Public Education, explains that the city established multiple privatized charter schools and then managed the district "like a stock portfolio—phasing out weak schools and schools that would become under-enrolled due to competition. The school district would keep on authorizing new charter schools to keep marketplace competition alive." It made schools into winners and losers by design, and the losing schools were always those serving communities with high concentrations of poverty, with the greatest challenges. In many cases, the schools were the one public institution of any real substance in a community, and Chicago Public Schools would come in and close them down, replacing them with charters in which the community, parents, and educators had no voice.

But the expansion of privatized charter schools accelerated under-enrollment in public schools in poor neighborhoods, and subsequently fifty "under-enrolled" schools on Chicago's South and West Sides were closed. The closures affected twenty-nine thousand students and eleven hundred staff. In 2015, twelve parents and education advocates held a thirty-four-day hunger strike to protest the shuttering of Dyett High School in Chicago's Bronzeville neighborhood. They won and the city agreed to reopen the school with $14.6 million in renovations. "We're tired of our children and our communities being demonized and being blamed for being underserved," said Jitu Brown, one of the leaders of the hunger strike.

Meanwhile, Chicago became ground zero for new "accountability standards" that measured student and teacher performance by test scores. But measuring student and teacher performance by scores on standardized tests merely forced teachers to teach to the test instead of actually changing the social, economic, and structural dynamics that improve educational outcomes. The result was that when Karen Lewis was elected head of the Chicago Teachers Union in 2010, Chicago's public schools—and most importantly, Chicago's public school students—were still struggling. That year, the graduation rate for the city's high schools was just 55 percent. Many other cities were struggling with similar challenges around their schools. But it was Karen Lewis who was the catalyzing force in a groundbreaking campaign not only to transform the trajectory of Chicago's public schools but to set a new tone nationwide.

What made Karen Lewis dangerous to the far right was that she didn't just want better wages for teachers—she wanted to transform the entire system for the better. She saw that public schools couldn't improve unless communities were strengthened, too. So she fought not just for teachers, but for housing, health care, and inclusion. Karen drew on and expanded a model of community-oriented unionism called "Bargaining for the Common Good"— bargaining not only around teachers' salaries and benefits but putting community-wide demands on the negotiating table.

Bear in mind, in 2012, 86 percent of Chicago public school students came from low-income families. Over ten thousand of the
district's students were homeless. As we discussed before, it's hard
for those children to walk into a classroom ready to learn and
achieve at the same level as their well-off peers. And just holding
teachers and young people to test-based standards isn't going to
change that—it's just going to lead to poor schools having even fewer
teachers. Karen understood that what was at stake was much bigger
than a contract fight. It was a power struggle over the future of public education.

As we explored in chapter 2, one thing that strengthens public
schools and communities as a whole is the community schools
model, including more classroom supports and wraparound services. That's why in their negotiation with the city in 2012, Karen
and her members were pushing not only for smaller class sizes and a
nurse and social worker in every school but for more resources to
help marginalized students, restorative justice programs that would
direct kids in crisis to counseling rather than the criminal justice
system, and city investments in housing to address the crisis facing
homeless students. And the union also pushed to end school privatization and stop the drastic budget cuts that were hurting working
families across Chicago. According to the Chicago Teachers Union,
the city's efforts to privatize Chicago's public schools and impose
standardized testing would "cheapen" the district and hurt the already struggling district by leading to teacher layoffs. The real answer was necessary investments to support struggling students.

In the private sector, when a union is bargaining a contract in a
contentious environment, it may decide to hold a vote to authorize a
strike. The right of private-sector workers to strike is protected under the National Labor Relations Act. But there is currently no fed-

eral law that protects the right of public-sector workers to strike, or even to collectively bargain, for that matter. Those rights are governed by a patchwork of state laws. So, for instance, in states like Illinois and California, public employees can form unions and decide to strike. In states like New York and Rhode Island, they can organize and collectively bargain but are prohibited from striking. And, as we'll see, in states like Wisconsin the right to organize has been severely restricted. In Texas, the right to collectively bargain is prohibited for all workers except police and firefighters. And just as the far right has undermined public education, they continue to try to erode the rights of workers to have a union or a voice at work. In the first few months of 2025 alone, Utah banned collective bargaining for public employees, including teachers, and legislators in states including South Dakota and Kentucky have advanced legislation that would further weaken their already weak labor rights. And in March 2025, President Trump signed an executive order undermining the collective bargaining rights of many federal workers.

Even when it's allowed under law, a strike isn't something to be undertaken lightly. And in the years leading up to 2012, labor strikes in the United States were relatively uncommon. In fact, nationwide, 2009 saw just five major strikes—the fewest number since the federal Bureau of Labor Statistics began tracking them. By September 2012, when the Chicago Teachers Union was weighing a strike, Chicago hadn't seen a labor strike in a quarter century.

Then–Chicago Mayor Rahm Emanuel got a new anti-union law passed requiring that, in order for the union's collective bargaining team to call for a strike, 75 percent of CTU's members had to approve the strike authorization. What was Karen Lewis's response? She told her members, "Brothers and sisters, if we don't have 75 percent of our members in favor of a strike, we shouldn't strike. A strike is not something you do lightly." When they finally had the vote, 90 percent of CTU members voted to authorize the strike.

For nine months leading up to the strike, Karen and her members worked tirelessly, going back and forth with the city and school management on a number of details pending in the contract, which also required complex state law to be taken into account. But when Karen and her union decided to strike, wages were not the only issue. The teachers went on strike because of the overemphasis on standardized tests that wouldn't actually measure student progress or help students achieve but only lead to 28 percent of teachers in the district losing their jobs as the systematic privatization of the district increased.

Remember, Chicago had become a testing ground for billionaire donors and some corporate-minded Democrats who wanted to introduce market-based competition to "reform" public education. Arne Duncan is a prime example. Now, Duncan seemed to genuinely want to help Chicago schools. He was born and raised in the city, his mom an educator who ran an after-school program for low-income Black students, a program Duncan worked at early in his career. But somewhere along the way, he bought into the idea that public schools would miraculously work better if they were run like corporations. Before Duncan was secretary of education for President Barack Obama, he was head of Chicago Public Schools. As Chicago education organizer Jitu Brown and education professors Eric Gutstein and Pauline Lipman write, Duncan was "the central messenger, manager, and staunch defender of corporate involvement in, and privatization of, public schools, closing schools in low-income neighborhoods of color with little community input, limiting local democratic control, undermining the teachers union, and promoting competitive merit pay for teachers." And he helped make Chicago "the incubator, test case and model for the neoliberal urban education agenda," explains Lipman.

The 2012 Chicago teachers' strike, writes William O'Keefe of the Illinois Policy Institute, "not only marked a pivotal moment for Chicago but also ignited a nationwide labor movement." "The strike was the first teacher work stoppage directly related to the unfair effects of corporate school policy," notes Kurt Hilgendorf of the Chicago Teachers Union. Reports Chicago Teachers Union Vice President Jackson Potter, "After facing 30 years of corporate education 'reform' that demonized teachers and led to massive privatization of public schools across the United States, teachers everywhere were ready to fight back."

What the city government didn't count on was that, hard though it was to have schools closed for seven days, polls showed the Chicago community supported the teachers in the strike. Parents joined teachers on the picket line, often bringing their kids. After all, parents knew that Karen and the Chicago Teachers Union were fighting for their students—which is why so many parents supported the strike. "I'm going to stay strong, behind the teachers," said one parent who joined the picket line with teachers. "My son says he's proud, 'You are supporting my teacher.'" As one striking teacher explained, "I am protesting because teachers have not been included in school reform talks, and sadly the only way to get our voices heard has been to strike. In the long run it will hurt our students more to give up this fight." Another teacher recounted a sign she saw on the picket lines that said, "Together we bargain—alone we beg." That's the power of unions.

The strike worked. According to Kurt Hilgendorf of the Chicago Teachers Union, "the strike and the resulting contract were clear victories for teachers and students." For instance, the union secured important pay raises, won commitments to hire additional teachers, and limited the impact of standardized testing.

Plus the Chicago Teachers Union inspired communities across the country to fight against corporate reform-oriented "austerity" budget cuts and privatization and, instead, advocate for community schools programs. Fed up with attacks on public schools and public school teachers, unions and communities joined together to demand more for our students, our teachers, and our schools. Strikes and protests erupted not only in reliably blue cities like Los Angeles, Oakland, and Denver but in red states like West Virginia, Oklahoma, and Arizona. Teachers, parents, and students showing up to protest wore red, hence the nickname for the movement, "Red for Ed." After decades of the far right dramatically underfunding schools, pushing privatization, and demonizing teachers—not to mention corporate Democrats often doing the same—parents, teachers, and communities across the nation were joining together to fight for the common good. Because that's what unions do. Just like teachers fight for what students need, unions fight for what communities need. And we all do better when *we all do better*.

WHY FASCISTS ATTACK UNIONS

Why do oligarchs, autocrats, and the far right hate unions so much? And what are the lengths they go to and strategies they use to try to undermine unions? To understand that, it's important to first understand how unions work.

On the one hand, they're like any other membership organization that people join because of shared interests. If you care about the environment and want more green space in your community, you might join a garden club or local environmental group. Well, if you care about your job and want to make sure you and other workers are treated fairly at work, you start a union or join one that already exists.

But unions have power that few other organizations do because, legally, they can represent groups of members in a workplace and bargain on behalf of those workers over the terms and conditions of work. And the right to do so—the right to form a union and collectively bargain with other workers—is protected under a mix of federal and state laws.

Unions are also unique in that they are democratic organizations. Each is organized differently depending on its constitution and bylaws, but in the AFT, we have chapters called "locals." They're basically organized around the employer that members work for. So, for instance, my local is Local 2—the United Federation of Teachers in New York City, where most of its members are educators working for the New York City Board of Education. All told, in the AFT, we have more than three thousand locals nationwide and those locals represent educators, health care workers, and public employees—about 1.8 million members in all.

Our union operates democratically. Locals have constitutions and elections. The members of the locals elect the leaders of their chapters. And in the AFT, we also have state federations that do a lot of lobbying and other representation services for the members in that state. All of the leaders are elected, including, in the case of national unions like mine, the members electing leaders of their national unions. I am elected to a two-year term by the members of the AFT at its biennial convention.

Together, we express shared interests with a shared voice. One of the best examples of this is through collective bargaining, which is the way that unions and the employers they work with arrive at a contract—where the terms and conditions of the working relationship are agreed upon. The way collective bargaining operates varies throughout the United States. Sometimes—like with the United Auto Workers and the "Big Three" U.S. car companies, or with the Teamsters and UPS—there is one national contract. All the employees represented by the auto workers at GM are covered by the same collective bargaining agreement, just like the machinists at Boeing and the Teamsters at UPS.

In the public sector, often the bargaining is much more localized. So for education, it is normally a local union like the United Federation of Teachers in New York City that bargains with the New York City public school district. And a stone's throw away, in White Plains, New York, the White Plains Teachers Association bargains with the local school district there. In addition, the way in which unions bargain is also varied. For example, some local unions use a lawyer to bargain with an employer, while some form a small committee of union leaders to do the bargaining. When I was president of the United Federation of Teachers local in New York City, I worked to change the way we bargained to create a very large bargaining committee of over three hundred people who were representative of all the different members and constituencies. Whatever the size or strategy, it's called "collective bargaining" because workers are coming together through their unions to negotiate as a group with employers on work-related issues. And workers have power in those negotiations because of their members joining together as one.

Unions make a powerful difference in the lives of working people. Unions raise wages for their members by an average of 10 to 15 percent. Over nine out of ten union members have employer-sponsored health benefits and paid sick days, significantly higher rates than for non-union workers. And union workers are more likely to have employer-sponsored retirement plans than non-union workers.

But, importantly, where there are strong unions, average wages are higher across the board even for non-unionized workers. For every 1 percent more that private workers are unionized, wages for non-union workers go up 0.3 percent. And the effect is even greater for workers without college degrees.

It's no surprise that fascists don't like unions. Unions make life better for all working people. Fascists rely on what political scientist Jean Hardisty called "mobilizing resentment," but that strategy doesn't work if there's no resentment to mobilize. Fascists need extreme economic inequality to provide the fertile ground for scapegoating immigrants and other vulnerable minorities. And the same playbook used to crush unions is deployed to silence journalists, demonize activists, and suppress voters—because fascism can't survive in a world where we, the people, have power, information, and opportunity.

Plus, of course, some fascists are oligarchs—or are aligned with oligarchs—who personally reap the benefits of wealth inequality. Elon Musk—remember, the wealthiest person in the world and the top supporter of Donald Trump's second presidential campaign—has profited by exploiting workers. Musk reportedly gloated about his employees trying to impress him by working twenty hours a day and sleeping in the office. And a U.S. appeals court ruled that Musk illegally threatened that Tesla workers would lose benefits if they unionized. He once said he disagrees with "the idea of unions" because they create "a lords and peasants sort of thing." Labor reporter Steven Greenhouse comments, "That the world's richest human dissed the idea of unions should certainly be seen as a selling point for unionizing. Musk's statement shows that he realizes that unions can be highly effective in harnessing the collective voice and power of workers." As a result of Musk's philosophy, non-unionized Tesla workers earn significantly less than auto workers covered by the United Auto Workers union—in some cases as much as 40 percent less. Meanwhile, amid mounting accusations of abuse against workers at SpaceX, Musk filed an audacious suit in federal court arguing that the National Labor Relations Board is unconstitutional. This is one of dozens of lawsuits that Musk's SpaceX, Jeff Bezos's Amazon, and other corporations have filed against the NLRB.

Look, no institution is perfect. That's why I work tirelessly to make the labor movement more effective, just like I work tirelessly to strengthen public schools. But while schools and unions face almost constant scrutiny, wealthy, powerful special interests are often let completely off the hook. For instance, when some of the largest private banks in America made massive mistakes, leading to the 2008 financial crisis, they weren't held accountable. They were bailed out and propped up. So bear in mind that when the friends of these bankers and other billionaire special interests attack unions, they don't really believe in "accountability" in any real sense. They just want to destroy the ability of unions to be a check on their unfettered power.

The fourth reason fascists fear teachers is because teachers belong to strong unions. Even amid attacks on unions in general, and public-sector unions in particular, teachers are the most unionized profession in the United States. And teachers organize to strengthen unions and the union movement as a whole. Unions increase economic opportunity and fairness for workers. Unions strengthen democracy. And unions—especially public school teachers' unions—

fight for what children and families need. And that includes fighting to defend public education. Fascists don't like any of that.

THE HISTORY AND LEGACY OF LABOR UNIONS

President Franklin Delano Roosevelt said, "It is one of the characteristics of a free and democratic modern nation that we have free and independent labor unions." Labor organizing, however, predates democracy. In ancient Egypt, tomb workers who went without pay for eighteen days put down their tools, marched together toward the city, and staged sit-ins. In the Middle Ages, merchants and craftspeople in Europe formed organizations called guilds that would collectively manage trade and prices.

The earliest forms of labor organizing in pre-revolutionary America were enslaved Blacks and enslaved Native Americans leading rebellions throughout the eighteenth and nineteenth centuries. In 1794, the first known union in the United States—a union of shoemakers—was founded in Philadelphia. Mill workers in Lowell, Massachusetts—including girls as young as twelve—formed the first union of working women in the nation, and in 1834 went on strike over wage cuts. In 1867, around three thousand Chinese laborers building the Transcontinental Railroad launched what was at the time the largest strike in the nation's history, stopping work to demand better wages.

The National Teachers Association was founded in 1857 when local teachers' unions in ten states came together to "advance the dignity, respectability, and usefulness of their calling." Later, my union—the AFT—was founded in 1916 when teachers groups in Gary, Indiana; Scranton, Pennsylvania; Washington, D.C.; Chicago; and

New York decided to join forces. They formed the AFT because they knew they could do even more to help their schools and their students by working together and using their collective voice. Over the years, we've grown to become one of the largest unions in the country, but that throughline remains the same—that we fight for what teachers and students need. (Remember, I used to run the United Federation of Teachers in New York City, which was the second AFT local in history and therefore is "AFT Local 2." The Chicago Teachers Union joined first, so it's "AFT Local 1." When she ran the Chicago Teachers Union, Karen Lewis would often tease me that she's number one and I'm number two!)

Unions have done more than raise wages for union and non-union workers. In the mid-1800s, Americans regularly worked twelve hours a day or even longer. Between 1890 and 1910, almost one out of every five children between the ages of ten and fifteen was working. And conditions were abysmal. As just one example, the nation was rocked in March 1911 when the Triangle Shirtwaist Factory in lower Manhattan caught fire. Poor ventilation meant the fire spread quickly and locked doors and a single faulty fire escape meant workers couldn't get out. That day, 146 burned alive or leapt from windows to their death.

But it was only because unions pressed for change that, in 1938, the federal government passed the Fair Labor Standards Act. The law established a maximum workweek of forty hours and required that anyone working more than that be paid overtime. Plus the law established a federal minimum wage and banned child labor. It would take over thirty more years for unions to win the Occupational Safety and Health Act in 1970, creating minimum workplace safety and health standards.

As the power and influence of unions grew, so did attacks from employers. It became common for businesses to "spy on, interrogate, discipline, discharge, and blacklist union members." So unions also pressed for and won the National Labor Relations Act. Enacted in 1935, the law guarantees workers "the right to self-organization, to form, join, or assist labor organizations, to bargain collectively through representatives of their own choosing, and to engage in other concerted activities for the purpose of collective bargaining or other mutual aid or protection." This is the foundation of labor rights—giving real voice and workplace democracy to millions of American workers who had for too long been powerless.

The National Labor Relations Act made it easier for workers to form unions if they wanted to—and it turns out they wanted to. As President Joe Biden often points out, "The middle class built America, and unions built the middle class." Unionization peaked in 1954, when 35 percent of American workers belonged to a union. But new unions kept being built and workers kept organizing. In 1962, Dolores Huerta, Cesar Chavez, and others started the United Farm Workers of America and, with it, a powerful movement for immigrant workers in America. "Once you see the outcomes and the results, and you see how many people are helped and benefitting," Huerta said, "you want to keep on doing it." Because as unionization goes up, incomes for working people rise, too. And, overall, income inequality goes down when unionization rises. It is incredibly powerful to look at historic charts of union membership versus income distribution in the United States. When unionization rates rise like a mountain, income inequality craters into a valley. Unions level the playing field. But, of course, the opposite is also true. When unionization declines, income inequality rises.

HOW FASCISTS UNDERMINE UNIONS

It's one thing for business owners or the government to disagree with labor unions about wages and other aspects of a contract negotiation. But attacks on the very existence of labor unions is a hallmark of fascism, as Jason Stanley explains. "Antipathy to labor unions is such a major theme of fascist politics that fascism cannot be fully comprehended without an understanding of it," writes Stanley.

"Fascism is most effective in times of severe economic inequality," explains journalist Spencer Bokat-Lindell. Teachers' unions, as we saw in chapter 3, work toward the exact opposite goal—fostering more opportunity for all. But fascism also relies on individuals in society feeling isolated, what philosopher Hannah Arendt called being "atomized." After all, when we don't know our neighbors, it's easier for fascist propaganda to turn us against each other. Unions show how our fates are linked and not only deliver better material conditions but make people feel connected to each other and engaged in their lives, jobs, and communities. Labor unions "promote solidarity across differences that fascism depends on exploiting," writes Bokat-Lindell. That's why, throughout history, fascists and their enablers have consistently sought to undermine unions and chip away at labor rights.

During Mussolini's rise to power in Italy, fascist goon squads laid siege to union offices across the country and beat and tortured trade leaders. In December 1922, Mussolini's supporters burned down the local trade union headquarters in the industrial city of Turin and killed eleven people. In May 1933, just three months after taking power, Hitler dissolved trade unions in Germany, seized all their records and assets, and jailed Germany's labor leaders. From Franco in Spain to Pinochet in Chile to Perón in Argentina, authoritarian leaders have habitually attacked labor leaders and dismantled organized unions.

In the United States, in 1947, anti-union politicians passed the Taft-Hartley Act, which limited the National Labor Relations Act and opened the door for states to pass anti-union "right to work" laws. Why? As with vouchers, it's impossible to disentangle the history of right-to-work laws from opposition to racial integration.

In the 1940s, members of the Congress of Industrial Organizations (CIO)—a federation of labor unions started by the United Mine Workers and others —launched a major effort to organize Southern workers. The CIO was racially integrated and was trying to not only organize Black and white workers in the South but lay siege to Jim Crow segregation. But the entrenched Southern political elite rose up and defeated the CIO's effort by stoking divisions between Black and white workers. Among them was a Texas man named Vance Muse.

Muse, proclaiming himself "a southerner and for white supremacy," was head of the explicitly racist, anti-Semitic, anti-Catholic Christian American Association. His organization distributed fliers arguing that unions force "white women and white men . . . into organizations with black African apes whom they will have to call 'brother.'" Other fliers accused labor unions, which were of course actually practicing cross-racial solidarity, of "trying to pit . . . black against white."

To try to permanently hobble the ability of Black and white workers to join together, build power, and challenge the segregationist status quo, Muse used an idea first floated by William Ruggles in a *Dallas Morning News* editorial. Ruggles even came up with the name—"right to work" laws—to try to cleverly obscure the fact that such laws actually profoundly limit the rights of workers to choose to form a union. Right-to-work laws found success in the Jim Crow South where most Black people couldn't vote and those who could were, like poor and working-class white people, prevented from voting because of poll taxes.

What followed was decades of concerted efforts to attack worker rights and erode union density. In 1971, Lewis Powell wrote a highly influential memo arguing that due to the rise of labor unions, the civil rights movement, and consumer rights organizations, "the American economic system is under broad attack." The memo was sent confidentially to the U.S. Chamber of Commerce but eventually leaked by a journalist. Powell argued that the United States was better off during the robber baron era of runaway corporate power and wealthy excess, before the reforms of the New Deal, and said that "constant surveillance" of news media and school textbooks was necessary to stop the increase in "anti-business views." Powell's memo would become the "blueprint for corporate power"—including guiding the ways in which big businesses and the billionaire class have tried to decimate unions ever since. Less than two months later, Powell was nominated to the Supreme Court, and eventually confirmed.

But a seminal moment came in 1981, when over twelve thousand members of the Professional Air Traffic Controllers Organization (PATCO) went on strike. President Ronald Reagan ordered the air traffic controllers to return to work and then fired more than eleven thousand who didn't. It was a significant shift in the labor movement. Historian Joseph McCartin has pointed out that although employers always had the legal power to fire striking workers, it was uncommon and frowned upon. But Reagan gave companies permission to unleash a generation of aggressive anti-union tactics—like firing union organizers and holding "captive audience" meetings with employees to spread disinformation about union drives. Corporate spending on anti-union consultants surged. Today, American companies spend an estimated $433 million per year on union-busting consulting firms. And they get what they pay for. Today, just 10 percent of the American workforce—one in ten workers—belongs to a union. Meanwhile, right-to-work laws that had spread across the South and Midwest mainly during the 1940s and 1950s found a new twenty-first-century champion in Scott Walker.

Walker, a Republican who was first elected governor of Wisconsin in 2010, was a sort of pioneer in proto-fascist American politics. When Donald Trump, J. D. Vance, Ron DeSantis, and others blame public schools and universities for "woke" indoctrination as a way to sow division and dismantle not only public education but all public institutions, they are following Scott Walker's playbook.

An investigation by *The New York Times* called Walker "a product of a loose network of conservative donors, think tanks and talk radio hosts who have spent years preparing the road for a politician who could successfully present their arguments for small government to a broader constituency." One of Walker's first acts in office was to enact legislation that severely restricted collective bargaining rights for Wisconsin public employees while also cutting benefits for public union workers. The measure was aimed at the state's teachers' union.

Some one hundred thousand Wisconsinites showed up at the state capitol to protest. Walker, who eventually compared the protesters to "radical Islamic terrorists," ignored the people's objections, as did the legislature. The anti-union bill became law. Shortly thereafter, Walker slashed public school funding by $800 million, adjusted for inflation, a whopping cut of 20 percent from the previous decade's peak.

Then Walker went after professors at the prestigious University of Wisconsin system. *The Chronicle of Higher Education* reports:

> He castigated faculty members as lazy and unindustrious, leading to the creation of a searchable database that tracked the number of hours individual professors spent in the classroom. Under pressure from critics angered by student protests against right-wing speakers on the Madison campus, the Board of Regents approved a policy that imposed penalties for students who interfered in the speech of other people. And, of course, Walker questioned the very purpose of college.

Walker removed tenure protections for University of Wisconsin professors and cut $250 million from the university's budget. He also secretly tried to change the very mission of the university. Embedded in state law, the "Wisconsin Idea" directs the University of Wisconsin to "search for truth" and "improve the human condition," but Walker wanted to replace those clauses with "meet the state's workforce needs." It was, arguably, an attack not only on the university but on Wisconsin's democratic ideals. "The Wisconsin Idea has always held that democracy requires an informed and engaged citizenry, and that academics and researchers should pursue the truth in order to serve that citizenry," wrote Wisconsin native John Nichols in *The Nation*.

For decades, the far right has argued that teachers' unions aren't fighting for what students and schools need but, rather, are standing in the way. So when Scott Walker radically undermined teachers' unions, did public education in Wisconsin actually improve as Walker and the far right promised it would? No. Walker literally said, "I am proud to be the pro-education governor because our reforms are working"—but that was a lie. Indeed, when Walker insisted that his policies improved public education in Wisconsin, the *Washington Post* fact checkers dinged him, citing "inconsistent performance among grade levels."

More than one in ten Wisconsin teachers left the profession altogether. The teachers who remained were less experienced—almost a quarter statewide had less than five years of teaching experience. Teacher pay plummeted. And Wisconsin districts statewide faced an "extreme shortage" of applicants for teacher vacancies. So, not surprisingly, student achievement declined.

But remember, fascists and their enablers don't actually want to solve problems. They want to create problems that divide and distract us so they can wield increasingly unchecked power. And in that regard, Walker got what he wanted. He didn't want to improve education for Wisconsin's children, he wanted to limit the ability of unions to block his extremist cuts to education and other public infrastructure. In 2010, 14.2 percent of Wisconsin workers were in a union. By 2020, just 8.7 percent were. And so of course the power and influence of unions declined as well. In 2009, the Wisconsin Education Association Council had seventeen lobbyists and spent $2.5 million to try to impact state policymaking. By 2019, they had just two lobbyists and a budget of $71,000.

Walker didn't just break the teachers' union—he broke Wisconsin. Wisconsin borders Minnesota, and their states and economies share many similarities, making for a good comparison. During the time Walker was governor, wages grew more slowly in Wisconsin than in neighboring Minnesota. Job growth was also slower in Wisconsin. So was economic growth as a whole. Remember, unions lift all boats. Hurting unions hurts everyone.

Walker survived a recall election, but in 2018, Tony Evers, the school superintendent for Wisconsin, ran against him. Education was at the center of the race, and Walker bizarrely tried to boast that he'd led "record investment" in the state's schools. Voters, frustrated with educational decline in the state, saw right through his lies. Walker was defeated. As this book was going to press, the Wisconsin state Supreme Court was considering the validity of Act 10, the law that undermined collective bargaining in Wisconsin. A lower court judge overturned the law in December 2024, ruling it was unconstitutional.

But the far-right strategy of attacking education, attacking inclusion, and attacking democracy by attacking teachers' unions unfortunately continues. In 2023, Florida's Republican Governor Ron DeSantis pushed for and won a new law to undermine the state's public-sector unions. The new union-busting law was bankrolled by the far-right anti-union Freedom Foundation—with funding from, among others, Betsy DeVos. The law made it harder for unions to collect dues and also increased the percentage of teachers who needed to vote to continue having a union—a process called "certification." Indeed, fifty-four public-sector unions were terminated, representing more than sixty-three thousand Florida workers. But when United Teachers of Dade was up for its certification vote in Miami-Dade County—the largest school district in the state—the Freedom Foundation went a step further. The far-right group tried to lure teachers to vote for a sham union it created, vowing to "spend whatever it takes" to defeat the teachers' union to advance their extremist, anti-union, anti-"woke" agenda. But their deception-filled campaign failed. United Teachers of Dade won recertification with an overwhelming 83 percent of the vote.

When unions are strong, America's middle class is strong, too. Between 1985 and 2011, when the proportion of union membership in the United States dropped by 8 percent, the number of middle-class households in the United States also dropped by 8 percent. In fact, between 1973 and 2007, data show that anywhere from a fifth to as much as one-third of the growth in economic inequality in the United States can be attributed to declines in union membership—"an effect comparable to the growing stratification of wages by education." You can see right there how the attacks on unions and the attacks on education connect.

Yet as economic inequality has skyrocketed and exploitation by billionaires and big business has skyrocketed, support for unions has risen. In 2024, seven out of ten Americans had a favorable view of unions—nearly the highest approval rating in sixty years. In fact, as confidence in every other major American institution—from the criminal justice system to Congress to TV news to the military—has fallen, trust in unions has increased.

Workers fight for unions because unions fight for working people. And teachers fight for unions because they know that teachers' unions fight for students. And we work together—as workers, as teachers, as Americans—because we know that together we can achieve things that would be impossible on our own.

THERE'S NO DEMOCRACY WITHOUT UNIONS

Unions build the middle class. And unions also build democracy. Historian Heather Cox Richardson talks about how "regular people having agency" is fundamentally disruptive to the fascist agenda that puts all power in a singular authoritarian leader. She adds that "people feeling as if they have agency and taking a stand for their rights" is the point of democracy. It's also the point of the labor movement. Instead of feeling isolated and "atomized" and outside of decision-making—where resentment and even conspiracy theories can fester—union members feel integral to systems of power and clear on their own power to make change. That's good for all of us as individuals and good for our nation as a whole.

Unions practice democracy internally by voting on leadership and contract negotiations. And they strengthen democracy in our nation not only by endorsing candidates but by encouraging people to vote. Union membership increases civic participation. In swing states like Pennsylvania and Michigan, an estimated one in five voters is a union member, and research shows that union members are at least 3 to 5 percent more likely to vote than non-union members. Political scientists Patrick Flavin and Benjamin Radcliff explain that belonging to a union is a form of "political participation in the workplace" that "translates beyond just the workplace and increases a member's likelihood of becoming involved in the political process and, ultimately, voting." But just like unions boost wages for all workers, not just union members, unions boost rates of voting for all Americans. Even non-union members living in states with strong unions are more likely to vote.

Plus, of course, unions take all that agency and engagement and voice and use it to fight for what our communities need. That's especially true for unions that represent teachers, which not only fight for members in negotiations over wages and benefits but also for what our students need to succeed. And it's what our nurse locals are also starting to do in our Code Red campaign for patients—

raising the alarm about staffing shortages in health care facilities. That's why collective bargaining agreements often include demands for things like smaller class sizes and more social workers in schools—because we know that helps our students thrive. And research shows that when teachers are unionized, yes, teacher salaries go up, but so does student achievement. Districts with strong teachers' unions tend to spend more money on public education, which benefits students and communities. Plus in our policy advocacy work, teachers meet with state legislators to explain, for instance, why voucher programs are bad and funding for special education is good. Teachers' unions give teachers a voice in politics and policy that affect schools and students. No wonder fascists find us so threatening. They want to destroy democracy, knowledge, and opportunity for all—and we're standing in their way. But in the fight for what's right, teachers never give up. There are so many brave, incredible teachers whose lives illustrate the point. Take Lucie Aubrac.

Lucie Aubrac was a brilliant young French woman who graduated from Paris's elite Sorbonne college and then, in 1938, attained her *agrégation* in history—the most competitive and prestigious higher degree in France and a rare achievement for women in that era. Lucie worked as a history teacher in a French high school, and eventually met and fell in love with a young Jewish engineer. Then Hitler invaded France.

When the Nazis took over the country and installed a puppet government in Vichy, Lucie became a leader in the French Resistance—again, a rarity among women at the time. Lucie still worked as a schoolteacher, but she also helped publish an underground newspaper, spread leaflets about the Nazi occupation, and delivered packages for the Resistance. In 1942, Nazis occupied most of France and the German Gestapo officer Klaus Barbie arrived in the country, where he would earn his horrific nickname as "the Butcher of Lyon." In 1943, Lucie's husband, Raymond, was caught up in a Gestapo raid and arrested. Barbie and his officers beat and tortured Raymond and he was sentenced to die.

Lucie had no idea how to free her husband. But, in her memoir, entitled *Outwitting the Gestapo*, Lucie describes how she hatched the plan with members of the General Confederation of Labour, one of the largest trade unions in France. The union's leaders were among those who helped Lucie learn how to use weapons during practice sessions in the countryside. And it was those same union leaders who joined her in a desperate but successful attack against the Gestapo to free her husband.

Lucie, pregnant with her second child, went to see Klaus Barbie in person. She told him she was pregnant but lied about being married to Raymond and pleaded for her "fiancé" to be released. When Barbie refused, Lucie found another Nazi officer and entreated him to at least let her and Raymond marry before Raymond's execution. During their "wedding" at Gestapo headquarters, Lucie communicated the escape plan to her husband. Hours later, she and the union leaders attacked a transport van and freed Raymond, along with more than a dozen other prisoners.

Lucie and her husband went into hiding and eventually escaped to London. But when France was liberated and the new French government announced that women would—for the first time ever—be able to vote, General Charles de Gaulle appointed a consultative assembly. He named Lucie a member, as a representative for the Resistance. Thus Lucie became one of the first women ever to serve in the French parliament. She was a groundbreaking democracy fighter in every way.

As during Lucie's time, there are ominous threats to democracy and opportunity around the globe. Voting is the first step in protecting democracy and opportunity, but creating and joining unions is even more powerful for working people—because collective power is the true antidote to authoritarianism. As the labor strategist Michael Podhorzer puts it, "Voting is like going to a restaurant and choosing between entrees on the menu. Collective power is like sitting at the table deciding what's on the menu." In a true democracy, more and more people have power not just in elections but in deciding how the economy and business and schools and every aspect of society are governed and run. That's the power of unions. And that's what truly threatens fascists.

The good news is that unions in the United States are growing, surging in both numbers and popularity. As I've already noted, support for unions has grown as Americans have become frustrated by the rise of billionaires and mega-corporations and fed up with leaders like Donald Trump who keep giving more tax cuts and privileges to the super-rich while squeezing the middle class. And unionization has grown, too. In 2021, there were 1,638 groups of employees filing paperwork with the National Labor Relations Board seeking elections to form new unions. But in 2022, 2,510 such petitions were filed—a 53 percent increase. Meanwhile, between 2002 and 2024, the AFT organized 185 new bargaining units across the fields of education, health care, and public services.

Authoritarians and the far right fear unions building power because that power is used to make people's lives better—to rebuild the middle class and ensure that more and more people have access to the American dream. Plus union power is used to increase wages and pensions and health insurance and other benefits. In the AFT we do all that and more. We use our power to create and spread lesson plans that promote critical thinking and knowledge instead of censorship. We use our power to proactively sit down with tech companies to write safe rules around social media and AI. We use our power to support elected leaders who increase funding for public education instead of defunding and undermining it. And we use our power to push for affordable housing and student debt relief and expanded child tax credits and other child- and family-friendly policies. Ultimately, fascists and their enablers oppose unions because we make our nation better for working families.

We've long known about the corporate elite's anti-union agenda. Delivering the Feller Memorial Labor Law Lecture at Berkeley Law in 2021, I said, "Many forces have conspired to erode union density in the United States for decades, starting fifty years ago with Lewis Powell's memo crafting the blueprint for corporate political and economic dominance, which Chambers of Commerce followed to the letter." Billionaires and their political shills "warn us" about unions and insist that corporations trying to squeeze out every penny of profit are really the ones who care about workers, just as the school privatizers trying to mine our tax dollars for profit allege that they're the ones who care about all kids. Even amid all the misinformation, do they really think we're dumb enough to believe them? Greedy private education corporations want to strip-mine our public schools and sell our students' hopes and dreams to the highest bidder. That was true before and, I fear, is only getting worse in an era of creeping oligarchy. And of course Elon Musk, who helped bankroll Trump's candidacy, has been appointed to a new position in charge of cutting "government waste"—where, among other things, the wealthiest man in the world has cut spending on childhood cancer research.

And while we don't yet know everything Trump will do—or try to do—in his second term as president, we know that prioritizing the billionaire class at the expense of ordinary Americans amounts to a great betrayal from the man who sold himself during the election as the savior of the working class. In his farewell address, President Biden issued an urgent—and accurate—warning: "Today, an oligarchy is taking shape in America of extreme wealth, power and influence that literally threatens our entire democracy, our basic rights and freedoms and a fair shot for everyone to get ahead."

The ultra-wealthy, ultra-right do not want students or teachers or poor people or workers to have any power or voice—not now, not ever. I don't know about you, but I think it's pretty clear which side to be on if you care about children, care about families, care about workers, and care about the future of our country. As Elizabeth Warren wrote in her 2014 memoir:

> No one is asking for a handout. All we want is a country where everyone pays a fair share, a country where we build opportunities for all of us; a country where everyone plays by the same rules and everyone is held accountable. And we have begun to fight for it. I believe in us. I believe in what we *can* do together, in what we *will* do together. All we need is a fighting chance.

Our simple goal, says Warren, is "an America that builds something better for the next kid and the kid after that and the kid after that." That's precisely what teachers' unions fight for.

Two years after the 2012 teachers' strike in Chicago, Karen Lewis was diagnosed with an aggressive and deadly form of brain cancer. But she kept leading the union while she battled for her life, not retiring until 2018. In 2021, when Lewis died at the age of sixty-seven, I was incredibly honored to speak at her memorial. Holding back tears remembering the woman who affectionately nicknamed me "mom," I said, "Karen built a movement that enabled agency and empowerment. Not alone—that is the point. The fight for dignity and respect, to be successful, had to become our collective fight for each other." Karen was the embodiment of the idea and the lesson that together we can do what is impossible to accomplish alone. As Chicago Teachers Union president Stacy Davis Gates says, Karen "knew that transformation only happens in the plural pronoun."

And as this book went to print in spring 2025, the Chicago Teachers Union announced a new tentative contract agreement with the city including a 4 percent cost-of-living pay increase for teachers, a commitment to hire more librarians and more teaching assistants, $10 million for sports programs, and expanding to seventy community schools across Chicago. It's a transformational contract that, in this case, didn't require a strike but did require decades of groundwork laid by Karen Lewis and Stacy Davis Gates and all the members of the Chicago Teachers Union.

Teachers' union leaders fight for what they believe in and believe in what they fight for. Because when teachers' unions fight, our students, our families, our schools, our communities, and our nation win.

CONCLUSION

THE WAY FORWARD—
FOR ALL

T eachers are heroes in the American story. So it's no wonder the villains are attacking us at every turn. We teach the next generation to read, write, and do math, of course, but also to think for themselves, problem solve, and understand and navigate the world around them. We teach young people to be persistent in the face of adversity. We teach them to have empathy and confidence and agency so they can pursue their dreams. These are invaluable skills for students—and invaluable schools for citizens. Knowledge, critical thinking, resilience, and the ability to relate to and work with others are essential for successful lives and successful nations. Indeed our founders understood that knowledge and education are key to the success of America and our democracy.

Public schools are more than physical structures. They are the manifestation of our civic values and ideals. The belief that in a free society, free education must be available and accessible to all. The idea that young people deserve opportunities to prepare for life, college, career, and citizenship. The understanding that, in a pluralistic society such as ours, people with different beliefs and backgrounds must learn to work together and bridge differences. And the principle, as the Founders believed, that an educated citizenry is essential to protect our democracy from demagogues.

It is, however, undeniable that a powerful group of autocrats, oligarchs, and far-right extremists are trying to undermine our nation's values by questioning what we teach and defunding and demeaning our public schools. They attack diversity, equity, and inclusion because they inherently believe some people are more worthy than others. They want to pit Americans against each other while they hoard all the wealth and power for a handful of elites. They want to dismantle the Department of Education to gut opportunity. They give taxpayer money to private schools and religious schools because they want to defund public schools. They attack critical thinking and rail against "indoctrination" because they want to control what all of us learn and think. And they foment culture wars to distract us from the all-out war they are waging on the American dream. They do not want to help students or help schools. They want to end public education as we know it.

Fascists and autocrats fear what teachers do because they know their brand of greed, hierarchy, and extremism cannot survive in a democracy of diverse, educated citizens. That's why, like fascists and oligarchs throughout history, extremists are targeting teachers and dismantling schools.

There are other challenges that confront educators, parents, and students—the epidemic of loneliness, the complex opportunities and threats of generative AI, the changing nature of work as we shift from the industrial model to more knowledge work. Yet instead of helping us solve these issues, fascists and their enablers will just keep creating more problems and distractions. Their ruthless agenda has a steep cost. Our nation's schoolchildren pay the price.

I am writing this book during the early days of Donald Trump's second presidency. Already he has taken big steps to fulfill his campaign promise of shuttering the Department of Education. The effects will be felt by kids in classrooms nationwide. The federal Department of Education provides about one dollar in education funding for every seven dollars paid for by state and local governments, but its funding overwhelmingly goes to help low-income students and students with disabilities. That includes a lot of rural schools in red states and red communities. Students in career and technical education programs and pursuing college rely on the Department of Education, too. And let's not forget that the agency was created by Congress and much of its spending and programs are required by Congress.

So what would be the consequence of getting rid of the Department of Education? According to AFT's research:

- Twenty-six million vulnerable kids in every school district—rural, suburban, and urban—would lose critical services designed to get them ahead and on grade level.
- Seven and a half million students with disabilities (15 percent of students) in every community would lose access to special education services funded by the federal government.
- Ten million students from working-class families could lose need-based Pell Grants or subsidized loans, increasing college costs for working-class families.
- Twelve million students across all fifty states would lose access to career and technical education programs designed to help them master the skills and knowledge required for employment in today's rapidly changing economy—and for the jobs Trump says he will create.

Just to drill down on one example, Title 1 is the federal program that provides additional funding to schools that serve low-income students. Losing that funding means already underresourced local schools will have to cut after-school programs and summer school and electives. The number of counselors and reading specialists will go down while class sizes will soar. To give just one specific example, in Mississippi—which gets over 20 percent of its funding from the federal government—cutting federal spending would likely jeopardize the state's incredible literacy program that's been heralded as a model for the rest of the nation and the world.

It's not a coincidence that extremists are trying to gut the federal role of education in the wake of a nationwide increase in white supremacist organizations and propaganda. Anti-LGBTQ hate and anti-Semitism have also increased in the United States. The Department of Education's Office for Civil Rights was established to ensure that school districts across the country do not violate civil rights laws so that our nation doesn't repeat the ugliness of segregation or discrimination. And yet instead of using the Department of Education to protect students from discrimination, the president who has repeatedly echoed racist conspiracy theories is using the Office for Civil Rights to punish schools for any efforts at diversity, equity, and inclusion. They're twisting and weaponizing the idea of diversity, equity, and inclusion to turn back the clock on the notion that anyone who doesn't look like their family came over on the *Mayflower* nevertheless deserves a fair shot at the American dream.

These attacks are not popular. In polling published on March 3, 2025, almost two-thirds of Americans opposed Trump's efforts to dismantle the Department of Education. And yet Trump and Musk's efforts reflect the broader far-right agenda to destroy the common good and remake our nation by otherizing immigrants and LGBTQ people and people of color. Meanwhile, the billionaire class wants to cut public programs like Medicaid, farm assistance, and public education so they can cut taxes, shrink government, and increase their disproportionate power and wealth. Consider Social Security, which was created to address rampant poverty among our nation's elderly and is now relied on by 97 percent of older Americans. When Elon Musk—the wealthiest man in the world given singular, unaccountable power to fire government workers and end spending—calls Social Security "the biggest Ponzi scheme of all time," that's not a misunderstanding, that's a strategy. Lie and smear to distract, destabilize, and defund. As reporter Peter Baker explains, Trump has over and over again demonstrated "a brazen willingness to advance distortions, conspiracy theories and outright lies to justify major policy decisions." Lies about "dangerous" teachers and misinformation about "woke" public schools have set the stage for drastic cuts in public spending on education.

And the right won't stop at K–12 schools. They're also attacking colleges and universities. As Cornell University president Michael I. Kotlikoff explains, "The impact of our universities derives in no small part from their ability to equip students with the skills to evaluate evidence critically, consider issues from multiple perspectives, participate meaningfully in the exchange of ideas, and grapple with the difficult and the complex—in short, to participate fully and capably in a modern democracy." Which is, of course, why the right is also attacking colleges and universities.

Long before he was elected vice president, Yale Law School graduate J. D. Vance spoke at the National Conservatism Conference in 2021. "If any of us want to do the things that we want to do for our country," Vance said, it is necessary to "aggressively attack the universities in this country." Then Vance did something surprising. He praised President Richard Nixon and repeated his famous quote, "Professors are the enemy."

In a 2023 campaign video, Donald Trump said a priority of his second administration is to go after academics at colleges and universities he accuses of being "obsessed with indoctrinating America's youth." Trump threatened to overhaul the college accreditation system with political appointees who would impose his agenda— "defending the American tradition in Western civilization" and firing what he called "Marxist diversity, equity and inclusion bureaucrats." "It's a bedrock principle that the federal government doesn't tell colleges what to teach," says the chairwoman of the Council of Regional Accrediting Commissions, Jamienne Studley. But early in his second term, the Trump administration canceled $400 million in grants to Columbia University saying it was "due to the school's continued inaction in the face of persistent harassment of Jewish students" and pressured the university to overhaul its policies and Middle Eastern studies department. *The New York Times* reports, "Harvard, Stanford, the University of Michigan and dozens of other schools face federal inquiries and fear similar penalties, and college administrators have said Columbia's response to the White House's demands may set a dangerous precedent."

Combatting anti-Semitism is absolutely vital—whether it reveals itself from the left or the right. That's why it's stunning when President Trump was silent when Elon Musk retweeted a post absolving Hitler of blame for the Holocaust or when he, along with Trump ally Steve Bannon, made a gesture that many interpreted as a Nazi salute. We must fight anti-Semitism and all forms of discrimination, not weaponize them. "We should be holding people accountable for actual crimes, not Orwellian thoughtcrimes," argues Jonathan Greenblatt, head of the Anti-Defamation League, speaking about immigrant students being detained and deported. "If we sacrifice our constitutional freedoms in the pursuit of security, we undermine the very foundation of the diverse, pluralistic society we seek to defend." Attacking pluralism and freedom of belief ultimately hurts everyone, especially minority groups like Jews.

Nevertheless, it's clear that Trump and his allies plan to try to constrain academic freedom and free speech in higher education while attacking students, faculty, and institutions who do not comply. In Florida, we already had an early warning of this agenda. Republican Governor Ron DeSantis is attempting to turn New College of Florida—the state's public honors college—into what's been described as a "beacon of conservatism." In one month alone, DeSantis removed six of the college's thirteen trustees and replaced them with far-right allies—including none other than Chris Rufo. The new board then forced out the college president and hired a DeSantis ally for that role, too. In the aftermath, faculty report the new administration at New College is changing core courses in ways that are "driven by conservative ideologues" and will "limit students' access to knowledge." Meanwhile, statewide, DeSantis has weakened faculty tenure protections at public universities, mandated Western civilization courses, and asked students to complete surveys about their political leanings. It's also worth noting reporting that shows Chris Rufo is directly influencing Musk's DOGE and Department of Education cuts and policies through his tweets. The people pledging to sow "universal public school distrust" are now helping set the agenda.

And while Trump ran for election in 2024 pretending to be an economic populist, his track record reveals his anti-worker agenda. In his first administration, President Trump abandoned a broad expansion of overtime protections for workers and tried to gut regulations that protect restaurant servers from having their tips taken by their employers. Trump weakened the Occupational Safety and Health Administration (OSHA), which sets and enforces standards for safety that keep workers safe. He repeatedly assaulted the union rights of federal workers and appointed anti-union leaders to leadership positions in the Department of Labor and the National Labor Relations Board. Trump even worked to undermine child labor law protections and make it easier for teens to work in high-risk, high-injury jobs. Since then, several states have weakened their child labor laws.

There's every indication to believe President Trump will be even more aggressively anti-union and anti-worker in his second term. As we discussed, Trump has stripped union rights from federal workers. During the 2024 campaign, Trump praised his billionaire backer Elon Musk for firing striking workers. And the second Trump administration has fired thousands of federal workers. As of April 2, 2025, Elon Musk—acting as Trump's special advisor—has overseen mass layoffs of nearly two hundred thousand federal workers. There is no transparency or oversight so no way of knowing precisely. Meanwhile, one-third of federal workers are veterans. And roughly one out of every four federal workers belongs to a union.

Musk has especially targeted agencies like the Federal Aviation Administration and the Consumer Financial Protection Bureau— agencies we rely on to keep our planes in the air while stopping credit card companies from charging sky-high fees, but which journalists have posited Musk is attacking because they regulate his own businesses.

Meanwhile, the Project 2025 blueprint contains clear threats to dismantle organized labor, suggesting that "Congress should also consider whether public-sector unions are appropriate in the first place." And Project 2025 proposes repealing wage protections, gutting labor agreements, making it easier for employers to engage in discriminatory behavior, and calling to "rein in" OSHA. And because of Trump's anti–collective bargaining executive order, about one million federal workers have lost their rights to a union contract and a voice at work.

This isn't, of course, all. The second Trump administration has also attacked the rule of law and broken so many other foundational norms that the first one hundred days of his presidency were as dizzying as they were dangerous. The second Trump administration has carried out mass deportations including deporting legal residents; ignored orders from the federal judiciary; pursued retribution against law firms that had been involved in cases against Trump; banned from the White House press pool news outlets whose coverage was deemed unfavorable; and cut funding for everything from food safety inspections to cancer research. Amid a deadly measles outbreak, Trump's anti-vaccine Secretary of Health and Human Services Robert F. Kennedy Jr. announced he was cutting ten thousand public health jobs across the government as well as local public health grants—which, among other things, resulted in canceling measles vaccine clinics that were targeting schools with low immunization rates. "Mass layoffs," noted one public health expert, "is not how you make America healthier." Nor is rampant economic uncertainty from broad tariffs how you make America wealthier. But as this book was going to print, there was not only no end in sight but the looming possibility that Trump could go on creating crises indefinitely. In late March 2025, Trump mused about a third term—which would involve either bending or breaking the United States Constitution.

These are actions right out of the authoritarian playbook—make people hopeless and helpless, to just silently obey, believing this will somehow "Make America Great Again." But the good news is people are not silent. The good news is we are not helpless. And the good news is that if we act as a community, communicate effectively, and fight not just in Congress but in courts and the court of public opinion, we will beat this corruption, cruelty, and chaos. That's why so many Americans have been showing up to nonviolently protest this administration's actions in communities nationwide.

Americans want a better life and more opportunity, not less. They want to be treated with dignity and respect, and want the same for others, too. From my lifetime of working with Americans across the political spectrum, I know this to be true. We are in a profoundly consequential fight between fear and hope, between anger and aspiration, between chaos and community. And I know, with every fiber of my being, that hope and aspiration and community always win—when we fight for them. Yes, the story of America has included too many dark chapters enabled by our worst impulses. But what makes our nation great isn't that we've always been perfect but we have fought for justice and have learned from our mistakes—that just as our forebearers forged a new nation to improve upon the one they fought for freedom, so too did our grandparents and our great-grandparents fight to make America more just, more fair, more equitable, more inclusive. An America of boundless opportunity. An America where the next generation has a pathway to the American dream. Just like we, in this moment, must fight for those values and that vision—and educate our children and grandchildren so that they, too, can continue to write the story of America that continues to reach toward hope and aspiration and opportunity and liberty and justice for all.

There is no question that fascists and their enablers will continue to pose an existential threat to our students, our nation, and everything we hold dear. Because fascists fear knowledge while teachers fight for and spread knowledge. Remember: Fascists attack teachers not because of anything we do wrong but because of everything we do right. Teachers teach critical thinking that strengthens democracy. Teachers create safe and welcoming communities that meet children's needs and promote pluralism, understanding, and inclusion. Teachers build opportunity for all. And teachers organize strong unions that give workers real power and a voice in our economy. As we've seen, these are unquestionably good things for students, for families, for communities, and for our nation—so much so that, no matter who they choose for president, the American people consistently side with teachers on these issues and more.

And while we can expect the far right to keep trying to spread disinformation and fan culture wars and attack the fundamental freedom to teach, we know teachers will continue, day in and day out, to show up and stand up for the needs of our students. I agree with President George H. W. Bush, who said, "Public service is a noble calling, and we need men and women of character to believe in their communities, in their states, and in their country." Teachers choose public service—to work as teachers in public schools—because they are public servants. Of course, like other government workers they could find jobs in the private sector, but they choose to dedicate their lives not to increasing profit but lifting up the public good. That's who teachers are. That's what teachers do.

Teachers like Marlena Simmons, now a teacher at White Plains High School in New York—just a stone's throw from where I grew up. Marlena started out as an aide and trained to become a teacher with the support of White Plains Teachers Association President Kara McCormick-Lyons. Today, Marlena runs a career and technical education program on "educator pathways" for students in high school to explore careers in education. They complete fieldwork in the local elementary school and learn about pedagogical strategies as well as reflecting on what their own perspectives as students teach them about the profession. With creative energy and inspiration, Marlena is training and supporting the next generation of teachers—which is more important than ever when our profession is facing existential threats.

Teachers like Damiano Mastrandrea, who helps run the Brooklyn STEAM (science, technology, engineering, art, and math) Center across eight high schools in Brooklyn, where I started my teaching career. The program teaches career pathways that include cybersecurity, construction technology, and computer-aided design and engineering.

In Texas, Karen Reyes, a formerly undocumented student, got temporary immigration status under the Deferred Action for Childhood Arrivals (DACA) program, became a teacher for deaf and hard-of-hearing students and works to support undocumented students and families under the threat of deportation. In New Lexington, Ohio, vocational agriculture teacher John Lindsey not only runs career and technical education programming but also leads a project with Future Farmers of America where students care for farm animals, test soil, and learn how to grow grapes and turn them into jelly. And in Rio Rancho, New Mexico, just days before the start of the new Trump administration, public school teachers weren't banning books, they were giving them away—240 educators and parents showing up at Ernest Stapleton Elementary School to help give away thirty thousand free books to support literacy and love of reading community-wide. In the face of fascist threats and attacks, these teachers and millions of other educators stand in the breach every single day because they care about their students and they care about the future of our country.

Throughout my time as president of the AFT, there have been several moments when former students of mine have been the ones introducing me at speaking events. If you're a teacher, you know exactly how proud I feel in those moments—not just seeing my students become successful, thriving adults but hearing them speak about how my class and my teaching helped set them on that path. Even if you're not a teacher, as a parent or godparent or neighbor, you know how rewarding it is to feel like you made a positive mark on a young person's future.

It was during one of those introductions that a former student of mine, Tamika Edwards, said, "The role of a teacher goes far beyond preparing a lesson plan, giving a lecture, or grading exams." Educators, said Tamika, "change the life trajectory of students." Now, as a parent of three students in the New York City public school system, Tamika said all she wants is for her children to learn what she learned—"the value of hard work and persistence, good citizenship, and maintaining high standards."

Teachers and parents want the same thing. We want the students in our lives to learn how to read and write and think for themselves and, eventually, find a passion they can turn into purpose. Whether it's a career or parenting or community leadership or chasing their American dream or all of the above. We want those who pursue careers to command jobs that come with good wages and respect. The American dream is one of the most revolutionary ideas in the history of humanity, but at its core, it's quite simple. We want our children to be able to know more, do more, and achieve more than ourselves. That's what I want for the young people in my life. And that's what every teacher I've ever met wants for every single one of their students.

In her final speech as our nation's First Lady, Michelle Obama delivered a powerful message to future generations. "I want our young people to know that they matter," she said. "Empower yourselves with a good education, then get out there and use that education to build a country worthy of your boundless promise." Boundless promise. That's the perfect way to capture the fundamental truth that every single child has potential and every single child deserves opportunity.

I have a poster in my office in Washington, D.C., that a member gave me when I was first elected president of the United Federation of Teachers in New York in 1998—the job I held before being elected AFT president. I look at it every time I am in the office. Here's what it says:

I INSPIRE
I ENCOURAGE
I EMPOWER
I NURTURE
I ACTIVATE
I MOTIVATE

I CHANGE THE WORLD.
I AM A TEACHER.

That's what we do. Inspire. Encourage. Empower. Nurture. Activate. Motivate. Every student. Every day. To change lives and change the world. Because teachers know about every child what every parent knows, too—that with the right support and right opportunities, they can do anything and be anything.

The idea of public education—from pre-kindergarten through college—is filled with boundless promise. Public education is an idea as old as democracy and inextricably linked with it. The radical idea that, instead of being a nation that gives power and knowledge only to kings, we invest in education for all and the common good. But like our democracy, our public schools are fragile. If we want them to achieve their full potential, they must also be supported and nurtured—not privatized, not demeaned, not starved.

I still believe in the power of public education because I believe in the United States of America and I know our story is only possible when we write it together. When we are all heroes in our story—all included, all with a voice, all with the power to decide our fate as individuals and as a nation. Progress isn't only possible, it is essential. We can and must protect America's future by preparing every child for real life in the real world—equipping them with engaging, hands-on learning and critical thinking skills, in safe and welcoming schools. Our brightest days are still ahead. And I know that letter by letter, number by number, dream by dream, teachers will keep showing up and standing up to equip the next generation of Americans—who will write their chapter of our nation's story. May our story never end.

ACKNOWLEDGMENTS

This book would not be possible without the contributions of so many of my mentors, colleagues, friends, and loved ones—far too many to name. Without them, I couldn't lead a 1.8-million-member-strong union—helping support the daily work of so many remarkable people who every day make a difference in the lives of Americans—let alone do so while also writing a book. I am indebted to the people listed here and so many, many more.

The leadership of the AFT was supportive from the start, including the AFT's other two officers, Secretary-Treasurer Fedrick Ingram and Executive Vice President Evelyn DeJesus—with whom I am incredibly fortunate to serve. Our union's vice presidents, our state and local presidents, and program and policy leaders provided valuable help and encouragement. There have been many moments in my life, especially in the last twenty-five years, when people have suggested I should write a book, and I want to thank Diane Ravitch, David Kusnet, Harold Levy, and Susan Amlung for being among those voices. I also want to thank current and former AFT staff Michelle Ringuette, Leo Casey, and Ori Korin for helping with some of the earliest formulations of what would become this book. Thank you to my team—including Tear Jones, our union's director of staff, Agnes Joseph, and, of course, Tom Petrillo, without whom I truly don't think I could survive.

So many other AFT colleagues helped at key points along the way, including but certainly not limited to Beth Antunez, Bob Brown, Leo Casey, Jen Chang, Andrew Crook, Leah Daughtry, Asher Huey, Leslee Hunter, Valerie Klayman, Maeve Kline, Monica Lucas, Calvin MacDowell, Dan McNeil, Jane Meroney, Bob Morgenstern, Brad Murray, Kelly Nedrow, John Ost, Mark Richard, Mary Catherine Ricker, Prescott Robinson, Marla Ucelli-Kashyap, and Rob Weil. Plus, of course, while my home union UFT is AFT Local 2 on paper, it's always number one in my heart. Thank you to Michael Mulgrew, Leo Casey, and the rest of my UFT family who have been anchors in every storm. I'm also so grateful for my brothers and sisters in the AFL-CIO, AFSCME, SEIU, UNITE-Here, and others, including Lee Saunders, Gwen Mills, Di Taylor, and Liz Shuler. And, of course, our sister union, the NEA. And none of this would have been possible without the tremendous leadership, mentoring, and legacy of Al Shanker and Sandy Feldman—who are my foundation stones—as well as Basil Paterson, Bill Scott, Harvey Nuland, Charles Moerdler, and Victor Gotbaum, some of my mentors and heroes in the labor movement writ large.

So many AFT members, school administrators, and students from around the country shared their thoughts and experiences, including but not limited to Debbie Elmore, Greg Cruey, Amanda Miller, Matt Thornsbury, and Pam Mundy. Thank you to the educators and students whose stories are the heart and soul of this book—Lillian Keys, Ryan Richman, Raphael Bonhomme, Abbey Clements, Bill Thompson, Jeff Adkins-Dutro, Kianna Pittman, Juliet King, Tameka Edwards, Marlena Simmons, Kara Lyons, Damiano Mastrandrea, Kayon Price, Karen Reyes, John Lindsey, the team in Rio Rancho, and of course the late great Karen Lewis. My thanks also to other makers of history, including David Hogg, Sari

Beth Rosenberg, Sarah Lerner, and Gayle Manchin. And of course thank you to *my* teachers—including Mr. Swift, Mr. Dillon, and my mother, Edith Weingarten, who taught public school for almost thirty years. Much like our democracy and the preservation of the American dream, this book would not be possible without these and so many other teachers.

The work of a number of brilliant scholars is cited throughout and I'm grateful for their research and wise words: Josh Cowen, Alex MacGillis, Eric Ward, Steve Greenhouse, Jonathan Kozol, Diane Ravitch, Jack Schneider, Jennifer Berkshire, and Valerie Strauss. I am also grateful to colleagues including Geoff Garin, Guy Moleneux, Maureen Salter, Ellie Engler, Paul Adler, Michael Bromwich, Amy Rutkin, Amy Spitalnick, Jo-Ann Mort, Faith Gay, Deb Katz, Steve Clemonts, Tina Flournoy, Minyon Moore, Patrick Gaspard, Luis Miranda, Neera Tanden, and Celinda Lake for their help in understanding this moment. And the scholarship and writing of deeply insightful historians have shaped so many of my views on fascism, authoritarianism, and democracy—and how this moment connects with the past. Thank you always to Timothy Snyder, Ruth Ben-Ghiat, Heather Cox Richardson, Jason Stanley, and Anne Applebaum.

This book would not have been possible without the incredibly thorough and pointed feedback and advice from early readers including Damon Silvers, Eric Ward, Ruth Ben-Ghiat, and Sari Beth Rosenberg. My AFT colleague Michael Powell has been encouraging me to write a book for almost as long as we've known each other and provided great advice throughout this process. Celia Lose, our senior writer at AFT who has worked with me for over fifteen years, was a constant source of profound insights, feedback, and edits at every step along the way. And writer Sally Kohn was indispensable as a day-to-day thought partner and collaborator.

My thanks to my literary agent, Richard Pine, for guiding me through the wild world of publishing a book. And my thanks to the fantastic team at Thesis, who have been just a dream to work with—including Adrian Zackheim, Helen Healey-Cunningham, Niki Papadopoulos, Megan Wenerstrom, and everyone else at Thesis and Penguin who helped get this book out into the world. And Emily Krieger did a brilliant, thorough job with fact checking, as did Charles Moerdler with his legal review.

Last, but never least, I want to thank my family and friends for their support and encouragement. They form my beloved community. There is not enough room to list everyone, but I am deeply grateful to a group of friends, including those we call "the Six"—three couples that get together regularly and cheer each other on: Sharon and me, Guy Rozenstrich and Stephen Hoerz, and Raun Rasmussen and Michelle Schreiber. (Michelle and I actually met on our first day of law school in September 1980, and we have been friends ever since.) Also thanks to our Inwood friends, including Kim Saverese and Scott Brown.

Education runs deep in my family. Initially, my sister, Dr. Jacki Weingarten Arams, became a doctor and I became a lawyer—but then we both eventually became teachers, the family business. We understood from our grandparents, particularly Harry and Ray Appelbaum, the importance of education and the importance of freedom and democracy. That's the lesson you learn when your grandparents escape the tyranny of authoritarianism. I also learned from my mom, who was a classroom teacher for three decades and whom I often called for advice on everything related to teaching and learning. And I learned from family members like my brother-in-law Ron Arams, and my father, Gabriel, who rooted us on. I will never forget the hours of discussion and debate with my dad, first over coffee, and eventually over bourbon.

I am also so grateful for a remarkable extended family, of siblings, children by marriage (Liba, Micah, and Molly), grandchildren, nieces and nephews (including Ryan, Jennifer, Ernie, Alex, and Emily) and grandnieces and grandnephews—all constantly nurtured by the love of my life, my wife, Rabbi Sharon Kleinbaum. Sharon always ensures that even in these dark and uncertain times, we see the light, we remain hopeful, we find joy, and we make time for our dog, Gracie, and for Shabbos. Thank you, always, Sharon.

And lastly I want to thank you for reading this book. Whether you're a teacher, a mom or a dad, a grandparent, a student, a policymaker, an activist, or just a concerned American who cares about kids and cares about our future, thank you for being part of our vibrant, diverse, democratic nation and doing everything you can to preserve its existence and ideals by supporting public education, public school teachers, the students we teach, and their families. If you made it this far in the book, you understand that especially in this moment, we need all of you. To sustain our democracy, we must all show up and speak out—from the streets to the ballot box, from the courts to the court of public opinion. You are an essential part of this fight. We're honored to have you join us on the right side of history to preserve public education, democracy, and broad-based opportunity. To learn more and get involved, please visit aft.org.

NOTES

INTRODUCTION

1 **signified that they "remained united":** "Why Did Norwegian Teachers Wear Paper Clips During World War II?," United States Holocaust Memorial Museum via Medium, August 19, 2021, https://medium.com/memory-action/why-did-norwegian -teachers-wear-paper-clips-during-world-war-ii-5a9aa379e293.

1 **upwards of twelve thousand refused:** Kourtney Juhl, "Norwegian Civil Resistance of the Nazi Occupation: 1940–1945," *The Cross Section*, November 11, 2019, https:// crosssection.gns.wisc.edu/2019/11/11/norwegian-civil-resistance-of-the-nazi -occupation-1940-1945/.

1 **beat teachers and students:** The Royal Norwegian Government's Press Representatives, *Norway's Teachers Stand Firm* (1942), https://www.ntnu.edu/documents /139226/1297048454/Norwegian+Teachers+Stand+Firm.pdf/24b5dd8e-9de8 -1b04-c9e1-d982ad3a5107?t=1697537105039.

1 **closed the schools:** Jasper Goldberg, "Norwegian Teachers Prevent Nazi Takeover of Education, 1942," Global Nonviolent Action Database, November 11, 2009, https://nvdatabase.swarthmore.edu/content/norwegian-teachers-prevent-nazi -takeover-education-1942.

2 **sent at least a thousand teachers:** *Norway's Teachers Stand Firm.*

2 **90 percent of schoolchildren attend:** Katherine Schaeffer, "U.S. Public, Private and Charter Schools in 5 Charts," Pew Research Center, June 6, 2024, https://www .pewresearch.org/short-reads/2024/06/06/us-public-private-and-charter -schools-in-5-charts. 83 percent of American school children attend traditional public schools and 7 percent attend public charter schools.

5 **from philosopher John Locke:** Brenee Goforth, "How John Locke Influenced the Declaration of Independence," JohnLocke.org, July 4, 2019, https://www.johnlocke .org/john-locke-and-the-declaration-of-independence.

5 **"I am sure the principal":** Peter King, *The Life of John Locke with Extracts from His Correspondence, Journals and Common-place Books* (Henry Colburn, 1829), 96, https://www.google.com/books/edition/The_Life_of_John_Locke/wwER AAAAYAAJ?hl=en&gbpv=1&bsq=principal.

5 **"I think I may say":** John Locke, *Some Thoughts Concerning Education* (Cambridge University Press, 1889), 1, https://archive.org/details/somethoughtsconc00lock uoft/page/n69/mode/2up?q=%22I+think+I+may+say%22.

5 **"Liberty cannot be preserved"**: John Adams, "A Dissertation on the Canon and the Feudal Law," *Papers of John Adams*, volume I, September 30, 1765, via Massachusetts Historical Society, accessed February 3, 2025, https://www.masshist.org/publica tions/adams-papers/index.php/view/ADMS-06-01-02-0052-0006.

5 **"The Good Education of Youth"**: Benjamin Franklin, "Proposals Relating to the Education of Youth in Pensilvania," 1747, via National Humanities Center, accessed February 3, 2025, https://nationalhumanitiescenter.org/pds/becomingamer/ideas /text4/franklinproposals.pdf.

5 **an early advocate**: "The Role of Education," Monticello.org, accessed February 3, 2025, https://www.monticello.org/the-art-of-citizenship/the-role-of-education.

5 **"Educate and inform the whole"**: Thomas Jefferson, "From Thomas Jefferson to Uriah Forrest, with Enclosure, 21 December 1787," via National Archives, accessed February 3, 2025, https://founders.archives.gov/documents/Jefferson/01-12-02-0490.

5 **That's why the motto**: "Democracy in Education, Education for Democracy—Remarks by AFT President Randi Weingarten, AFT TEACH 2019," AFT, July 11, 2019, https:// www.aft.org/press/speeches/democracy-education-education-democracy.

6 **"Wars are won by"**: Editorial Board, "The Authoritarian Endgame on Higher Education," *New York Times*, March 15, 2025, https://www.nytimes.com/2025/03/15 /opinion/trump-research-cuts.html.

7 **Rufo gave a speech**: "Chris Rufo | Laying Siege to the Institutions | Livestream April 5, 2022," posted by Hillsdale College, YouTube, https://www.youtube.com/watch?v =W8Hh0GqoJcE.

7 **conservative Hillsdale College**: "Why We Study the Constitution," Hillsdale College, accessed March 6, 2025, https://www.hillsdale.edu/constitution-/.

7 **legal construct called critical race theory**: Kimberlé Williams Crenshaw, "King Was a Critical Race Theorist Before There Was a Name for It," *Los Angeles Times*, January 17, 2022, https://www.latimes.com/opinion/story/2022-01-17/critical-race -theory-martin-luther-king.

7 **"turn it toxic"**: Christopher F. Rufo (@realchrisrufo), "We have successfully frozen their brand—'critical race theory'—into the public conversation and are steadily driving up negative perceptions. We will eventually turn it toxic . . . ," X, March 15, 2021, https://x.com/realchrisrufo/status/1371540368714428416.

7 **examines the persistence of racism**: Gloria Oladipo, "'Just the Tip of the Iceberg': Kimberlé Crenshaw Warns Against Rightwing Battle over Critical Race Theory," *The Guardian*, March 4, 2023, https://www.theguardian.com/us-news/2023/mar /04/critical-race-theory-kimberle-crenshaw-segregation-us-democracy.

7 **"the perfect villain"**: Moira Weigel, "Christopher Rufo's Troubling Path to Power," *New Republic*, November 27, 2023, https://newrepublic.com/article/176809/chris topher-rufos-troubling-path-power.

7 **repeatedly spread false claims**: Laura Meckler and Josh Dawsey, "Republicans, Spurred by an Unlikely Figure, See Political Promise in Targeting Critical Race Theory," *Washington Post*, June 21, 2021, https://www.washingtonpost.com/educa tion/2021/06/19/critical-race-theory-rufo-republicans.

8 **"I get asked"**: Dave Weigel and Shelby Talcott, "Mike Pompeo: 'The Most Dangerous Person in the World Is Randi Weingarten,'" *Semafor*, November 21, 2022, https:// www.semafor.com/article/11/21/2022/mike-pompeo-2024-trump.

8 **"North Korea test-launched":** "North Korea's Missile Activity in 2022," International Institute for Strategic Studies, December 2022, https://www.iiss.org/sv/publications/strategic-comments/2022/north-koreas-missile-activity-in-2022.

8 **"If you ask, 'Who's the most'":** Weigel and Talcott, "Mike Pompeo."

9 **then-President Donald Trump incited:** "Report: The Committee on House Administration's January 6 Investigative Activities in the 118th Congress," Committee on House Administration, 119th Congress, First Session, U.S. House of Representatives, January 2025, https://democrats-cha.house.gov/sites/evo-subsites/democrats-cha.house.gov/files/evo-media-document/2025_01_06_January_6_Report_CHA.pdf.

9 **a "terrorist organization":** Erik W. Robelen, "Furor Lingers over Paige's Union Remark," *Education Week*, March 3, 2004, https://www.edweek.org/policy-politics/furor-lingers-over-paiges-union-remark/2004/03.

9 **as "union bullies":** Peter Montgomery, "DeVos Slams 'Union Bullies' for Opposing Her Plan to Send Federal Tax Dollars to Private and Religious Schools," People For, October 1, 2019, https://www.peoplefor.org/rightwingwatch/post/devos-slams-union-bullies-for-opposing-her-plan-to-send-federal-tax-dollars-to-private-and-religious-schools.

9 **increase in school shootings:** "Study Quantifies Dramatic Rise in School Shootings and Related Fatalities Since 1970," American College of Surgeons, March 6, 2024, https://www.facs.org/media-center/press-releases/2024/study-quantifies-dramatic-rise-in-school-shootings-and-related-fatalities-since-1970.

9 **youth suicide rates:** Eva Cornman, "Youth Suicide Is on the Rise: Yale Aims to Save Lives," Yale School of Medicine, September 11, 2024, https://medicine.yale.edu/news-article/youth-suicide-is-on-the-rise-yale-aims-to-save-lives.

9 **and child poverty:** "Record Rise in Poverty Highlights Importance of Child Tax Credit; Health Coverage Marks a High Point Before Pandemic Safeguards Ended," Center on Budget and Policy Priorities, September 12, 2023, https://www.cbpp.org/press/statements/record-rise-in-poverty-highlights-importance-of-child-tax-credit-health-coverage.

10 **want to destroy public education altogether:** Kathryn Joyce, "The Guy Who Brought Us CRT Panic Offers a New Far-Right Agenda: Destroy Public Education," *Salon*, April 8, 2022, https://www.salon.com/2022/04/08/the-guy-brought-us-crt-panic-offers-a-new-far-right-agenda-destroy-public-education.

10 **Trump repeatedly alleged:** Matt Lavietes, "Trump Repeats False Claims That Children Are Undergoing Transgender Surgery During the School Day," NBC News, September 9, 2024, https://www.nbcnews.com/nbc-out/out-politics-and-policy/trump-false-claims-schools-transgender-surgeries-rcna170217.

10 **"We don't have any evidence":** Hannah Natanson and Moriah Balingit, "Teachers Who Mention Sexuality Are 'Grooming' Kids, Conservatives Say," *Washington Post*, April 5, 2022, https://www.washingtonpost.com/education/2022/04/05/teachers-groomers-pedophiles-dont-say-gay.

11 **a concrete plan to reopen schools:** "A Plan to Safely Reopen America's Schools and Communities: Guidance for Imagining a New Normal for Public Education, Public Health and Our Economy in the Age of COVID-19," AFT, 2020, https://www.aft.org/sites/default/files/media/2020/covid19_reopen-america-schools.pdf.

11 **do what many countries in:** Sharon Otterman and Eliza Shapiro, "Europe Keeps Schools Open, Not Restaurants. The U.S. Has Other Ideas," *New York Times*, published November 13, 2020, updated August 19, 2021, https://www.nytimes.com/2020 /11/13/nyregion/covid-indoor-dining-school-closings.html.

11 **the Chancellor's District:** Dorothy Callaci, "The Weingarten Years," United Federation of Teachers, accessed March 6, 2025, https://www.uft.org/your-union/our -history/weingarten-years.

11 **the Teacher Union Reform Network:** Rachel M. Cohen, "When Unions Lead Education Reform," *In These Times*, November 9, 2017, https://inthesetimes.com/article /unions-teachers-aft-nea-turn-workers-labor-movement.

11 **pioneering new projects and initiatives:** Randi Weingarten, "Connecting Through Community Schools," *Forward*, April 29, 2024, https://forward.com/sponsored /607336/connecting-through-community-schools.

11 **and career and technical education:** "Career and Tech Ed Take Center Stage at Collaborative Conference," AFT, January 1, 2024, https://www.aft.org/news/career-and -tech-ed-take-center-stage-collaborative-conference.

13 **"ultranationalism of some variety":** Jason Stanley, *How Fascism Works: The Politics of Us and Them* (Random House, 2018), xxviii.

13 **"It's hard to create":** Natalia Gumenyuk, "Timothy Snyder: 'The Idea That It Is Offensive to Call a Fascist a Fascist Is Weird,'" Life in War, February 18, 2024, https:// lifeinwar.com/en/publications/timoti-snyder-interview.

14 **"The task of generalizing about":** Stanley, *How Fascism Works*, xxviii.

15 **Iran's Cultural Revolution:** "The 1980 Cultural Revolution and Restrictions on Academic Freedom in Iran," Iran Press Watch, March 4, 2020, https://iranpresswatch .org/post/20819/1980-cultural-revolution-restrictions-academic-freedom-iran.

15 **From Russia to:** Lorenzo Tondo, "Moscow Forcing Teachers in Occupied Ukraine to follow Russian Curriculum," *The Guardian*, July 1, 2022, https://www.theguardian .com/world/2022/jul/01/moscow-forcing-teachers-in-ukraine-to-sign-up-to -russian-curriculum.

15 **to Indonesia to:** "Academic Freedom in Indonesia: Dismantling Soeharto-Era Barriers," Human Rights Watch, 1 September 1998, https://www.refworld.org/reference /countryrep/hrw/1998/en/21796.

15 **to Hungary to:** Jennifer Rankin, "Hungary Passes Law Banning LGBT Content in Schools or Kids' TV," *The Guardian*, June 15, 2021, https://www.theguardian.com /world/2021/jun/15/hungary-passes-law-banning-lbgt-content-in-schools.

15 **Chile, fascist and:** Sebastián Uchida Chávez, "Chile's Nationwide Teacher Strike Has Thousands Taking to the Streets," *Jacobin*, July 11, 2019, https://jacobin.com/2019 /07/chile-teacher-strike-student-movemen.

15 **In the Reconstruction era:** Eric Foner, "Reconstruction," *Britannica*, February 15, 2025, https://www.britannica.com/event/Reconstruction-United-States-history.

15 **one of the first things:** Ethan Roy and James E. Ford, "Deep Rooted: A Brief History of Race and Education in North Carolina," EdNC, August 11, 2019, https://www .ednc.org/deep-rooted-a-brief-history-of-race-and-education-in-north-carolina.

15 **Journal of Freedom reported:** "Journal of Freedom (Raleigh, N.C.) 1865–186?," Library of Congress, accessed March 7, 2025, https://www.loc.gov/item/sn88074095.

15 **"The Freedmen . . . has got":** Ethan Roy and James E. Ford, "Deep Rooted: A Brief History of Race and Education in North Carolina," EdNC, August 11, 2019, https://

www.ednc.org/deep-rooted-a-brief-history-of-race-and-education-in-north-carolina."

15 **"determined to hold onto":** Roy and Ford, "Deep Rooted."

15 **"nearly every colored church":** "Reconstruction in America—Chapter 2: Freedom to Fear," Equal Justice Initiative, accessed March 7, 2025, https://eji.org/report/reconstruction-in-america/freedom-to-fear/#fighting-for-education.

15 **the mob said:** Roy and Ford, "Deep Rooted."

15 **Congress passed a series of laws:** "The Rise and Fall of Jim Crow—Jim Crow Stories: The Enforcement Acts (1870–71)," *Thirteen* (PBS), accessed March 7, 2025, https://www.thirteen.org/wnet/jimcrow/stories_events_enforce.html.

15 **"Education," said Frederick Douglass:** Frederick Douglass, "Blessings of Liberty and Education," Teaching American History, September 3, 1894, https://teachingamericanhistory.org/document/blessings-of-liberty-and-education.

16 **beginning in 1873:** "Compromise of 1877," History.com, March 17, 2011, updated November 27, 2019, https://www.history.com/topics/us-presidents/compromise-of-1877.

16 **"the political practice of publicizing":** *American Heritage Dictionary*, "McCarthyism," accessed February 3, 2025, https://ahdictionary.com/word/search.html?q=McCarthyism.

16 **About six hundred teachers:** Maureen Kudlik, Micah Ariel, Jessica Martinez, and Vince Sandri, "McCarthyism in Education," in *Constructing a Culture*, March 14, 2016, accessed February 3, 2025, https://scalar.usc.edu/works/constructing-a-culture/mccarthyism-in-education.

16 **Bryant was outraged:** "1977: Anita Bryant Founds 'Save Our Children,' and Starts Organized Opposition to the Movement for Lesbian and Gay Rights," PBS, accessed February 3, 2025, https://www.pbs.org/outofthepast/past/p5/1977.html.

16 **Florida's "Don't Say Gay" law:** "Florida Teachers Can Discuss LGBTQ Topics Under 'Don't Say Gay' Law, Settlement Says," NPR, March 11, 2024, https://www.npr.org/2024/03/11/1237730819/florida-dont-say-gay-law-settlement-lgbtq.

16 **recent book bans:** Danielle Prieur, "Florida Department of Education Releases List of over 700 Banned Books in K-12 Schools," Central Florida Public Media, November 11, 2024, https://www.cfpublic.org/education/2024-11-11/florida-list-banned-books-schools.

16 **follow the same repressive pattern:** Linda Robertson and Devoun Cetoute, "How Anita Bryant's Miami Anti-Gay Campaign Pioneered Today's Parental Rights Movement," *Miami Herald*, January 13, 2025, https://www.miamiherald.com/news/local/community/miami-dade/article298335973.html.

17 **Donald Trump was once quoted:** Michael Tackett and Maggie Haberman, "Trump Once Said Power Was About Instilling Fear. In That Case, He Should Be Worried," *New York Times*, February 4, 2019, https://www.nytimes.com/2019/02/04/us/politics/fear-trump.html.

17 **middle-class jobs were hollowed out:** David Autor, "The Shrinking Share of Middle-Income Jobs," EconoFact, March 14, 2022, https://econofact.org/the-shrinking-share-of-middle-income-jobs.

17 **moved their manufacturing overseas:** Jeff Faux, "NAFTA's Impact on U.S. Workers," *Working Economics Blog*, Economic Policy Institute, December 9, 2013, https://www.epi.org/blog/naftas-impact-workers.

17 **not because more immigrants came:** Daniel Costa and Heidi Shierholz, "Immigrants Are Not Hurting U.S.-Born Workers," *Working Economics Blog*, Economic Policy Institute, February 20, 2024, https://www.epi.org/blog/immigrants-are -not-hurting-u-s-born-workers-six-facts-to-set-the-record-straight.

17 **don't end at the schoolhouse door:** Chris Duncombe, *Unequal Opportunities: Fewer Resources, Worse Outcomes for Students in Schools with Concentrated Poverty*, Commonwealth Institute, October 2017, https://thecommonwealthinstitute.org/wp -content/uploads/2017/10/unequal_opportunities.pdf.

17 **decades of disinvestment:** Julien Lafortune, *Understanding the Effects of School Funding*, Public Policy Institute of California, May 2022, https://www.ppic.org /publication/understanding-the-effects-of-school-funding/#:~:text=Several %20years%20of%20sustained%20spending,%E2%86%92.

18 **"fascist to the core":** Ruby Cramer, "Trump is 'fascist to the core,' Milley says in Woodward book," *Washington Post*, October 12, 2024, https://www.washington post.com/nation/2024/10/12/mark-milley-donald-trump-fascist.

18 **his former boss is "an authoritarian":** Michael S. Schmidt, "As Election Nears, Kelly Warns Trump Would Rule Like a Dictator," *New York Times*, October 22, 2024, updated November 6, 2024, https://www.nytimes.com/2024/10/22/us/politics/john -kelly-trump-fitness-character.html.

18 **as Anne Applebaum reports:** Anne Applebaum, "America's Future Is Hungary," *The Atlantic*, March 31, 2025, https://www.theatlantic.com/magazine/archive/2025/05 /viktor-orban-hungary-maga-corruption/682111.

18 **who has weakened:** Leila Fadel, Arezou Rezvani, and Milton Guevara, "Former U.S. Ambassador to Hungary Discusses Democratic Decay Under Viktor Orbán," NPR, February 25, 2025, https://www.npr.org/2025/02/25/nx-s1-5294699/former-u-s -ambassador-to-hungary-discusses-democratic-decay-under-pm-orban.

18 **"we could learn from":** Kaia Hubbard, "Hungary's Far-Right PM Viktor Orbán Has Made 'Some Smart Decisions,' Sen. JD Vance Says," CBS News, May 19, 2024, https://www.cbsnews.com/news/jd-vance-viktor-orban-smart-decisions-face -the-nation.

18 **"Trump is now performing":** Masha Gessen, "Donald Trump's Fascist Performance," *New Yorker*, June 3, 2020, https://www.newyorker.com/news/our-columnists/don ald-trumps-fascist-performance.

19 **110 bills were introduced:** "America's Censored Classrooms," PEN America, November 9, 2023, https://pen.org/report/americas-censored-classrooms-2023.

21 **most unionized profession in the nation:** "Union Members—2024," News Release, Bureau of Labor Statistics, January 28, 2025, https://www.bls.gov/news.release /pdf/union2.pdf.

21 **belong to unions:** "Total Number of Public School Teachers and Percentage of Public School Teachers in a Union or Employees' Association, by Selected School Characteristics: 2015–16," *National Teacher and Principal Survey*, National Center for Education Statistics, accessed February 3, 2025, https://nces.ed.gov/surveys/ntps /tables/Table_TeachersUnion.asp.

22 **railing against COVID closures:** Jo Napolitano, "74 Interview: Moms for Liberty Co-Founder Tina Descovich on Her Group's Stunning Growth, Facing Threats Herself as a School Board Member and Googling Koch Brothers," *The 74*, November 1, 2021, https://www.the74million.org/article/74-interview-moms-for-liberty-cofounder

-tina-descovich-on-her-groups-stunning-growth-facing-threats-herself-as-a
-school-board-member-and-googling-koch-brothers.

22 **won thirty-three school board races:** Valerie Strauss, "Voters Drub Moms for Liberty 'Parental Rights' Candidates at the Ballot," *Washington Post*, November 10, 2023, https://www.washingtonpost.com/education/2023/11/10/voters-reject-moms-for-liberty.

22 **multimillion-dollar budget:** Ali Swenson, "Moms for Liberty Reports over $2 Million in Revenue, with Bulk of Contributions from Two Donors," Associated Press, November 17, 2023, https://apnews.com/article/moms-for-liberty-donors-revenue-gop-schools-70d733e024d81f7ad054b0f321e67647.

22 **ACLU filed a formal complaint:** "ACLU-PA Files Federal Complaint Alleging Widespread Discrimination in Central Bucks School District," ACLU Pennsylvania, October 6, 2022, https://www.aclupa.org/en/press-releases/aclu-pa-files-federal-complaint-alleging-widespread-discrimination-central-bucks.

22 **Office for Civil Rights investigated:** Emily Rizzo, "U.S. Department of Education Will Investigate Central Bucks School District, following ACLU Complaint Alleging 'Hostile' Environment for LGBTQ Kids," WHYY, October 22, 2022, https://whyy.org/articles/us-department-of-education-investigating-central-bucks-school-district-after-aclu-complaint.

22 **close when the weather is too hot:** "Nine Central Bucks Schools Will Close Early Because of Heat," TAPinto, September 6, 2023, https://www.tapinto.net/towns/doylestown/sections/education/articles/nine-central-bucks-schools-will-close-early-because-of-heat.

22 **spent $1.5 million of taxpayer money:** "Democrats Who Swept Moms for Liberty off School Board Fight Superintendent's $700,000 Exit Deal," *Politico*, November 23, 2023, https://www.politico.com/news/2023/11/23/democrats-who-swept-moms-for-liberty-off-school-board-fight-superintendents-700-000-exit-deal-00128561.

23 **more than $3 billion:** John Rogers et al., "The Cot of Conflict: The Fiscal Impact of Culturally Divisive Conflict on Public Schools in the United States," UCLA Institute for Democracy, Education, and Access et al., 2024, https://idea.gseis.ucla.edu/publications/files/costs-of-conflict-report.

23 **by a margin of less than a hundred votes:** "Municipal Election Summary," Bucks County, PA, November 2, 2021, https://www.buckscounty.gov/ArchiveCenter/ViewFile/Item/434.

23 **were resoundingly defeated:** Strauss, "Voters Drub Moms for Liberty 'Parental Rights' Candidates."

23 **won race after race:** Brooke Schultz and Geoff Mulvihill, "Liberal and Moderate Candidates Take Control of School Boards in Contentious Races Across US," Associated Press, November 8, 2023, https://apnews.com/article/school-board-elections-moms-liberty-progressives-1e439de49b0e8498537484fb031f66a6.

23 **"want public money to pay":** Diane Ravitch, "'Their Kind of Indoctrination,'" *New York Review of Books*, January 11, 2025, https://www.nybooks.com/online/2025/01/11/their-kind-of-indoctrination/?srsltid=AfmBOor5zlJYQ0feh910baBlk1pUSNgxiVLoUU8980kdjWK_Ap5WdTKr.

23 **Freud called this projection:** *Britannica*, "projection," accessed February 3, 2025, https://www.britannica.com/science/projection-psychology.

25 **blueprint for a second Trump presidency:** Rachel M. Perera, Jon Valant, and Katharine Meyer, "Project 2025 and Education: A Lot of Bad Ideas, Some More Actionable Than Others," Brookings, August 12, 2024, https://www.brookings.edu/articles/project-2025-and-education-a-lot-of-bad-ideas-some-more-actionable-than-others.

25 **affecting Head Start:** Shannon Pettypiece, "Head Start Child Care Programs Are Still Unable to Access Federal Money After Trump's Funding Freeze," NBC News, February 5, 2025, https://www.nbcnews.com/politics/donald-trump/head-start-childcare-programs-are-still-unable-access-federal-money-tr-rcna190791.

25 **and school lunches:** Ashley Parks, "School Lunches at Risk After Donald Trump's Federal Funding Freeze: NYC Official," *Newsweek*, January 28, 2025, https://www.newsweek.com/school-lunches-risk-after-donald-trump-federal-funds-freeze-2022389.

25 **as well as Medicaid:** Megan Cerullo, "What Does Trump's Federal Funding Freeze Mean for People Who Get Aid?," CBS News, January 29, 2025, https://www.cbsnews.com/news/federal-funding-freeze-student-loans-snap-medicaid.

25 **misleading attacks on "diversity, equity and inclusion":** Samia M. Kirmani et al., "Federal Court Blocks Provisions of Trump Administration's 'Illegal DEI' Executive Orders," JacksonLewis, February 24, 2025, https://www.jacksonlewis.com/insights/federal-court-blocks-provisions-trump-administrations-illegal-dei-executive-orders.

25 **called "a big con job":** Nandita Bose and Kanishka Singh, "Trump Says He Wants Education Department to Be Closed Immediately," Reuters, February 13, 2025, https://www.reuters.com/world/us/trump-says-he-wants-education-department-be-closed-immediately-2025-02-12.

26 **"young, inexperienced engineers":** Vittoria Elliott, "The Young, Inexperienced Engineers Aiding Elon Musk's Government Takeover," *Wired*, February 2, 2025, https://www.wired.com/story/elon-musk-government-young-engineers.

26 **a research operation that tracks the progress:** Collin Binkley and Bianca Vázquez Toness, "DOGE Cuts $900 Million from Agency That Tracks American Students' Academic Progress," Associated Press, February 11, 2025, https://apnews.com/article/ies-musk-doge-education-cuts-4461d7bdbe9d55c5a411d8465999b011.

26 **took down applications for:** Adam Minsky, "Department of Education Takes Down Key Student Loan Forgiveness and Repayment Applications," *Forbes*, February 24, 2025, https://www.forbes.com/sites/adamminsky/2025/02/24/department-of-education-takes-down-key-student-loan-forgiveness-and-repayment-applications.

26 **tried to access the personal data:** Melanie Hanson, "Student Loan Debt Statistics," Education Data Initiative, January 15, 2025, https://educationdata.org/student-loan-debt-statistics.

26 **issued an executive order to shutter:** "Executive Order 14242 of March 20, 2025, Improving Education Outcomes by Empowering Parents, States, and Communities," 90 F.R 13679 (2025), https://www.federalregister.gov/documents/2025/03/25/2025-05213/improving-education-outcomes-by-empowering-parents-states-and-communities.

26 **curtail collective bargaining:** "Executive Order 14251 of March 27, 2025, Exclusions from Federal Labor-Management Relations Programs," 90 FR 14553 (2025), https://www.govinfo.gov/app/details/FR-2025-04-03/2025-05836.

26 **Congress created it:** "S. 200—96th Congress (1979–1980): An Act to Establish a Department of Education, and for Other Purposes," https://www.congress.gov/bill /96th-congress/senate-bill/210.

26 **every single school voucher ballot measure:** Eli Hager and Jeremy Schwartz, "Despite Trump's Win, School Vouchers Were Again Rejected by Majorities of Voters," ProPublica, November 9, 2024, https://www.propublica.org/article/school-vouchers -2024-election-trump.

26 **wealthy donors and interest groups:** Lily Klam, "The Dangers of Federal School Vouchers: H.R. 9462 and Its Impact on Public Education," First Focus Campaign for Children, January 6, 2025, https://firstfocus.org/update/the-dangers-of-federal -school-vouchers-h-r-9462-and-its-impact-on-public-education.

27 **rejected high-stakes testing:** Michael Jonas, "Voters in Massachusetts End MCAS Graduation Test Requirement," *Rhode Island Current*, November 6, 2024, https://rhodeislandcurrent.com/2024/11/06/voters-end-mcas-graduation-test -requirement.

27 **the state constitution to increase:** Trevor Myers, "Utah Voters Pass Both Constitutional Amendments in November Election," ABC 4, November 5, 2024, updated November 6, 2024, https://www.abc4.com/news/politics/election/utah-voters-pass -both-constitutional-amendments-in-november-election.

27 **passed a $10 billion bond:** John Fensterwald and Michael Burke, "California Voters Say Yes to $10 Billion School Construction Bond," *EdSource*, November 6, 2024, https://edsource.org/2024/california-election-result-prop-2/721799.

27 **passed funding increases:** "Students Win with Pro-Public Education Measures Passed Across State," Florida Education Association, November 5, 2024, https:// feaweb.org/release/election-release.

27 **cities from Detroit:** Lori Higgins, "Detroit's Proposal S School Millage Election Passes Decisively," *Chalkbeat*, November 6, 2024, https://www.chalkbeat.org/de troit/2024/11/06/dps-proposal-s-millage-proposal-election-2024.

27 **to Toledo, Ohio:** Melissa Burden, "TPS Voters Approve Issue 19 Allowing for New Opportunities at Scott Park," *Toledo Blade*, November 5, 2024, https://www.tole doblade.com/local/politics/2024/11/05/tps-voters-approve-issue-19-tax-levy -new-opportunities-scott-park-public-schools/stories/20241105125.

27 **to Bozeman, Montana:** Alex Sakariassen, "Levy Requests Produce Mixed Results for Montana's Largest Districts," *Montana Free Press*, May 8, 2024, https://mon tanafreepress.org/2024/05/08/montana-large-district-levy-results-2024.

27 **68 percent of Americans:** "OpinionatED: Voters Views on Education in 2024," All 4 Ed, accessed February 5, 2025, https://all4ed.org/publication/voters-views-on -education-in-2024.

28 **budget crisis in New York City:** Martin Tolchin, "Nyquist and Shanker Assail Proposed US. Education Budget," *New York Times*, May 23, 1973, https://www.nytimes .com/1973/05/23/archives/nyquist-and-shanker-assail-proposed-us-education -budget-cuts-in.html.

29 **one of my high school teachers, Mr. Dillon:** "The Union Is the Solution: Our Moment Is Now—Keynote by AFT President Randi Weingarten, AFT 2008 Convention," AFT, July 14, 2008, https://www.aft.org/press/speeches/convention-keynote -2008.

1: TEACHERS TEACH CRITICAL THINKING

31 **Henryk Goldszmit was born:** Commissioner for Human Rights, "Janusz Korczak: The Child's Right to Respect," Council of Europe, November 2009, https://www.coe.int/t/commissioner/source/prems/publicationkorczak_en.pdf.

31 **director of an orphanage:** "Dom Sierot (Children's Home)," Korczakianum, accessed February 4, 2025, https://korczakianum.muzeumwarszawy.pl/en/about-the-museum/korczakianums-seat.

32 **In 1938, Jewish students:** "Jewish Children Banned from German Schools," Zachor Holocaust Remembrance Foundation, accessed February 4, 2025, https://www.zachorfoundation.org/timeline/jewish-children-banned-from-german-schools.

32 **In 1940, when the Nazis:** "Warsaw," United States Holocaust Memorial Museum, accessed February 4, 2025, https://encyclopedia.ushmm.org/content/en/article/warsaw.

32 **carried a favorite toy or game:** Dina Kraft, "Martyred Protector of Children Still Remembered by His Charges," *New York Times*, February 3, 2008, https://www.nytimes.com/2008/01/23/world/africa/23iht-letter.1.9429262.html.

32 **is indoctrination of youth:** "Indoctrinating Youth," United States Holocaust Memorial Museum, accessed February 4, 2025, https://encyclopedia.ushmm.org/content/en/article/indoctrinating-youth.

33 **"All the Nazi or Fascist schoolbooks":** Umberto Eco, "Ur-Fascism," *New York Review*, June 22, 1995, https://www.nybooks.com/articles/1995/06/22/ur-fascism.

33 **"should be allowed to grow":** "Janusz Korczak: The Child's Right to Respect."

34 **"the only Guardian of true liberty":** James Madison, "From James Madison to George Thompson, 30 June 1825," National Archives, accessed February 4, 2025, https://founders.archives.gov/documents/Madison/04-03-02-0562.

34 **"The American people owe it":** James Madison, "From James Madison to William T. Barry, 4 August 1822," National Archives, accessed February 4, 2025, https://founders.archives.gov/documents/Madison/04-02-02-0480.

34 **founded in 1635:** "BLS History," Boston Latin School, accessed February 4, 2025, https://www.bls.org/apps/pages/index.jsp?uREC_ID=206116&type=d.

34 **funded by public money:** "First Public School Site," National Park Service, via Archive.org, https://web.archive.org/web/20210115170614/https://www.nps.gov/places/first-public-school-site.htm.

34 **until 337 years later, in 1972:** "BLS History."

34 **"Education," argued Mann:** Roslin Growe and Paula S. Montgomery, "Educational Equity in America: Is Education the Great Equalizer?," *The Professional Educator* XXV, no. 2 (Spring 2023): 23, https://files.eric.ed.gov/fulltext/EJ842412.pdf.

34 **"Universal, taxpayer-supported schooling":** Jennifer C. Berkshire and Jack Schneider, *The Education Wars: A Citizen's Guide and Defense Manual* (New Press, 2024), 136–37.

35 **"Democracy cannot succeed unless":** Franklin D. Roosevelt, "Message for American Education Week," September 27, 1938, American Presidency Project, https://www.presidency.ucsb.edu/documents/message-for-american-education-week.

35 **"Only an educated and informed people":** President John F. Kennedy, "Remarks in Nashville at the 90th Anniversary Convocation of Vanderbilt University, May 18, 1963," John F. Kennedy Presidential Library and Museum, https://www.jfklibrary

.org/archives/other-resources/john-f-kennedy-speeches/vanderbilt-university
-19630518.

35 **"Without knowledge and understanding":** Diane Ravitch, *The Death and Life of the Great American School System: How Testing and Choice Are Undermining Education* (Basic Books, 2016), 238.

35 **"For the mind does not":** Plutarch, "On Listening to Lectures," *Moralia*, reproduced at https://penelope.uchicago.edu/Thayer/E/Roman/Texts/Plutarch/Moralia /De_auditu*.html#copyright.

35 **"it is manifest that education":** Aristotle, *The Politics*, trans. Benjamin Jowett (Clarendon Press, 1885), Book Eight, Part One, via https://contextus.org/Aristotle %2C_The_Politics%2C_Book_Eight%2C_Part_One.2?lang=en.

35 **"Universal teaching must precede":** Colin MacCabe, "Reading the Screen," *Prospect*, May 19, 1996, https://www.prospectmagazine.co.uk/opinions/55053/reading -the-screen.

36 **research from around the world:** Edward L. Glaeser, Giacomo Ponzetto and Adrei Shleifer, "Why Does Democracy Need Education?," National Bureau of Economic Research, March 2006, https://www.nber.org/system/files/working_papers/w12128 /w12128.pdf.

36 **"education is a prerequisite factor":** Nicholas Apergis, "Education and Democracy: New Evidence from 161 Countries," *Economic Modelling* 71 (April 2018): 59–76, https://www.sciencedirect.com/science/article/abs/pii/S0264999317313561#.

36 **A 2019 poll across Europe:** Richard Wike et al., "European Public Opinion Three Decades After the Fall of Communism: 3. Democratic Satisfaction," Pew Research Center, October 14, 2019, https://www.pewresearch.org/global/2019/10/14/demo cratic-satisfaction.

36 **higher levels of education are correlated:** Jeffrey M. Jones, "Postsecondary Education Linked to Volunteerism, Better Health," Gallup, August 30, 2023, https://news .gallup.com/poll/510254/postsecondary-education-linked-volunteerism-better -health.aspx.

36 **made 22 percent less in 2019:** Steven Rattner, "Donald Trump Will Do Nothing to Bring Back Our Dying American Dream," *New York Times*, November 25, 2024, https://www.nytimes.com/2024/11/25/opinion/donald-trump-economy -millennial-genx-working-class.html.

37 **From 1969 to 2021:** Katherine Schaeffer, "Single-Party Control in Washington Is Common at the Beginning of a New Presidency, but Tends Not to Last Long," Pew Research Center, February 3, 2021, https://www.pewresearch.org/short-reads /2021/02/03/single-party-control-in-washington-is-common-at-the -beginning-of-a-new-presidency-but-tends-not-to-last-long.

37 **in 2022, when Democrats gained:** Harry Enten, "How Joe Biden and the Democratic Party Defied Midterm History," CNN, November 13, 2022, https://www.cnn .com/2022/11/13/politics/democrats-biden-midterm-elections-senate-house/in dex.html.

37 **the violent crime rate:** Bill Hutchinson, "US Stats Show Violent Crime Dramatically Falling, So Why Is There a Rising Clash with Perception?," ABC News, March 22, 2024, https://abcnews.go.com/US/us-stats-show-violent-crime-dramatically-falling -rising/story?id=108042096.

37 **"On Joe Biden's watch"**: Megan Lebowitz and Nigel Chiwaya, "Trump Claims Crime Rates Are Soaring. The Numbers Indicate Otherwise," NBC News, March 28, 2024, https://www.nbcnews.com/politics/donald-trump/trumps-claims-crime-rates -clash-police-data-rcna145353.

37 **murder rate increased by 30 percent**: John Gramlich, "What We Know About the Increase in U.S. Murders in 2020," Pew Research Center, October 27, 2021, https:// www.pewresearch.org/short-reads/2021/10/27/what-we-know-about-the -increase-in-u-s-murders-in-2020.

37 **But polling showed that**: Clifford Young, Sarah Feldman, and Bernard Mendez, "The Link Between Media Consumption and Public Opinion," Ipsos, October 18, 2024, https://www.ipsos.com/en-us/link-between-media-consumption-and-public -opinion.

37 **"Americans are being buried"**: "Full Transcript of President Biden's Farewell Address," *New York Times*, January 15, 2025, https://www.nytimes.com/2025/01/15 /us/politics/full-transcript-of-president-bidens-farewell-address.html.

38 **"people are often attracted"**: Anne Applebaum, *Twilight of Democracy: The Seductive Lure of Authoritarianism* (Anchor Books, 2020), 106.

38 **"What makes it possible"**: Hannah Arendt, "Hannah Arendt: From an Interview," *New York Review of Books*, October 26, 1978, https://www.nybooks.com/articles /1978/10/26/hannah-arendt-from-an-interview.

38 **"goal of education is to create"**: Eleanor Duckworth, "Piaget Rediscovered," *Journal of Research in Science Teaching* 2, no. 3 (1964): 175, https://onlinelibrary.wiley .com/doi/epdf/10.1002/tea.3660020305.

38 **Martin Luther King Jr. wrote an essay**: Martin Luther King Jr., "The Purpose of Education," *Maroon Tiger*, January–February 1947, Martin Luther, Jr. Research and Education Institute, Stanford University, https://kinginstitute.stan ford.edu/king-papers/documents/purpose-education.

39 **"Democracies die more often"**: David Smith, "'An End of American Democracy': Heather Cox Richardson on Trump's Historic Threat," *The Guardian*, October 7, 2023, https://www.theguardian.com/books/2023/oct/07/american-democracy -heather-cox-richardson-trump-biden.

39 **"Authoritarian regimes have become more"**: Sarah Repucci and Amy Slipowitz, "Freedom in the World 2022: The Global Expansion of Authoritarian Rule," Freedom House, February 2022, https://freedomhouse.org/sites/default/files/2022 -02/FIW_2022_PDF_Booklet_Digital_Final_Web.pdf.

39 **still refusing to admit**: Ryan J. Reilly, "Trump Refuses to Acknowledge His 2020 Loss and Dodges Debate Question About His Jan. 6 Actions," NBC News, September 10, 2024, https://www.nbcnews.com/politics/justice-department/trump-refuses -acknowledge-2020-loss-dodges-debate-question-jan-6-actio-rcna170540.

40 **"you're not going to have to vote"**: Maggie Astor, "Trump Declines to Back Away from 'You Don't Have to Vote Again' Line," *New York Times*, July 30, 2024, https://www.nytimes.com/2024/07/30/us/politics/trump-christians-vote -ingraham.html.

40 **"I don't want everybody to vote"**: Roger Bybee, "Smoking Gun: Voter Suppression, in Their Own Words," *Progressive*, February 9, 2022, https://progressive.org/maga zine/smoking-gun-voter-suppression.

40 **"damage or destroy democracy"**: Ruth Ben-Ghiat, "The New-Old Authoritarianism," *Project Syndicate*, June 7, 2024, https://www.project-syndicate.org/onpoint /how-authoritarian-leaders-dismantle-democracy-trump-orban-netanyahu -meloni-by-ruth-ben-ghiat-2024-06-1-2024-06.

40 **billionaire Trump enabling:** Stephen Pastis, "Trump's Net Worth Rose $3.6 Billion This Year—Despite Wild Fluctuations in His Wealth," *Forbes*, December 25, 2024, https://www.forbes.com/sites/stephenpastis/2024/12/25/trumps-net-worth -rose-36-billion-this-year-despite-wild-fluctuations-in-his-wealth.

40 **Elon Musk, the wealthiest:** Dan Moskowitz, "The 10 Richest People in the World," *Investopedia*, February 3, 2025, https://www.investopedia.com/articles/invest ing/012715/5-richest-people-world.asp.

40 **on track to be the wealthiest:** Peter Charalambous, Laura Romero, and Soo Rin Kim, "Trump Has Tapped an Unprecedented 13 Billionaires for His Administration. Here's Who They Are," ABC News, December 17, 2024, https://abcnews.go.com/US/trump -tapped-unprecedented-13-billionaires-top-administration-roles/story?id=116872968.

40 **"worth at least $382 billion":** Laura Mannweiler, "All the President's Billionaires: The Extraordinary Wealth in Trump's Proposed Administration," *US News and World Report*, December 10, 2024, https://www.usnews.com/news/national-news /articles/how-many-billionaires-are-in-trumps-administration-and-what-is -their-worth#google_vignette.

40 **"On the whole, higher levels of education":** Anthony P. Carnevale et al., "The Role of Education in Taming Authoritarian Attitudes," McCourt School of Public Policy Center on Education and the Workforce, Georgetown University, 2020, https://files .eric.ed.gov/fulltext/ED609008.pdf.

40 **"The more education you have":** Amy Erica Smith and Mollie J. Cohen, "Here's What Citizens Who Vote for Authoritarians Have in Common," *Washington Post*, November 2, 2016, https://www.washingtonpost.com/news/monkey-cage/wp/2016/11/02 /heres-what-citizens-who-vote-for-authoritarians-like-trump-have-in-common.

40 **"education causes democracy":** Edward L. Glaeser, Giacomo Ponzetto, and Adrei Shleifer, "Why Does Democracy Need Education?," National Bureau of Economic Research, March 2006, 4, https://www.nber.org/system/files/working_papers/wl 2128/wl2128.pdf.

40 **in 2017, the *Financial Times*:** Billy Ehrenberg-Shannon and Aleksandra Wisniewska, "How Education Level Is the Biggest Predictor of Support for Geert Wilders," *Financial Times*, March 2, 2017, https://www.ft.com/dutchvoting.

41 **"We won with poorly educated":** Melissa Fares and Gina Cherelus, "Trump Loves 'the Poorly Educated' . . . and Social Media Clamors," Reuters, February 24, 2016, https://www.reuters.com/article/idUSKCN0VX2DE.

41 **"I started using the word":** Alexandra Hutzler, "Trump Now Says Bringing Down Grocery Prices, as He Promised, Will Be 'Very Hard,'" ABC News, December 13, 2024, https://abcnews.go.com/Politics/trump-now-bringing-grocery-prices-promised -hard/story?id=116763207.

41 **"It's hard to bring things down":** Rob Wile, "Trump Says It Will Be 'Hard' to Bring Down Grocery Prices, Pins Hopes on Lower Energy Costs and Better Supply Chains," NBC News, December 12, 2024, https://www.nbcnews.com/business/con sumer/trump-says-hard-bring-grocery-prices-down-why-rcna183960.

41 **second-term proposals, including tariffs:** Megan Cerullo, "Trump's Proposed Tariffs Could Raise U.S. Grocery Prices, Analysis Finds," CBS News, November 21, 2024, https://www.cbsnews.com/news/trump-tariffs-inflation-grocery-store-food-prices.

41 **mass deportations, would:** Matt Egan and Maya Blackstone, "Grocery Prices Are High. Trump's Mass Deportations Could Make Matters Worse," CNN, November 18, 2024, https://www.cnn.com/2024/11/18/economy/economy-trump-deportation-grocery-inflation/index.html.

41 **the price of eggs went up:** Nathan Bomey and Kelly Tyko, "Egg Shortages, Higher Prices Spike as Bird Flu Grows," *Axios*, January 21, 2025, https://www.axios.com/2025/01/21/bird-flu-egg-prices-avian-influenza-trump.

42 **"The authoritarian follower":** Bob Altemeyer, *The Authoritarians* (Cherry Hill, 2006), 104, https://theanarchistlibrary.org/mirror/b/ba/bob-altemeyer-the-authoritarians.a4.pdf.

42 **Research conducted in 2004 and 2007:** Darrell Meece, "One State, Two State, Red State, Blue State: Education Funding Accounts for Outcome Differences," Paper presented to biennial meeting of the Conference on Human Development, Indianapolis, April 2008, https://files.eric.ed.gov/fulltext/ED503486.pdf.

42 **"His plans for his second term":** Diane Ravitch, "'Their Kind of Indoctrination,'" *New York Review of Books*, January 11, 2025, https://www.nybooks.com/online/2025/01/11/their-kind-of-indoctrination/?srsltid=AfmBOor5zlJYQ0feh910baBlk1pUSNgxiVLoUU8980kdjWK_Ap5WdTKr.

42 **unprecedented federal control:** Orion Rummler, "'Patriotic Education': Trump Orders Federal Push to Monitor K-12 Curriculum," *The 19th*, January 30, 2025, https://19thnews.org/2025/01/trump-transgender-education-curriculum.

42 **to be used instead for private school:** Erica Meltzer, "Trump Executive Order Seeks to Steer Federal Funds to Private School Vouchers," *Chalkbeat*, January 29, 2025, https://www.chalkbeat.org/2025/01/30/trump-private-school-choice-executive-order-steers-federal-money-to-vouchers.

42 **education "back to the states":** Anna North, "America's Kids Are Already Suffering Under Trump's Education Policies," *Vox*, March 4, 2025, https://www.vox.com/policy/402336/department-of-education-trump-musk-doge-schools.

43 **dramatically improve literacy rates:** Sharon Lurye, "Kids' Reading Scores Have Soared in Mississippi 'Miracle,'" Associated Press, May 17, 2023, https://www.pbs.org/newshour/education/kids-reading-scores-have-soared-in-mississippi-miracle.

43 **approach called Reading Universe:** "Partner Organizations," Reading Universe, accessed March 7, 2025, https://readinguniverse.org/about/partner-organizations.

43 **required every school:** Ja'han Jones, "Oklahoma Schools Chief Tries—and Fails—to Force-Feed Students Pro-Trump Propaganda," MSNBC, November 18, 2024, https://www.msnbc.com/the-reidout/reidout-blog/ryan-walters-oklahoma-video-trump-bibles-rcna180668&sa=D&source=docs&ust=1738776271856245&usg=AOvVaw3zyKOSP9LnLo3o0HLwC9sn.

43 **buy Trump Bible editions:** Jennifer Palmer, Paul Monies, and Heather Warlick, "State Education Department Seeks Bids for 55,000 Classroom Bibles," Oklahoma Watch, October 3, 2024, https://oklahomawatch.org/2024/10/03/state-education-department-seeks-bids-for-55000-classroom-bibles.

43 **"teaching kids to hate their country"**: Murray Evans, "Ryan Walters Attempts to Connect Teachers' Unions with New Orleans Terror Attack," *The Oklahoman*, January 3, 2025, https://www.oklahoman.com/story/news/education/2025/01/03/new -orleans-terror-attack-ryan-walters-oklahoma-video-posted-twitter-x /77441453007.

43 **dozens of bomb threats**: Shaquille Brewster, Peter Shaw, and Daniella Silva, "Springfield Children 'Fearful' amid Dozens of Bomb Threats After False Migrant Rumors," NBC News, September 19, 2024, https://www.nbcnews.com/news/us -news/springfield-children-fearful-dozens-bomb-threats-false-migrant-rumors -rcna171825.

44 **"more than 3,000 books"**: "ACLU Supports Bill to Block Book Bans," ACLU, February 8, 2024, https://www.aclu.org/press-releases/aclu-supports-bill-to-block-book -bans.

44 **gun violence is the leading cause**: Deidre McPhillips, "As Guns Rise to Leading Cause of Death Among US Children, Research Funding to Help Prevent and Protect Victims Lags," CNN, February 7, 2024, https://www.cnn.com/2024/02/07/health /gun-deaths-injury-research-funding/index.html.

44 **extraordinary lengths to block**: "Armed and Dangerous: How the Gun Lobby Enshrines Guns as Tools of the Extreme Right," Everytown for Gun Safety, September 30, 2020, https://everytownresearch.org/report/extreme-right.

44 **Nazis ransacked the Institute**: Irene Katz Connelly, "It Was a Pioneering Trans Library—Until the Nazis Burned It," *Forward*, June 7, 2023, https://forward.com /culture/549587/trans-book-burning-library-gay-pride.

44 **the first book burning**: Dianna E. Anderson, "Bigotry and Nationalism Launched Nazi Book Burning," EveryLibrary, May 25, 2022, https://action.everylibrary.org /bigotry_and_nationalism_launched_nazi_book_burning.

44 **The Nazi government also closed down**: "Nazi Propaganda and Censorship," United States Holocaust Memorial Museum, accessed February 5, 2025, https://encyclope dia.ushmm.org/content/en/article/nazi-propaganda-and-censorship.

44 **eventually rounded up and jailed**: "Gay People," Holocaust Memorial Day Trust, accessed February 5, 2025, https://hmd.org.uk/learn-about-the-holocaust-and -genocides/nazi-persecution/gay-people.

44 **trans Germans and**: Laurie Marhoefer, "Transgender Life and Persecution Under the Nazi State: *Gutachten* on the Vollbrecht Case," *Central European History* 65, no. 4 (2023): 595–601, https://www.cambridge.org/core/journals/central-european -history/article/transgender-life-and-persecution-under-the-nazi-state -gutachten-on-the-vollbrecht-case/0779A24B130C4F0CA64DB639FA6DBF46.

45 **undermined sex education for decades**: Patti Verbanas, "U.S. Adolescents Are Receiving Less Sex Education in Key Topics Than 25 Years Ago," Rutgers University, November 4, 2021, https://www.rutgers.edu/news/us-adolescents-are-receiving-less -sex-education-key-topics-25-years-ago.

45 **One story about *It's Perfectly Normal***: "Parents' Guide to *It's Perfectly Normal: Changing Bodies, Growing Up, Sex, and Sexual Health*," Common Sense Media, accessed February 5, 2025, https://www.commonsensemedia.org/book-reviews/its -perfectly-normal-changing-bodies-growing-up-sex-and-sexual-health.

45 **"There were heroes in this case"**: Suzanne Trimel, "PEN America Mourns the Death of Children's Book Author Robie Harris, a Champion of Free Expression and

the Right to Read," PEN America, January 19, 2024, https://pen.org/pen-america
-mourns-the-death-of-childrens-book-author-robie-harris-a-champion-of-free
-expression-and-the-right-to-read.

46 **majority of Americans oppose:** Kiara Alfonseca, "How Americans Feel About Book Bans, Restrictions: Survey," ABC News, August 21, 2024, https://abcnews.go.com /US/americans-feel-book-bans-restrictions-survey/story?id=112991794.

46 **"oppose efforts to have books removed from":** "Voters Oppose Book Bans in Libraries," American Library Association, accessed March 7, 2025, https://www.ala.org /advocacy/voters-oppose-book-bans-libraries.

46 **given away more than ten million free books:** "AFT Gives Away 10 Million Books to Help Create a Generation of Joyful, Confident Readers," AFT, May 11, 2024, https:// www.aft.org/press-release/aft-gives-away-10-million-books-help-create -generation-joyful-confident-readers.

46 **a copy of** *Freedom Soup*: Tami Charles, *Freedom Soup* (Candlewick Press, 2021).

47 **written with the help of:** Emily Rizzo, "The Central Bucks School District Is Buying Books to Consider Banning Them from Libraries," WHYY, February 7, 2023, https://whyy.org/articles/central-bucks-school-district-buying-books-consider -banning.

47 **only one copy:** Jo Ciavaglia, "Central Bucks School District Orders Librarians to Remove Two LGBTQ+ Themed Books," *Bucks County Courier Times*, May 12, 2023, https://www.phillyburbs.com/story/news/local/2023/05/12/central-bucks -school-district-s-remove-2-lgbtq-themed-books-from-libraries-book-ban-pa /70211562007.

47 **But extremists were apparently:** Maddie Hanna, "A PAC vilifying Central Bucks Dems is warning voters about sexually explicit images by mailing out explicit images," September 1, 2023, https://www.inquirer.com/education/central-bucks -books-ban-pac-stop-bucks-extremism-20230901.html#loaded.

47 **is to spread anti-LGBTQ hate:** "Moms for Liberty's Network of Anti-LGBTQ Associates," GLAAD, December 15, 2023, https://glaad.org/moms-for-liberty -connections-anti-lgbt-groups; "Moms for Liberty," Southern Poverty Law Center, accessed February 5, 2025, https://www.splcenter.org/resources/extremist-files /moms-liberty.

47 **In 2023, in that district:** Kenny Cooper, "How Democrats Flipped a Central Bucks School Board Embroiled in Controversy," WHYY, November 8, 2023, https://whyy .org/articles/central-bucks-school-board-elections-democrats-sweep.

48 **nationwide, Moms for Liberty:** Strauss, "Voters Drub Moms for Liberty 'Parental Rights' Candidates."

48 **"the number of countries moving toward":** "The Global State of Democracy 2022: Forging Social Contracts in a Time of Discontent," International Institute for Democracy and Electoral Assistance, 2022, https://www.idea.int/democracytracker /sites/default/files/2022-11/the-global-state-of-democracy-2022.pdf.

48 **"substantially less democratic":** Brian Klass, "The Red States Experimenting with Authoritarianism," *The Atlantic*, April 18, 2023, https://www.theatlantic.com /ideas/archive/2023/04/america-democracy-autocracy-laboratories/673751.

48 **the first modern presidential candidate:** Joel Shannon, "No Presidential Candidate in Modern History Has Refused to Concede, but There's No Law That Requires It," *USA Today*, November 7, 2020, https://www.southcoasttoday.com/story/news

/2020/11/07/no-presidential-candidate-in-modern-history-has-refused-to
-concede-but-theres-no-law-that-requires-i/43015015.

48 **refuse to concede the results:** Edward Helmore and Martin Pengelly, "Donald
Trump Refuses to Concede Defeat as Recriminations Begin," *The Guardian*, November 7, 2020, https://www.theguardian.com/us-news/2020/nov/07/donald
-trump-refuses-to-concede-defeat-as-recriminations-begin.

48 **Trump spread lies about the election:** Nicholas Riccardi and David Klepper, "Trump
and His Allies Double Down on Election Lies After Indictments for Trying to Undo
2020 Results," Associated Press, August 21, 2023, https://apnews.com/article/trump
-indictment-2020-election-lies-georgia-misinformation-4b2269d68dad3024
bd5afa711478505a.

48 **egged on election denialism:** Tal Axelrod, "A Timeline of Donald Trump's Election
Denial Claims, Which Republican Politicians Increasingly Embrace," ABC News,
September 8, 2022, https://abcnews.go.com/Politics/timeline-donald-trumps
-election-denial-claims-republican-politicians/story?id=89168408.

48 **was still denying the results:** Reilly, "Trump Refuses to Acknowledge His 2020
Loss."

49 **"lit that fire":** Mary Clare Jalonick et al., "Jan. 6 Report: Trump 'Lit That Fire' of
Capitol Insurrection," Associated Press, December 23, 2022, https://apnews.com
/article/jan-6-committee-final-report-trump-bcfea6162fe9cfa0d120e86d069af0e4.

49 **As of May 2023:** Ben Kamisar, "Almost a Third of Americans Still Believe the 2020
Election Result Was Fraudulent," NBC News, June 20, 2023, https://www.nbcnews
.com/meet-the-press/meetthepressblog/almost-third-americans-still-believe
-2020-election-result-was-fraudule-rcna90145.

49 **spread false accusations of voter fraud:** Julia Ingram, "When Trump's Victory Became Clear, Online Claims of Election Fraud Quieted," CBS News, November 8, 2024,
https://www.cbsnews.com/news/trump-victory-online-claims-election-fraud
-quieted.

49 **a 2017 poll found that:** Richard Wike, Katie Simmons, Bruce Stokes, and Janell Fet-
terolf, "Globally, Broad Support for Representative and Direct Democracy: 2. Democracy Widely Supported, Little Backing for Rule by Strong Leader or Military,"
Pew Research Center, October 16, 2017, https://www.pewresearch.org/global/2017
/10/16/democracy-widely-supported-little-backing-for-rule-by-strong-leader
-or-military.

49 **A 2024 poll was even more:** "One Leader Under God: The Connection Between Authoritarianism and Christian Nationalism in America," PRRI, September 10, 2024,
https://www.prri.org/research/one-leader-under-god-the-connection-between
-authoritarianism-and-christian-nationalism-in-america.

49 **threatening to use the military:** Leila Fadel, Tom Bowman, and Carrie Johnson,
"Trump Threatens to Use the Military and DOJ to Go After Those Who Are Dis-
loyal," NPR, October 21, 2024, https://www.npr.org/2024/10/21/nx-s1-5155005
/trump-threatens-to-use-the-military-and-doj-to-go-after-those-who-are-dis
loyal.

49 **promising to abolish:** Steve Inskeep and Taylor Haney, "What Trump's Pledge to
Close Dept. of Education Means for Students, GOP-Led States," NPR, November 15,
2024, https://www.npr.org/2024/11/14/nx-s1-5181966/a-look-at-the-potential-impact
-of-shutting-down-the-department-of-education.

50 **Republicans in Congress proposed massive cuts:** Bobby Kogan and Alan Cohen, "Budget Committee Republicans Are Moving to Take Away Food and Health Care from Americans," Center for American Progress, February 12, 2025, https://www .americanprogress.org/article/budget-committee-republicans-are-moving-to -take-away-food-and-health-care-from-americans.

50 **made $8 million per day:** Laerke Christensen, "What we know about rumor Musk makes $8M per day from US government contracts," Snopes, February 18, 2025, https://www.snopes.com/news/2025/02/18/musk-8-million-a-day.

50 **started dismantling federal agencies:** William Gavin, "Elon Musk's DOGE Is Going After the Agencies That Regulate His Companies," *Quartz*, February 21, 2025, https://www.yahoo.com/news/elon-musks-doge-going-agencies-134200086.html.

50 **"Trump has been conditioning":** Peter Baker, "'Trump's America': Comeback Victory Signals a Different Kind of Country," *New York Times*, November 6, 2024, https://www.nytimes.com/2024/11/06/us/politics/trump-america-election-victory .html.

50 **"One major reason":** Richard Haass, "Why We Need Civics," *The Atlantic*, January 22, 2023, https://www.theatlantic.com/ideas/archive/2023/01/american-identity -democracy-civics-education-requirement/672789.

51 **the first official motto:** "e pluribus unum," Dictionary.com, accessed March 6, 2025, https://www.dictionary.com/browse/e-pluribus-unum.

51 **Ryan Richman is a high school:** Ethan Dewitt, "As They Await State Guidance, Teachers Consider How 'Divisive Concepts' Law Will Affect Lesson Plans," *New Hampshire Bulletin*, July 12, 2021, https://newhampshirebulletin.com/2021/07/12 /as-they-await-state-guidance-teachers-consider-how-divisive-concepts-law-will -affect-lesson-plans.

52 **what he called "divisive concepts":** "Executive Order 13950 of September 22, 2020, Combating Race and Sex Stereotyping, 85 FR 60683 (2020), https://www.federal register.gov/documents/2020/09/28/2020-21534/combating-race-and-sex-stereo typing.

52 **in at least twenty states:** Sarah Schwartz, "Who's Really Driving Critical Race Theory Legislation? An Investigation," *Education Week*, July 19, 2021, https://www.ed week.org/policy-politics/whos-really-driving-critical-race-theory-legislation-an -investigation/2021/07.

52 **The law itself:** Local 8027, AFT-New Hampshire, AFL-CIO et al v. NH Department of Education, Commissioner et al, No. 1:2021cv01077—Document 63 (D. N. H. 2023), https://law.justia.com/cases/federal/district-courts/new-hampshire/nhdce/1 :2021cv01077/58483/63.

52 **created a website:** "Fighting to Teach Honest History in New Hampshire," AFT, December 16, 2021, https://www.aft.org/news/fighting-teach-honest-history-new -hampshire.

52 **a $500 bounty:** Holly Ramer, "Governor Condemns Tweet Offering a 'Bounty' on Teachers," Associated Press, November 18, 2021, https://apnews.com/article/edu cation-race-and-ethnicity-racial-injustice-new-hampshire-b231854bde76495a806 d76355991857d.

53 **"The new teaching law":** Dewitt, "As They Await State Guidance."

53 **arguing that the law was:** "Fighting to Teach Honest History."

53 **"New Hampshire law thus requires"**: Local 8027, AFT-New Hampshire, AFL-CIO et al. v. Frank Edelblut, in his Official Capacity as Commissioner of the Department of Education ("DOE") et al., No. 1:21-cv-01063—Complaint (D. N. H., filed December 13, 2021), https://www.aft.org/sites/default/files/media/2021/aft_nh_complaint _final.pdf.

54 **a federal judge ruled**: Local 8027, AFT-N.H., AFL-CIO, et al., v. Frank Edelblut, Commissioner, N.H. Department of Education, et al., No. 1:2021cv01077PB (D. N. H, May 28, 2024), https://static.politico.com/3d/a4/6481c73f42d7bf1904a2a761ec2f /case-1-21-cv-01077-pb-ruling-52824.pdf.

54 **"I swore never to be silent"**: Elie Wiesel, "Acceptance Speech," The Nobel Prize, December 10, 1986, https://www.nobelprize.org/prizes/peace/1986/wiesel/accep tance-speech.

55 **"I won't be badgered into whitewashing"**: Dewitt, "As They Await State Guidance."

55 **"We must start teaching our children"**: Valerie Cury, "Youngkin Kicks Off Education Agenda in Loudoun," *Blue Ridge Leader & Loudon Today*, July 3, 2021, https:// blueridgeleader.com/youngkin-kicks-off-education-agenda-in-loudoun.

56 **"tapping into culture war fights"**: Will Wessert and Sarah Rankin, "Republican Glenn Youngkin Wins Election for Governor in Virginia," Associated Press, November 3, 2021, https://www.pbs.org/newshour/politics/republican-glenn-youngkin-wins -election-for-governor-in-virginia.

56 **from teaching "divisive concepts"**: Matthew Barakat and Sarah Rankin, "Youngkin Looks to Root Out Critical Race Theory in Virginia," Associated Press, February 15, 2022, https://apnews.com/article/education-richmond-race-and-ethnicity-racial -injustice-virginia-8ad5da65b9cb05265f2b8081c41827cd.

56 **"erasing perspectives and events"**: Jason Stanley, *Erasing History* (One Signal, 2024), 3.

56 **insurrection as "a day of love"**: Dan Barry and Alan Feuer, "'A Day of Love': How Trump Inverted the Violent History of Jan. 6," *New York Times*, January 5, 2025, https:// www.nytimes.com/2025/01/05/us/politics/january-6-capitol-riot-trump.html.

56 **delete the Department of Justice's case records**: Scott MacFarlane, "Judges in Jan. 6 Cases and Watchdog Groups Recoil at Justice Department's Deletion of Records," CBS News, February 1, 2025, https://www.cbsnews.com/news/jan-6-judges-react -doj-deleting-records.

56 **a new curriculum for Florida public schools**: "Florida's State Academic Standards— Social Studies, 2023," Florida Department of Education, 2023, https://www.fldoe .org/core/fileparse.php/20653/urlt/6-4.pdf.

57 **"They're probably going to show"**: Kevin Sullivan and Lori Rozsa, "DeSantis Doubles Down on Claim That Some Blacks Benefited from Slavery," *Washington Post,* July 22, 2023, https://www.washingtonpost.com/politics/2023/07/22/desantis -slavery-curriculum.

57 **Harris fired back in response**: Eugene Daniels, Ryan Lizza, and Rachael Bade, "Playbook: Harris Slams DeSantis over Slavery Curriculum," *Politico*, July 22, 2023, https://www.politico.com/newsletters/playbook/2023/07/22/harris-slams-desantis -over-slavery-curriculum-00107701.

57 **as "woke indoctrination"**: Juliana Kim, "Florida Says AP Class Teaches Critical Race Theory. Here's What's Really in the Course," NPR, January 2, 2023, https://

www.npr.org/2023/01/22/1150259944/florida-rejects-ap-class-african-american
-studies.

57 **"lacks educational value"**: Patricia Mazzei and Anemona Hartocollis, "Florida Rejects A.P. African American Studies Class," *New York Times*, January 19, 2023, https://www.nytimes.com/2023/01/19/us/desantis-florida-ap-african-american
-studies.html.

57 **at much higher rates:** "Florida 2nd in Nation for AP Performance, According to New College Board Report," Florida College Access Network, March 9, 2021, https://flor
idacollegeaccess.org/news/florida-2nd-in-nation-for-ap-performance-according
-to-new-college-board-report.

57 **"among the most aggressive states"**: Russell Contreras and Sommer Brugal, "Educators Wrestle with New Limits on Teaching Black History," *Axios*, February 1, 2024, https://www.axios.com/2024/02/01/teachers-black-history-month-crt-backlash.

58 **to "bring school back to the states"**: Kristina Watrobski, "Trump calls to 'Bring School Back to the States' amid Education Department Uncertainty," News Channel 9 ABC, February 19, 2025, https://newschannel9.com/news/nation-world/trump-calls-to
-bring-school-back-to-the-states-amid-education-department-uncertainty-trump
-elon-hannity-interview-doge-schools-students-crisis-in-the-classroom.

58 **federal law limits the role:** "20 USC 1232a: Prohibition Against Federal Control of Education," accessed March 6, 2025, https://uscode.house.gov/view.xhtml?req=(ti
tle:20%20section:1232a%20edition:prelim).

58 **in an April 3, 2025, memorandum:** Michael C. Bender, "Trump Administration Threatens to Withhold Funds from Public Schools," *New York Times*, April 3, 2025, https://www.nytimes.com/2025/04/03/us/politics/public-school-funding-trump
-dei.html.

58 **launched a comprehensive study:** "American Lesson Plan: Teaching US History in Secondary Schools," American Historical Association, 2024, https://www.histori
ans.org/wp-content/uploads/2024/09/American-Lesson-Plan-1.pdf.

59 **Research shows that inclusive curricula:** "Ninth-Grade Ethnic Studies Helped Students for Years, Stanford Researchers Find," Stanford, September 6, 2021, https://
news.stanford.edu/stories/2021/09/research-finds-sustained-impact-ethnic-studies
-class.

59 **The AHA study also reported:** Dana Goldstein, "History Teachers Are Replacing Textbooks with the Internet," *New York Times*, September 19, 2024, https://www.ny
times.com/2024/09/19/us/social-studies-curriculum.html.

59 **Research by RAND found:** Ashley Woo et al., "Walking on Eggshells—Teachers' Responses to Classroom Limitations on Race- or Gender-Related Topics: Findings from the 2022 American Instructional Resources Survey," RAND, January 25, 2023, https://www.rand.org/pubs/research_reports/RRA134-16.html.

59 **A 2023 survey by RAND found:** Ashley Woo, Melissa Kay Diliberti, and Elizabeth D. Steiner, "Policies Restricting Teaching About Race and Gender Spill Over into Other States and Localities: Findings from the 2023 State of the American Teacher Survey," RAND, February 15, 2024, https://www.rand.org/pubs/research_reports
/RRA1108-10.html.

60 **federal No Child Left Behind law:** U.S. Congress, House, *No Child Left Behind Act of 2001*, H.R. 1, 107th Congress, January 8, 2002, became Public Law No. 107–110, https://www.congress.gov/bill/107th-congress/house-bill/1.

60 **education reporter Valerie Strauss notes:** Valerie Strauss, "It Looks Like the Beginning of the End of America's Obsession with Student Standardized Tests," *Washington Post*, June 21, 2020, https://www.washingtonpost.com/education/2020/06/21/it -looks-like-beginning-end-americas-obsession-with-student-standardized-tests.

60 **Even a majority of Trump voters:** "OpinionatED: Voters' Views on Education in 2024," All 4 Ed, accessed February 5, 2025, https://all4ed.org/publication/voters -views-on-education-in-2024.

60 **civics knowledge has been in decline:** Rebecca Winthrop, "The Need for Civic Education in 21st-Century Schools," Brookings, June 4, 2020, https://www.brookings .edu/articles/the-need-for-civic-education-in-21st-century-schools.

60 **As of 2024, more than one-third:** "Annenberg Civics Knowledge Survey," Annenberg Public Policy Center, University of Pennsylvania, 2024, https://www.annen bergpublicpolicycenter.org/political-communication/civics-knowledge-survey.

60 **About one in five Americans:** "A Majority of Americans Can't Recall Most First Amendment Rights," Annenberg Public Policy Center, University of Pennsylvania, September 12, 2024, https://www.annenbergpublicpolicycenter.org/most-americans -cant-recall-most-first-amendment-rights.

60 **as civics scores have dropped:** Sarah D. Sparks, "It's Not Just U.S. Students. Civics Scores Have Dropped Around the World," *Education Week*, November 28, 2023, https://www.edweek.org/policy-politics/its-not-just-u-s-students-civics-scores -have-dropped-around-the-world/2023/11.

60 **"You go into a focus group":** Hilary McQuilkin and Meghna Chakrabarti, "What Motivates American Voters?," WBUR, November 8, 2024, https://www.wbur.org /onpoint/2024/11/08/american-voters-economy-values-republican-polls-trump -election.

61 **"Only eight states":** Richard Haass, "Why We Need Civics," *The Atlantic*, January 22, 2023, https://www.theatlantic.com/ideas/archive/2023/01/american-identity -democracy-civics-education-requirement/672789.

61 **Bonhomme is an elementary:** Raphael Bonhomme, "The Trail to Experiential Learning," AFTVoices.org, September 18, 2023, https://aftvoices.org/the-trail-to -experiential-learning-23b52be3cfee.

62 **We The People civics competition:** "We the People," Center for Civic Education, accessed February 5, 2025, https://www.civiced.org/we-the-people.

62 **when we won first place:** Hon. Major R. Owens, "A Point-of-Light for All Americans: The Clara Barton High School Bill of Rights Team," *Congressional Record* 141, no. 99 (June 16, 1995), https://www.govinfo.gov/content/pkg/CREC-1995-06-16/html/CREC -1995-06-16-pt1-PgE1270-2.htm.

63 **When I spoke at the Democratic National Convention:** "Randi Weingarten Speaks at the 2024 Democratic National Convention | DNC Day 4," posted by Democratic National Convention, YouTube, https://www.youtube.com/watch?v=lTfnjuZH2J4.

63 **"to teach children what":** Richard D. Kahlenberg and Clifford Janey, "Putting Democracy Back into Public Education," The Century Foundation, November 10, 2016, https://tcf.org/content/report/putting-democracy-back-public-education.

63 **"If we want democracy":** Susan Hopgood and Fred van Leeuwen, "On Education & Democracy: 25 Lessons from the Teaching Profession," Education International, July 2019, https://issuu.com/educationinternational/docs/eiwc8_oneducationand democracy.

63 **In 2003, the AFT published:** "Education for Democracy: A Statement Signed by over 100 Distinguished Leaders," *American Educator*, Fall 2003, https://www.aft.org/sites/default/files/Democracy.pdf.

64 **"The process of education has naturally":** Wieman v. Updegraff, 344 U.S. 183 (1952), https://supreme.justia.com/cases/federal/us/344/183.

64 **Congresswoman Barbara Jordan noted:** Barbara Jordan, "The Americanization Ideal," *New York Times*, September 11, 1995, https://www.nytimes.com/1995/09/11/opinion/the-americanization-ideal.html.

2: TEACHERS FOSTER SAFE AND WELCOMING COMMUNITIES

67 **at a segregated school:** "LBJ in Cotulla," LBJ Museum, accessed February 6, 2025, https://lbjmuseum.com/exhibits/online-exhibits/lbj-in-cotulla.

67 **whom he witnessed diving:** Melissa Block, "LBJ Carried Poor Texas Town with Him in Civil Rights Fight," NPR, April 11, 2014, https://www.npr.org/2014/04/11/301820334/lbj-carried-cotulla-with-him-in-civil-rights-fight.

67 **"I shall never forget":** "LBJ in Cotulla."

67 **just like the 90 percent of teachers today:** James Powel, "Study: More Than 90 Percent of Teachers Spend out of Pocket for Back-to-School Supplies," *USA Today*, August 26, 2023, https://www.usatoday.com/story/news/education/2023/08/26/teachers-spending-out-pocket-classrooms-asking-amazon-donations/70569670007.

67 **teachers spent on average:** Caroline Bauman and Owen Berg, "Teachers: Are You Buying School Supplies with Your Own Money?," *Chalkbeat*, July 17, 2024, https://www.chalkbeat.org/2024/07/17/teachers-spending-money-on-back-to-school-supplies-survey.

68 **paid 26 percent less than:** "Teacher Pay Fell Further Behind in 2022," Economic Policy Institute, September 29, 2023, https://www.epi.org/press/teacher-pay-fell-further-behind-in-2022-teachers-made-26-4-less-than-other-similarly-educated-professionals.

68 **Johnson also organized:** "LBJ in Cotulla."

68 **took notice and named LBJ:** "LBJ in Cotulla."

68 **"You never forget what poverty":** Lyndon B. Johnson, "Special Message to the Congress: The American Promise," The American Presidency Project, March 15, 1965, https://www.presidency.ucsb.edu/documents/special-message-the-congress-the-american-promise.

68 **"Freedom is the right":** Lyndon B. Johnson, "Commencement Address at Howard University: 'To Fulfill These Rights,'" The American Presidency Project, June 4, 1965, https://www.presidency.ucsb.edu/documents/commencement-address-howard-university-fulfill-these-rights.

69 **adrienne maree brown says:** "How to Make Loving Corrections with adrienne maree brown," *We Can Do Hard Things*, season 2, episode 354, Audacy, October 15, 2024, https://podcasts.apple.com/us/podcast/how-to-make-loving-corrections-with-adrienne-maree-brown/id1564530722?i=1000673112584.

71 **"The true engine of supremacy":** Eric Ward, interview, March 3, 2025.

72 **and "bursting at the seams":** "Sell-Out Conference Shrugs Off Anti-Fa," *American Renaissance*, July 31, 2017, accessed February 6, 2025, https://www.amren.com/features/2017/07/sell-conference-shrugs-off-anti-fa.

72 **"Klansmen, neo-Nazis":** "American Renaissance," Southern Poverty Law Center, accessed February 6, 2025, https://www.splcenter.org/resources/extremist-files/american-renaissance.

72 **"Blacks and whites are different":** "Jared Taylor," Southern Poverty Law Center, accessed February 6, 2025, https://www.splcenter.org/resources/extremist-files/jared-taylor.

72 **"acting in the interests":** Jonathan Mahler, "Donald Trump's Message Resonates with White Supremacists," *New York Times*, February 29, 2016, https://www.nytimes.com/2016/03/01/us/politics/donald-trump-supremacists.html.

72 **a "white advocate":** Jason Wilson, "Trump Ally Laura Loomer Called Herself 'White Advocate,' Audio Reveals," *The Guardian*, September 14, 2024, https://www.theguardian.com/us-news/2024/sep/14/trump-ally-laura-loomer-audio.

73 **a racist conspiracy theory:** David Bauder, "EXPLAINER: White 'Replacement Theory' Fuels Racist Attacks," Associated Press, May 16, 2022, https://apnews.com/article/great-white-replacement-theory-explainer-c86f309f02cd14062f301ce6b9228e33.

73 **"not human" and are "poisoning the blood":** Amanda Terkel and Megan Lebowitz, "From 'Rapists' to 'Eating the Pets': Trump Has Long Used Degrading Language Toward Immigrants," NBC News, September 19, 2024, https://www.nbcnews.com/politics/donald-trump/trump-degrading-language-immigrants-rcna171120.

73 **"a lot of these illegal immigrants":** Jude Joffe-Block and Odette Yousef, "How Trump Is Relying on a Racist Conspiracy Theory to Question Election Results," NPR, September 13, 2024, https://www.npr.org/2024/09/13/g-s1-22583/trump-great-replacement-conspiracy-theory.

73 **"drown traditional, classic Americans":** Media Matters Staff, "Newt Gingrich: The Left Is Bringing Immigrants to the United States 'to Get Rid of the Rest of Us,'" Media Matters, August 4, 2021, https://www.mediamatters.org/newt-gingrich/newt-gingrich-left-bringing-immigrants-united-states-get-rid-rest-us.

73 **During the 2017 "Unite The Right" rally:** Yair Rosenberg, "'Jews Will Not Replace Us': Why White Supremacists Go After Jews," *Washington Post*, August 14, 2017, https://www.washingtonpost.com/news/acts-of-faith/wp/2017/08/14/jews-will-not-replace-us-why-white-supremacists-go-after-jews.

73 **an "attack" on America:** Nicholas Confessore, "'America Is Under Attack': Inside the Anti-D.E.I. Crusade," *New York Times*, January 20, 2024, https://www.nytimes.com/interactive/2024/01/20/us/dei-woke-claremont-institute.html.

74 **why in February 2024:** Sahil Kapur and Frank Thorp V, "Republicans Kill Border Bill in a Sign of Trump's Strength and McConnell's Waning Influence," NBC News, February 7, 2024, https://www.nbcnews.com/politics/congress/republicans-kill-border-bill-sign-trumps-strength-mcconnells-waning-in-rcna137477.

74 **would have secured the border:** American Immigration Council Staff, "What Is the 'Bipartisan Border Bill' and How Would It Change the US Immigration System?," Immigration Impact, November 1, 2024, https://immigrationimpact.com/2024/11/01/what-is-the-bipartisan-border-bill.

74 **"The border is a very important":** Sahil Kapur and Frank Thorp V, "'Immoral': Some Republicans Rebuke Efforts to Kill Immigration Deal to Help Trump," NBC News, January 25, 2024, https://www.nbcnews.com/politics/congress/immoral-republicans-rebuke-efforts-kill-immigration-deal-help-trump-rcna135732.

74　**a batch of leaked emails:** Confessore, "'America Is Under Attack.'"

74　**"The core of what we oppose":** Confessore, "'America Is Under Attack.'"

74　**"Our sexual culture will not":** Io Y. Gilman, "The Fight over DEI Arrives at Harvard," *Harvard Crimson*, February 24, 2024, https://www.thecrimson.com/article/2024/2/24/dei-scrut.

74　**"protect and promote historical":** "KCEA—Home," Keystone Christian Education Association, accessed February 6, 2025, https://www.kcea.com.

75　**"pluralism, world peace":** Dr. Norman C. Marks, "The State of State Education," Keystone Christian Education Association, 1994, https://www.kcea.com/uploads/1/4/2/2/142236856/3_the_state_of_state_education.pdf.

75　**"designed to appeal":** Karen Francisco and Carol Burris, "A Sharp Turn Right: A New Breed of Charter Schools Delivers the Conservative Agenda," Network for Public Education, July 2023, https://networkforpubliceducation.org/wp-content/uploads/2023/06/Sharp-Turn-Right-FINAL-6.6.23.pdf.

75　**treated "more gently":** Bonnie Peltier, as Guardian of A.P., a minor child; Erika Booth, as Guardian of I.B., a minor child et al. v. Charter Day School, Inc., Robert P. Spencer, in his capacity as member of the Board of Trustees of Charter Day School, Inc., et al., No. 20–1001 (4th Cir. 2022), https://www.justice.gov/crt/case-document/file/1515051/dl?inline=.

75　**routinely spread false rumors:** Taylor Lorenz, "How Libs of TikTok Became a Powerful Presence in Oklahoma Schools," *Washington Post*, February 24, 2024, https://www.washingtonpost.com/technology/2024/02/24/libs-tiktok-oklahoma-nonbinary-teen-death.

76　**received bomb threats for six:** Matt Lavietes, "Libs of TikTok Creator Accused of Inspiring School Bomb Threats Named to Oklahoma Library Board," NBC News, January 23, 2024, https://www.nbcnews.com/nbc-out/out-news/libs-tik-tok-bomb-threats-oklahoma-library-committee-rcna135369.

76　**retweeted Raichik's post:** Ryan Walters (@RyanWalters_), "Democrats say it doesn't exist. The liberal media denies the issue. Even some Republicans hide from it. Woke ideology is real and I am here to stop it." X, August 22, 2023, https://x.com/RyanWalters_/status/1693977016045912308.

76　**appointing her to:** Taylor Lorenz, "How Libs of TikTok Became a Powerful Presence in Oklahoma Schools," *Washington Post*, February 24, 2024, https://www.washingtonpost.com/technology/2024/02/24/libs-tiktok-oklahoma-nonbinary-teen-death.

76　**signed a law in 2022 preventing:** Bevan Hurley, "Oklahoma Banned Trans Students from Bathrooms. Now Nex Benedict Is Dead After a Fight at School," *The Independent*, February 20, 2024, https://www.the-independent.com/news/world/americas/nex-benedict-dead-oklahoma-b2501844.html.

76　**label of a "stochastic terrorist":** Lorenz, "How Libs of TikTok Became a Powerful Presence in Oklahoma Schools."

76　**documented how tweets from Raichik:** Zach Montague, "On X, Conservative Activists Find a Direct Pipeline to Musk's Team," *New York Times*, February 26, 2025, https://www.nytimes.com/2025/02/26/us/politics/elon-musk-doge-x-accounts-activists.html.

76　*Vice* **reports that:** Tess Owen, "Schools Report Bomb Threats Following Libs of TikTok Anti-LGBTQ Posts," *Vice*, October 4, 2023, https://www.vice.com/en/article/schools-report-bomb-threats-following-libs-of-tiktok-anti-lgbtq-posts.

77 **"the fact that the U.S. population":** "Cultural Issues and the 2024 Election—1. Racial Attitudes and the 2024 Election," Pew Research Center, June 6, 2024, https://www.pewresearch.org/politics/2024/06/06/racial-attitudes-and-the-2024-election.

78 **doubled down by trying to end:** Collin Binkley, "Trump Administration Gives Schools a Deadline to End DEI Programs or Risk Losing Federal Money," Associated Press, February 18, 2025, https://apnews.com/article/dei-critical-race-theory-colleges-diversity-db8317ad37931558dd5a396cf5ab3d42.

78 **support LGBTQ rights:** "LGBTQ+ Rights," Gallup, accessed February 6, 2025, https://news.gallup.com/poll/1651/gay-lesbian-rights.aspx.

78 **believe in racial equality:** "New Public Agenda Report: Americans Widely Agree on Racial Equality, but Differ over the Impacts of Racism and How to Address It," Public Agenda, June 15, 2023, https://publicagenda.org/news/new-public-agenda-report-americans-widely-agree-on-racial-equality-but-differ-over-the-impacts-of-racism-and-how-to-address-it.

78 **advance women's equality:** Juliana Menasce Horowitz and Ruth Igielnik, "A Century After Women Gained the Right to Vote, Majority of Americans See Work to Do on Gender Equality," Pew Research Center, July 7, 2020, https://www.pewresearch.org/social-trends/2020/07/07/a-century-after-women-gained-the-right-to-vote-majority-of-americans-see-work-to-do-on-gender-equality.

78 **"overcoming racism requires changes":** "New Public Agenda Report: Americans Widely Agree on Racial Equality, but Differ over the Impacts of Racism and How to Address It."

78 **71 percent of Americans favor:** "School Integration Survey Findings," Lake Research Partners, April 26, 2024, https://drive.google.com/file/d/1aPQO41T7tv7Z5dr72-MGvmXGI7XedTi1/view?pli=1.

79 **lost about three-quarters of its population:** "Population of McDowell County," Population.us, accessed March 2, 2025, https://population.us/county/wv/mcdowell-county.

79 **Jobs left the county:** Eduardo Porter, "A Fading Coal County Bets on Schools, but There's One Big Hitch," *New York Times*, June 14, 2021, https://www.nytimes.com/2021/06/14/business/economy/west-virginia-county-teachers.html.

79 **almost half of the students:** "In Rural W.Va., Schools Rethink Their Role," KTAR News, May 8, 2013, https://ktar.com/uncategorized/in-rural-wva-schools-rethink-their-role/217545.

79 **highest rates of opioid addiction:** Sari Horwitz, Steven Rich, and Scott Higham, "Opioid Death Rates Soared in Communities Where Pain Pills Flowed," *Washington Post*, July 17, 2019, https://www.washingtonpost.com/investigations/opioid-death-rates-soared-in-communities-where-pain-pills-flowed/2019/07/17/f3595da4-a8a4-11e9-a3a6-ab670962db05_story.html.

79 **highest opioid death rate:** Jim Malatras, "The Growing Drug Epidemic in New York," Rockefeller Institute of Government, April 2017, https://rockinst.org/issue-area/growing-drug-epidemic-new-york.

79 **more than forty-five times the national average:** Holly Hedegaard, Arialdi M. Miniño, and Margaret Warner, "Drug Overdose Deaths in the United States, 1999–2017," NCHS Data Brief, No. 329, November 2018, Centers for Disease Control, accessed March 1, 2025, https://www.cdc.gov/nchs/data/databriefs/db329-h.pdf.

79 **median household income:** "McDowell County, WV," Data USA, accessed March 1, 2025, https://datausa.io/profile/geo/mcdowell-county-wv.

79 **national median of $74,580:** Gloria Guzman and Melissa Kollar, "Income in the United States: 2022," Census Bureau, September 2023, https://www.census.gov /content/dam/Census/library/publications/2023/demo/p60-279.pdf.

79 **one-third of the county:** "McDowell County, WV."

79 **three times the national average:** "McDowell County, WV."

79 **In 2022, the suicide rate:** Matthew Young, "CDC statistics show West Virginia has second-lowest life expectancy in U.S., higher murder-rate than New York," RealWV, May 22, 2023, https://therealwv.com/2023/05/22/cdc-statistics-show-west -virginia-has-second-lowest-life-expectancy-in-u-s-higher-murder-rate-than -new-york.

79 **almost twice the national average:** Young, "CDC statistics show West Virginia has second-lowest life expectancy in U.S., higher murder-rate than New York."

80 **"carry burdens that hang":** Lyndsey Layton, "Teachers Union Leads Effort That Aims to Turn Around West Virginia School System," *Washington Post*, December 15, 2011, https://www.washingtonpost.com/local/education/teachers-union-leads-effort -that-aims-to-turn-around-west-virginia-school-system/2011/12/14/gIQA5pxywO _story.html.

80 **"armed with a turnaround":** Layton, "Teachers Union Leads Effort."

81 **first new multistory construction:** Roxy Todd, "New Housing Complex Aims to Bring More Teachers to McDowell: Is It Working?," WV Public Broadcasting, January 21, 2022, https://wvpublic.org/new-housing-complex-aims-to-bring-more -teachers-to-mcdowell-is-it-working.

82 **In McDowell, we cut the dropout rate:** "Reconnecting McDowell Accomplishments," AFT, July 2017, https://www.aft.org/sites/default/files/media/2017/mcdowell _accomplishments_051719.pdf.

82 **A comprehensive analysis:** Anna Maier, Julia Daniel, Jeannie Oakes, and Livia Lam, "Community Schools as an Effective School Improvement Strategy: A Review of the Evidence," Learning Policy Institute and National Education Policy Center, December 2017, https://learningpolicyinstitute.org/media/137/download?inline& file=Community_Schools_Effective_REPORT.pdf.

83 **went on strike to expand:** Louis Freedberg, "Los Angeles Teachers Return to Class After Voting to End Strike," *EdSource*, January 22, 2019, https://edsource.org/2019/ agreement-reached-on-la-school-strike-teachers-expected-to-return-to-class-on -wednesday/607523.

83 **pledged to create thirty new:** Sonali Kohli, "What's in the Deal to End the LAUSD Teachers' Strike? A Look at the Details," *Los Angeles Times*, January 22, 2019, https://www.latimes.com/local/education/la-me-edu-lausd-strike-deal-details -20190122-story.html.

85 **On December 14, 2012:** Nicole Asbury, "After School Shootings, Teachers Struggle for Years with Trauma," *Washington Post*, June 20, 2022, https://www.washington post.com/education/2022/06/20/teacher-trauma-school-shooting-uvalde -parkland.

85 **armed with an AR-15-style assault weapon:** Rick Rojas, Karen Zraick and Troy Closson, "Sandy Hook Families Settle with Gunmaker for $73 Million Over Massa-

cre," *New York Times*, February 15, 2022, https://www.nytimes.com/2022/02/15/nyregion/sandy-hook-families-settlement.html.

85 **fired 154 rounds:** Mary Ellen Clark and Noreen O'Donnell, "Newtown School Gunman Fired 154 Rounds in Less Than 5 Minutes," Reuters, March 28, 2013, https://www.reuters.com/article/business/newtown-school-gunman-fired-154-rounds-in-less-than-5-minutes-idUSL2N0CK0KN.

85 **killed twenty-six people:** Lauren Frias, Azmi Haroun, and Michal Kranz, "It's Been a Decade Since the Sandy Hook Shooting. Here Are the Names and Pictures of the 27 Victims, Including 20 Children, Who Were Murdered That Day," *Business Insider*, December 14, 2022, https://www.businessinsider.com/who-were-the-victims-of-the-sandy-hook-shooting-2017-12.

85 **leading cause of death for children:** Silvia Villarreal et al., "Gun Violence in the United States 2022 Examining the Burden Among Children & Teens," Center for Gun Violence Solutions, Johns Hopkins Bloomberg School of Public Health, September 2024, https://publichealth.jhu.edu/sites/default/files/2024-09/2022-cgvs-gun-violence-in-the-united-states.pdf.

86 **twenty-seven school shootings in the United States:** Jaclyn Diaz, "27 School Shootings Have Taken Place So Far This Year," NPR, May 25, 2022, https://www.npr.org/2022/05/24/1101050970/2022-school-shootings-so-far.

86 **In one video they made:** "Randi Weingarten's AFT: One of the Greatest Threats to Our Children," posted by NRATV, YouTube, https://www.youtube.com/watch?v=nfmZoBfvtR4.

87 **a strong majority of Americans:** Madison Fernandez, "Study Shows Majority of Gun Owners Support Specific Gun Safety Policies," *Politico*, October 19, 2022, https://www.politico.com/news/2022/10/19/gun-owners-support-safety-policies-00062335.

87 **AFT members like Anne Marie Murphy:** Mike Elk, "A Grief-Stricken Randi Weingarten Engages Hesitant Unions on Gun Control in Wake of Sandy Hook," *In These Times*, December 20, 2012, https://inthesetimes.com/article/randi-weingarten-calls-for-labor-to-take-up-gun-control.

87 **have called to roll back:** Nathan Layne, "Trump Vows to Undo Biden Gun Restrictions if Re-Elected," Reuters, February 9, 2024, https://www.reuters.com/world/us/trump-vows-undo-biden-gun-restrictions-if-re-elected-2024-02-10.

88 **"get over it":** Jillian Frankel and Zoë Richards, "Trump Tells Supporters 'We Have to Get Over It' After Iowa School Shooting," NBC News, January 5, 2024, https://www.nbcnews.com/politics/donald-trump/trump-tells-supporters-get-iowa-school-shooting-move-forward-rcna132610.

88 **"for entertainment and for sport":** Roque Planas, "Trump Tells Parents of School Shooting Victims We Need More Guns 'For Entertainment,'" *HuffPost*, October 17, 2024, https://www.huffpost.com/entry/trump-tells-school-shooting-victims-parents-we-need-guns-for-entertainment_n_6711590de4b0e33eefb22e3c.

88 **has extensive plans for book bans:** "Project 2025 and Its Threat to Free Expression," PEN America, September 12, 2024, https://pen.org/report/project-2025.

88 **expand unfettered access to guns:** "The Role of Guns in Project 2025, Explained," Brady Campaign to Prevent Gun Violence, accessed March 1, 2025, https://elections.bradyunited.org/resources/project-2025-guns.

88 **I am so grateful:** "About," Teachers Unify to End Gun Violence, accessed March 1, 2025, https://www.teachersunify.org/about.

89 **higher rates of anxiety, depression, and suicide:** Carol Graham, "The Kids Are Not OK, but Education Innovations Provide Hope," *American Educator*, Winter 2024–2025, https://www.aft.org/ae/winter2024-2025/graham.

89 **the 2024 World Happiness Report:** Victoria Bisset, "America's Happiness Score Drops amid a Youth 'Midlife Crisis,'" *Washington Post*, March 20, 2024, https://www.washingtonpost.com/wellness/2024/03/20/us-world-happiness-report-youth.

89 **Economist Carol Graham:** Graham, "The Kids Are Not OK."

89 **Research shows that teens who spend:** "Likes vs. Learning: The Real Cost of Social Media for Schools," AFT, American Psychological Association, Design It For Us, Fairplay, and ParentsTogether, 2023, https://www.aft.org/sites/default/files/media/documents/2023/LikesVSLearning_Report.pdf.

89 **increasing eating disorders:** Dennis Thompson, "Social Media Linked to Eating Disorders in Kids and Young Teens," *US News & World Report*, September 13, 2024, https://www.usnews.com/news/health-news/articles/2024-09-13/social-media-linked-to-eating-disorders-in-kids-and-young-teens.

89 **suicidal thoughts:** Rosemary Sedgwick et al., "Social Media, Internet Use and Suicide Attempts in Adolescents," *Current Opinion in Psychiatry* 36, no. 6 (2019): 534–41, https://pmc.ncbi.nlm.nih.gov/articles/PMC6791504.

89 **and anxiety and:** Fengxia Lai et al., "Relationship Between Social Media Use and Social Anxiety in College Students: Mediation Effect of Communication Capacity," *International Journal of Environmental Research and Public Health* 20, no. 4 (February 18, 2023): 3657, https://pmc.ncbi.nlm.nih.gov/articles/PMC9966679.

89 **decreasing self-esteem:** Jacqui Taylor-Jackson and Ahmed A Moustafa, "The Relationships Between Social Media Use and Factors Relating to Depression," *The Nature of Depression* (October 16, 2020): 171–82, https://pmc.ncbi.nlm.nih.gov/articles/PMC7562923.

89 **Nearly half of teens:** Emily A. Vogels, "Teens and Cyberbullying 2022," Pew Research Center, December 15, 2022, https://www.pewresearch.org/internet/2022/12/15/teens-and-cyberbullying-2022.

89 **rates of exposure to bullying:** Daisy Mui Hung Kee, Maryam Ammar Lutf Al-Anesi, and Sarah Ammar Lutf Al-Anesi, "Cyberbullying on Social Media Under the Influence of COVID-19," *Global Business and Organizational Excellence* 41, no. 6 (July 6, 2022): 11–22, https://pmc.ncbi.nlm.nih.gov/articles/PMC9350190.

89 **In polling conducted:** Vogels, "Teens and Cyberbullying 2022."

89 **the more time young people:** Amanda L. Giordano, Elizabeth A. Prosek, and Joshua C. Watson, "Understanding Adolescent Cyberbullies: Exploring Social Media Addiction and Psychological Factors," *Journal of Child and Adolescent Counseling* 7, no. 1 (2021): 42–55, https://www.tandfonline.com/doi/abs/10.1080/23727810.2020.1835420?journalCode=ucac20.

89 **increasing the amount of time:** Eun Jung Choi, Gabrielle K. C. King, and Emma G. Duerden, "Screen Time in Children and Youth During the Pandemic: A Systematic Review and Meta-Analysis," *Global Pediatrics* 6 (December 2023), https://www.sciencedirect.com/science/article/pii/S2667009723000465.

89　**a nationwide epidemic:** Amanda Seitz, "Loneliness Poses Risks as Deadly as Smoking: Surgeon General," Associated Press, May 2, 2023, https://apnews.com/article /surgeon-general-loneliness-334450f7bb5a77e88d8085b178340e19.

90　**Survey data of fifteen- and sixteen-year-olds:** Tara Bahrampour, "Teens Around the World Are Lonelier Than a Decade Ago. The Reason May Be Smartphones," *Washington Post*, July 20, 2021, https://www.washingtonpost.com/local/social-issues /teens-loneliness-smart-phones/2021/07/20/cde8c866-e84e-11eb-8950-d73b3e 93ff7f_story.html.

90　**Murthy himself blames:** Seitz, "Loneliness Poses Risks as Deadly as Smoking."

90　**"Up to 95% of youth":** "Social Media and Youth Mental Health: The U.S. Surgeon General's Advisory," United States Department of Health and Human Services, 2023, https://www.hhs.gov/sites/default/files/sg-youth-mental-health-social-media -advisory.pdf.

90　**72 percent of high school teachers:** Jenn Hatfield, "72% of U.S. High School Teachers Say Cellphone Distraction Is a Major Problem in the Classroom," Pew Research Center, June 12, 2024, https://www.pewresearch.org/short-reads/2024/06/12/72 -percent-of-us-high-school-teachers-say-cellphone-distraction-is-a-major-problem -in-the-classroom.

90　**59 percent of parents:** "Dealing with Devices: The Parent-Teen Dynamic," Common Sense Media, accessed March 1, 2025, https://www.commonsensemedia.org/tech nology-addiction-concern-controversy-and-finding-balance-infographic.

90　**50 percent of teenagers:** "Dealing with Devices."

90　**almost two in five say:** Monica Anderson, Michelle Faverio, and Eugenie Park, "How Teens and Parents Approach Screen Time," Pew Research Center, March 11, 2024, https://www.pewresearch.org/internet/2024/03/11/how-teens-and-parents -approach-screen-time.

90　**one in four teens:** Anderson, Faverio, and Park, "How Teens and Parents Approach Screen Time."

90　**almost three-quarters of teens:** Anderson, Faverio, and Park, "How Teens and Parents Approach Screen Time."

91　**Meta's own internal research:** Kolbe Nelson, "Facebook Knew Instagram Was Pushing Girls to Dangerous Content: Internal Document," CBS News, December 11, 2022, https://www.cbsnews.com/news/facebook-instagram-dangerous-content-60 -minutes-2022-12-11.

91　**the best seats at his inauguration:** Ali Swenson, "Trump, a Populist President, Is Flanked by Tech Billionaires at His Inauguration," Associated Press, January 20, 2025, https://apnews.com/article/trump-inauguration-tech-billionaires-zuckerberg -musk-wealth-0896bfc3f50d941d62cebc3074267ecd.

91　**we can count on the opposite:** Paige Gross, "Trump Tech Appointees Point to a Deregulated Industry, Tech Players Say," *Ohio Capital Journal*, January 6, 2025, https://ohiocapitaljournal.com/2025/01/06/trump-tech-appointees-point-to -a-deregulated-industry-tech-players-say.

92　**the U.S. Senate passed:** "Senate Overwhelmingly Passes Children's Online Privacy Legislation," U.S. Senate Committee on Commerce, Science, & Transportation, United States Senate, July 30, 2024, https://www.commerce.senate.gov/index.php /2024/7/senate-overwhelmingly-passes-children-s-online-privacy-legislation.

92 **overwhelming bipartisan support:** Scott Wong et al., "Senate Passes the Most Significant Child Online Safety Bills in Decades," NBC News, July 30, 2024, https://www.nbcnews.com/politics/congress/senate-poised-pass-significant-child-online-safety-bills-decades-rcna164259.

92 **"give parents new tools":** Wong et al. "Senate Overwhelmingly Passes Children's Online Privacy Legislation."

92 **Meta, the trillion-dollar technology behemoth:** Brian Baker, "Trillion-Dollar companies: 10 Most Valuable Mega-Cap Stocks," Bankrate, December 16, 2024, https://www.bankrate.com/investing/trillion-dollar-companies.

92 **succeeded in stopping:** Ruth Reader, "Mark Zuckerberg and Meta Got a Big Win. They Have the House GOP to Thank," *Politico Pro*, December 24, 2024, https://subscriber.politicopro.com/article/2024/12/mark-zuckerberg-meta-congress-bill-00195958.

92 **the social media platform X:** Ramishah Maruf, "Elon Musk-Owned X Settles Lawsuit with Donald Trump over January 6 Suspension," CNN, February 12, 2025, https://www.cnn.com/2025/02/12/business/x-settlement-musk-trump-jan-6/index.html.

92 **enacted state laws:** Louis Freedberg, "California Acts to Protect Children from 'Addictive' Social Media," *EdSource*, September 23, 2024, https://edsource.org/2024/california-acts-to-protect-children-from-addictive-social-media/719340.

92 **filed or joined lawsuits:** "Likes vs. Learning: The Real Cost of Social Media for Schools," AFT, American Psychological Association, Design It for Us, Fairplay, and ParentsTogether, 2023, https://www.aft.org/sites/default/files/media/documents/2023/LikesVSLearning_Report.pdf.

93 **Lillian Keys grew up:** Lillian Keys, interview, March 11, 2021.

94 **There's Michael Shunney:** "Meet Our Heroes on the Frontlines of COVID-19," AFT, accessed March 3, 2025, https://www.aft.org/press/nyt/meet-our-heroes-frontlines-covid-19.

94 **Wretha Rawls Thomas and Denetris Jones:** "Connecting to Community One Partner at a Time," AFT Voices, AFT, December 14, 2022, https://aftvoices.org/connecting-to-community-one-partner-at-a-time-48c02d3cdd00.

94 **There's Clare Berke:** Clare Berke, "These Students Learn by Doing," AFT Voices, AFT, April 2, 2024, https://aftvoices.org/these-students-learn-by-doing-a25bc8daa7ec.

95 **1.2 million school-aged students:** "Nationwide, More Children Live in the State of Homelessness Than in Most American States," National Alliance to End Homelessness, August 27, 2024, https://endhomelessness.org/resource/nationwide-more-children-live-in-the-state-of-homelessness-than-in-most-american-states.

95 **overdose death rates have tripled:** "The Opioid Epidemic in the United States," State Health Access Data Assistance Center, accessed March 6, 2025, https://www.shadac.org/opioid-epidemic-united-states.

96 **During the 2022–2023 school year, over:** "Table 204.10. Number and Percentage of Public School Students Eligible for Free or Reduced-Price Lunch, by State: Selected School Years, 2000–01 Through 2022–23," Digest of Education Statistics, National Center for Education Statistics, 2023, accessed March 3, 2025, https://nces.ed.gov/programs/digest/d23/tables/dt23_204.10.asp.

96 **Donald Trump tried to kick:** Saul Elbein, "Walz Pick Highlights Partisan Divisions on Free School Lunches," *The Hill*, August 10, 2024, https://thehill.com/homenews/campaign/4820875-universal-school-meals-partisan-divide.

96 **Republican governors have turned:** Elbein, "Walz Pick Highlights Partisan Divisions."

97 **in Salt Lake City:** Amanda Holpuch, "Utah School District Apologises After Meals Taken Away from Pupils," *The Guardian*, January 30, 2014, https://www .theguardian.com/world/2014/jan/30/utah-school-district-meals-taken-away -pupils.

97 **issued an executive order to close:** "Executive Order 14242 of March 20, 2025, Improving Education Outcomes by Empowering Parents, States, and Communities," 90 F.R. 13679 (2025), https://www.federalregister.gov/documents/2025/03/25/2025 -05213/improving-education-outcomes-by-empowering-parents-states-and -communities.

97 **in part goes to support:** Laura Meckler and Annabelle Timsit, "Trump Pledged to Close the Education Department. What Would That Mean?," *Washington Post*, November 12, 2024, https://www.washingtonpost.com/education/2024/11/12/trump -close-education-department-proposal-explained.

97 **Both the Project 2025 blueprint:** Evie Blad, "How Trump Could Roll Back Access to Free School Lunches," *Education Week*, November 26, 2024, https://www.edweek .org/policy-politics/how-trump-could-roll-back-access-to-free-school-lunches /2024/11.

97 **and Congressional Republicans' 2025 budget:** Kate Grumke, "Hundreds of Thousands of Midwest Kids Would Lose Free School Meals Under Potential Federal Budget Cut," *Harvest Public Media*, January 29, 2025, https://www.kcur.org/news /2025-01-29/midwest-kids-free-school-meals-potential-budget-cut.

97 **"sponge off of the government":** Lauren Irwin, "Republican Suggests Students Get Jobs to Pay for Lunches," *The Hill*, January 29, 2025, https://thehill.com/home news/house/5112987-ritch-mccormick-funding-freeze-school-lunch.

97 **Almost ten million school-aged children:** Sarah D. Sparks, "More Children Are Living in Poverty. What This Means for Schools," *Education Week*, September 12, 2024, https://www.edweek.org/leadership/more-children-are-living-in-poverty-what -this-means-for-schools/2024/09.

97 **More than half of students in poverty:** "How Does Hunger Affect Learning?," No Kid Hungry, April 24, 2023, https://www.nokidhungry.org/blog/how-does-hunger-affect -learning.

97 **Almost half of students living below:** Sarah D. Sparks, "Rx for Reading Gaps: Screen All Students Early for Vision Problems," *Education Week*, January 25, 2024, https:// www.edweek.org/leadership/rx-for-reading-gaps-screen-all-students-early-for -vision-problems/2024/01.

98 **"Our schools cannot be improved":** Diane Ravitch, *The Death and Life of the Great American School System* (Basic Books, 2016): 244.

98 **"Study after study":** "Making Strides on School Integration," *School Administrator Magazine*, School Superintendents Association, April 1, 2022, https://www.aasa .org/resources/resource/making-strides-on-school-integration.

99 **"education is the only valid passport":** "Lyndon Baines Johnson Quotes," LBJ Museum, accessed March 3, 2025, https://lbjmuseum.com/exhibits/online-exhibits /lyndon-baines-johnson-quotes.

99 **"unless the whole of American society":** Martin Luther King Jr., *Where Do We Go from Here: Chaos or Community* (Beacon Press, 1968): 51.

99 **"The Great Society is a place"**: Lyndon B. Johnson, "Remarks at the University of Michigan," May 22, 1964, American Presidency Project, https://www.presidency .ucsb.edu/documents/remarks-the-university-michigan.

3: TEACHERS CREATE OPPORTUNITY

101 **Robert Russa Moton was**: "Moton School Strike and Prince Edward County School Closings," Encyclopedia Virginia, accessed March 3, 2025, https://encyclopediavir ginia.org/entries/moton-school-strike-and-prince-edward-county-school-clo sings.

102 **built tar-paper shacks**: Jeff Feinstein, "Column: This Little Known Site Is the Birthplace of the Student Civil Rights Movement," PBS, April 29, 2016, https://www .pbs.org/newshour/education/column-this-little-known-site-is-the-birthplace -of-the-student-civil-rights-movement.

102 **Originally designed to hold**: "Moton School Strike and Prince Edward County School Closings."

102 **"had no plumbing"**: Feinstein, "Column: This Little Known Site."

102 **"These structures were cold"**: Joan Johns Cobbs, *Brown v. Board* at 65: Joan Johns Cobbs Remembers the Day Her Sister Led a Student Protest That Went On to Change the Course of American History," *The 74*, May 14, 2019, https://www.the 74million.org/article/brown-v-board-at-65-joan-johns-cobbs-remembers-the -day-her-sister-led-a-student-protest-that-went-on-to-change-the-course-of -american-history.

102 **"no dedicated gymnasium"**: "Moton School Strike and Prince Edward County School Closings."

102 **In 1951, Barbara Johns**: "Biography: Barbara Rose Johns Powell, 1935–1991," Robert Russa Moton Museum, accessed March 6, 2025, https://motonmuseum.org /learn/biography-barbara-rose-johns-powell.

102 **several years before the Montgomery**: "Eastern National Publishes *The Moton School Story: Children of Courage*," Eastern National, November 14, 2012, https:// easternnational.org/wp-content/uploads/2015/05/11142012-Press-Release-Moton -Book-Press-Release.pdf.

102 **in April 1951, Barbara led**: "Barbara Johns (1935–1991)," Virginia Changemakers, accessed March 6, 2025, https://edu.lva.virginia.gov/changemakers/items/show/121.

103 **landmark *Brown v. Board of Education* case**: Brown v. Board of Education of Topeka, 347 U.S. 483 (1954), https://supreme.justia.com/cases/federal/us/347/483.

103 **in reality, Prince Edward County**: "Moton School Strike and Prince Edward County School Closings."

104 **Economist John N. Friedman**: John N. Friedman, "School Is for Social Mobility," *New York Times*, September 1, 2022, https://www.nytimes.com/2022/09/01/opin ion/us-school-social-mobility.html#:~.

104 **if students in low-income countries**: "Education for People and Planet: Creating Sustainable Futures for All," Global Education Monitoring Report Team, UNESCO, 2016, https://unesdoc.unesco.org/ark:/48223/pf0000245752.

104 **"many of their peers"**: Ron Haskins, "Education and Economic Mobility," Economic Mobility Project, Brookings Institution, 2016, https://www.brookings.edu/wp -content/uploads/2016/07/02_economic_mobility_sawhill_ch8.pdf.

104 **"With the right level of investment":** Friedman, "School Is for Social Mobility."

104 **"A world-class education":** Ezra Mechaber, "Staying Competitive Through Education: The President and American Business Leaders Announce New Commitments," Obama White House Archives, July 18, 2011, https://obamawhitehouse
.archives.gov/blog/2011/07/18/staying-competitive-through-education-president
-and-american-business-leaders-announ.

105 **"Access to education does":** Diane Ravitch, "The Dark History of School Choice,"
New York Review, January 14, 2021, https://www.nybooks.com/articles/2021/01/14
/the-dark-history-of-school-choice.

105 **American dream is out of reach:** Gabriel Borelli, "Americans Are Split over the State
of the American Dream," Pew Research Center, July 2, 2024, https://www.pewre
search.org/short-reads/2024/07/02/americans-are-split-over-the-state-of-the
-american-dream.

105 **"all children, regardless of background":** "The Nation's Education Agenda," AFT,
January 2023, https://www.aft.org/sites/default/files/media/documents/2023/slides
_national-education-survey_Jan2023.pdf.

106 **"Education is the key":** "Education is the key to unlock the golden door of freedom.—George Washington Carver," Library of Congress, accessed March 3, 2025,
https://www.loc.gov/item/2023634980/?ref%3Damericanpurpose.com.

106 **"In 1955 and 1956":** Nancy MacLean, "'School Choice' Developed as a Way to Protect Segregation and Abolish Public Schools," *Washington Post*, September 27, 2021,
https://www.washingtonpost.com/outlook/2021/09/27/school-choice-developed
-way-protect-segregation-abolish-public-schools.

106 **In 1954, Gallup found:** Joseph Carroll, "Race and Education 50 Years After *Brown v.
Board of Education*," Gallup, May 14, 2004, https://news.gallup.com/poll/11686
/race-education-years-after-brown-board-education.aspx.

107 **"The mixing of races":** Sara Rimer, "Resistance to Racial Integration," Equal Justice Initiative, December 18, 2024, https://eji.org/news/resistance-to-racial-inte
gration.

107 **"If we must choose":** "Segregation in America: Segregationists," Equal Justice Initiative, accessed March 3, 2025, https://segregationinamerica.eji.org/segregation
ists#full.

107 **shut down all of the county's schools:** "Prince Edward County School Closings."

107 **cancel school taxes:** Chris Ford, Stephenie Johnson, and Lisette Partelow, "The
Racist Origins of Private School Vouchers," Center for American Progress, July
12, 2017, https://www.americanprogress.org/article/racist-origins-private-school
-vouchers.

107 **created a whites-only private school:** "Civil Rights Movement in Virginia: The Closing of Prince Edward County's Schools," Virginia Museum of History & Culture,
accessed March 3, 2025, https://virginiahistory.org/learn/civil-rights-movement
-virginia/closing-prince-edward-countys-schools.

107 **created a voucher program:** Ford, Johnson, and Partelow, "The Racist Origins of
Private School Vouchers."

107 **in Prince Edward County until 1964:** "Timeline," Robert Russa Moton Museum, accessed March 6, 2025, https://motonmuseum.org/learn/timeline.

107 **yet another Supreme Court case:** Griffin v. School Board, 377 U.S. 218 (1964), https://
supreme.justia.com/cases/federal/us/377/218.

107 **only allocated $189,000:** Ford, Johnson, and Partelow, "The Racist Origins of Private School Vouchers."

107 **economist Milton Friedman:** Nancy MacLean, "How Milton Friedman Aided and Abetted Segregationists in His Quest to Privatize Public Education," Institute for New Economic Thinking, September 27, 2021, https://www.ineteconomics.org /perspectives/blog/how-milton-friedman-aided-and-abetted-segregationists -in-his-quest-to-privatize-public-education.

108 **Friedman, notably, went on:** Maurice Earls, "Pinochet's Free-Market Fascism Mixed Economic Reform with Brutal Repression," *Irish Times*, October 24, 2008, https://www.irishtimes.com/opinion/pinochet-s-free-market-fascism-mixed -economic-reform-with-brutal-repression-1.900621.

108 **"largely found to have exacerbated":** Amaya Garcia, "Chile's School Voucher System: Enabling Choice or Perpetuating Social Inequality?" New America, February 9, 2017, https://www.newamerica.org/education-policy/edcentral/chiles-school -voucher-system-enabling-choice-or-perpetuating-social-inequality.

108 **"Father of Economic Freedom":** Andrew Peek, Tim Kane, and William Beach, "Milton Friedman, the Father of Economic Freedom," The Heritage Foundation, https://www.heritage.org/trade/report/milton-friedman-the-father-economic -freedom.

108 **the institution that produced:** Spencer Chretien, "Project 2025," The Heritage Foundation, January 31, 2023, https://www.heritage.org/conservatism/commen tary/project-2025.

109 **billionaire Koch family:** Connie Matthiessen, "Who's Funding the Latest Conservative Assault on Public Education?," *Inside Philanthropy*, July 27, 2021, https://www .insidephilanthropy.com/home/2021-7-27-whos-funding-the-latest-conservative -attack-on-public-education.

109 **In 1980, David Koch ran:** Nicholas Confessore, "1980 Report Showing That David Koch Spent $2,086,000 on the Clark-Koch Presidential Campaign," Koch Docs, accessed March 6, 2025, https://kochdocs.org/2019/08/21/libertarian-party-1980 -presidential-campaign.

109 **"We advocate the complete":** William Rasberry, "Incompetent Teachers," *Washington Post*, November 5, 1981, https://www.washingtonpost.com/archive/politics /1981/11/06/incompetent-teachers/208c55ef-ae94-4f60-88bf-c530f94f88de.

109 **"religious education is fundamental":** Josh Cowan, interview, November 12, 2024.

109 **"Our desire is to":** Emily McFarlan Miller, "Betsy DeVos: 5 Faith Facts to Know About the Education Secretary," Religion News Service, via *USA Today*, February 7, 2017, https://www.usatoday.com/story/news/nation/2017/02/07/5-faith-facts-betsy -devos/97601374.

110 **"the church—which ought to":** Benjamin Wermund, "Trump's Education Pick Says Reform Can 'Advance God's Kingdom,'" *Politico*, December 2, 2016, https://www .politico.com/story/2016/12/betsy-devos-education-trump-religion-232150.

110 **"more and more churches":** Wermund, "Trump's Education Pick Says Reform Can 'Advance God's Kingdom.'"

110 **were not enrolled:** Mark Lieberman, "Most Students Getting New School Choice Funds Aren't Ditching Public Schools," *Education Week*, October 4, 2023, https:// www.edweek.org/policy-politics/most-students-getting-new-school-choice-funds -arent-ditching-public-schools/2023/10.

110 **earn over $200,000 per year:** Carl Davis, "Tax Avoidance Continues to Fuel School Privatization Efforts," Institute on Taxation and Economic Policy, March 3, 2023, https://itep.org/tax-avoidance-fuels-school-vouchers-privatization-efforts.

110 **among the top 10 percent:** Elise Gould and Jori Kandra, "Inequality in Annual Earnings Worsens in 2021," Economic Policy Institute, December 21, 2022, https://www.epi.org/publication/inequality-2021-ssa-data.

110 **backed Abbott's successful push:** Joe Lovinger, "Billionaires Swoop In to Fund Abbott's Texas School-Voucher Push," Bloomberg, January 14, 2025, https://www.bloomberg.com/news/articles/2025-01-14/billionaires-swoop-in-to-fund-abbott-s-texas-school-voucher-push?srnd=homepage-americas&embedded-checkout=true.

110 **oust Republicans in the state legislature:** Jimmy Cloutier, "National 'School Choice' Movement Ousts Anti-Voucher Republicans in Texas Runoffs," Open Secrets, May 31, 2024, https://www.opensecrets.org/news/2024/05/national-school-choice-movement-ousts-anti-voucher-republicans-in-texas.

110 **"This is, at the end of the day":** Lovinger, "Billionaires Swoop In to Fund Abbott's Texas School-Voucher Push."

111 **"The risks of universal vouchers":** Alec MacGillis, "How Religious Schools Became a Billion-Dollar Drain on Public Education," *New Yorker*, January 13, 2025, https://www.newyorker.com/magazine/2025/01/20/religious-education-public-schools-vouchers-taxes-catholic-church-ohio.

111 **billions in taxpayer dollars:** Laura Meckler and Michelle Boorstein, "Billions in Taxpayer Dollars Now Go to Religious Schools via Vouchers," *Washington Post*, June 3, 2024, https://www.washingtonpost.com/nation/2024/06/03/tax-dollars-religious-schools.

111 **"The church is supposed to direct":** Jeff Cercone, "Fact Check: Boebert Says 'the Church Is Supposed to Direct the Government,'" WRAL News, July 8, 2022, https://www.wral.com/story/fact-check-boebert-says-the-church-is-supposed-to-direct-the-government/20365965.

111 **"Congress shall make no law":** "The United States Constitution," National Constitution Center, accessed March 5, 2025, https://constitutioncenter.org/the-constitution/full-text.

111 **"wall of separation":** Nicholas Rathod, "The Founding Fathers' Religious Wisdom," Center for American Progress, January 8, 2008, https://www.americanprogress.org/article/the-founding-fathers-religious-wisdom.

111 **believed faith would thrive:** Rathod, "The Founding Fathers' Religious Wisdom."

112 **nations which officially establish:** Dan Koev, "The Influence of State Favoritism on Established Religions and Their Competitors," *Politics and Religion* 16, no. 1 (April 29, 2022): 129–59, https://www.cambridge.org/core/journals/politics-and-religion/article/abs/influence-of-state-favoritism-on-established-religions-and-their-competitors/4C4A242102F5D4AC0EA33E2CC234976A.

112 **"America has had a strong wall":** Randi Weingarten and Sharon Kleinbaum, "The Bible Simply Doesn't Belong in Texas Public Schools," *Houston Chronicle*, December 8, 2024, https://www.houstonchronicle.com/opinion/outlook/article/texas-schools-bible-aft-19964263.php.

113 **the example of Arizona:** "Arizona School Vouchers, Explained," Arizona Center for Economic Progress, July 1, 2023, https://azeconcenter.org/arizona-school-vouchers-explained.

113   **made them "universal":** Bob Christie, "Arizona OKs Biggest US School Voucher Plan, Faces Challenge," Associated Press, July 7, 2022, https://apnews.com/article/educa tion-arizona-doug-ducey-school-vouchers-7c5d7eb0498e5e7234d7eeb726027506.

113   **65 percent of Arizonans voted:** "Arizona Proposition 305, Expansion of Empowerment Scholarship Accounts Referendum (2018)," Ballotpedia, accessed March 5, 2025, https://ballotpedia.org/Arizona_Proposition_305,_Expansion_of_Empow erment_Scholarship_Accounts_Referendum_(2018).

113   **Republicans ignored the will:** "Arizona School Vouchers, Explained."

113   **Three out of four students:** "Universal Vouchers: The Verdict Is In," Save Our Schools Arizona Network, January 17, 2024, https://www.sosaznetwork.org/2024 /universal-vouchers-the-verdict-is-in.

113   **goes to the wealthiest zip codes:** "Universal Vouchers: The Verdict Is In."

113   **a $1.4 billion budget shortfall:** Jacques Billeaud and Jonathan J. Cooper, "Arizona Lawmakers Pass Budget Closing $1.4 Billion Deficit," Associated Press, June 16, 2024, https://apnews.com/article/arizona-budget-deficit-cuts-hobbs-legislature-f84e 9144310146ceb0f58c742af53973.

114   **"Voucher programs have been in place":** Diane Ravitch, "*'Their* Kind of Indoctrination,'" *New York Review*, January 11, 2025, https://www.nybooks.com/online/2025 /01/11/their-kind-of-indoctrination.

114   **"This is the goal":** Diane Ravitch (@DianeRavitch), "This is the goal of the privatizers. Starve public schools. Everyone gets a voucher and public schools go away," X, March 21, 2024, https://x.com/DianeRavitch/status/1770871541980434623.

114   **Nationwide, while state funding:** "NEWS: New Report on the Coordinated Effort by Billionaires to Dismantle the American Public School System," U.S. Senate Committee on Health, Education, Labor & Pensions, June 25, 2024, https://www.help .senate.gov/dem/newsroom/press/news-new-report-on-the-coordinated-effort -by-billionaires-to-dismantle-the-american-public-school-system.

114   **school vouchers have been rejected by voters every time:** Eli Hager and Jeremy Schwartz, "Despite Trump's Win, School Vouchers Were Again Rejected by Majorities of Voters," *ProPublica*, November 9, 2024, https://www.propublica.org/article/ school-vouchers-2024-election-trump.

114   **by wide margins:** Hager and Schwartz, "Despite Trump's Win."

115   **parents want more non-college pathways:** Zach Hrynowski, "Nearly Half of U.S. Parents Want More Noncollege Paths," Gallup, April 7, 2021, https://news.gallup .com/poll/344201/nearly-half-parents-noncollege-paths.aspx.

115   **about two out of five high school graduates:** "61.4 Percent of Recent High School Graduates Enrolled in College in October 2023," U.S. Bureau of Labor Statistics, May 10, 2024, https://www.bls.gov/opub/ted/2024/61-4-percent-of-recent-high -school-graduates-enrolled-in-college-in-october-2023.htm.

115   **children in career and technical education:** "New Research from Advance CTE Indicates Families in Career Technical Education More Satisfied with Education, Prepared for College," Advance CTE, April 28, 2021, https://careertech.org/news/new -research-from-advance-cte-indicates-families-in-career-technical-education -more-satisfied-with-education-prepared-for-college.

115   **students who participate:** Rachel Rosen and Joshua Malbin, "Career and Technical Education: A Summary of the Evidence," MRDC, November 2024, https://www .mdrc.org/work/publications/career-and-technical-education-summary-evidence.

115 **"The number of Americans":** Steve Rattner (@SteveRattner), "The number of Americans earning more than their parents has been steadily decreasing over the last 80 years . . . ," X, November 7, 2024, https://x.com/SteveRattner/status /1854489701912092809.

116 **the right technical training:** Steve Lohr, "How High School Graduates Can Improve Their Earnings Potential," *New York Times*, November 21, 2024, https://www.ny times.com/2024/11/21/business/high-school-graduates-earnings.html.

116 **it turns out that career and technical education:** Te-Ping Chen, "The Schools Reviving Shop Class Offer a Hedge Against the AI Future," *Wall Street Journal*, March 1, 2025, https://www.wsj.com/us-news/education/high-school-shop-class-revival-24d7a525.

116 **82 percent of voters:** "Public Perspectives," National Skills Coalition, accessed March 5, 2025, https://nationalskillscoalition.org/public-perspectives.

116 **775 times more supporting colleges and universities:** "Government Funding for Universities," IBIS World, July 11, 2024, https://www.ibisworld.com/us/bed/gov ernment-funding-for-universities/4073.

116 **than career and technical education apprenticeship programs:** Dr. Robert Lerman, "How the U.S. Is Barely Tapping the Potential of Apprenticeships," *Fast Company*, April 15, 2023, https://www.fastcompany.com/90873199/how-the-u-s-is-barely-tap ping-the-potential-of-apprenticeships.

116 **CHIPS and Science Act:** "The CHIPS and Science Act: Here's What's In It," Mc-Kinsey, October 4, 2022, https://www.mckinsey.com/industries/public-sector/our -insights/the-chips-and-science-act-heres-whats-in-it.

116 **manufacturing tractors in Peoria:** Paul Gordon, "Caterpillar Marks 100 Years of Business in Peoria Area," *Rockford Register Star*, February 16, 2010, https:// www.rrstar.com/story/news/2010/02/16/caterpillar-marks-100-years-business /44625923007.

116 **large track-type tractors there:** "Caterpillar U.S. Locations," Caterpillar, accessed March 5, 2025, https://www.caterpillar.com/en/company/global-footprint/americas /united-states.html.

117 **Jeff Adkins-Dutro, the:** "Pathways to Prosperity: Peoria Federation of Teachers, Local 780," AFT Innovation Fund, AFT, 2017, https://www.aft.org/sites/default /files/media/2017/if_peoria-pathways_2017.pdf.

117 **"One day we visited":** Kianna Pittman, "What CTE Means to Me," *American Educator*, Fall 2022, https://www.aft.org/ae/fall2022/pittman.

118 **Micron is building:** Randi Weingarten and Michael Mulgrew, "STEM Training Of-fers Hope for Communities Across the Country," *Newsweek*, December 26, 2024, https://www.newsweek.com/stem-training-offers-hope-communities-across -country-opinion-2005366.

118 **created a pilot program:** "Micron Partnership Opens New Career Pathways for Stu-dents," AFT, December 12, 2023, https://www.aft.org/news/micron-partnership -opens-new-career-pathways-students.

119 **Lincoln-West School of Science and Health:** Pamela Hummer, "Creating a Healthy Community: How a High School in a Hospital Launches Careers and Enhances Well-Being," *American Educator*, Spring 2024, https://www.aft.org/ae/spring2024 /hummer.

119 **In Switzerland, for instance:** Diane Elliott and Batia Katz, "Three Lessons from the Swiss Apprenticeship Model to Inform Our Post-COVID-19 Recovery," Urban

Institute, July 20, 2020, https://www.urban.org/urban-wire/three-lessons-swiss
-apprenticeship-model-inform-our-post-covid-19-recovery.

119 **more than eight out of ten voters:** "New Poll: Over Two Thirds of Voters Want Candidates Who Will Invest in Skills Training," National Skills Coalition, May 13, 2024,
https://nationalskillscoalition.org/news/press-releases/public-perspectives.

120 **"front and center":** Matthew Dembicki, "McMahon: Workforce Pell and More CTE,"
Community College Daily, American Association of Community Colleges, February 13,
2025, https://www.ccdaily.com/2025/02/mcmahon-workforce-pell-and-more-cte.

120 **I agree. And:** Randi Weingarten, "Stop Trying to Make Everyone Go to College,"
New York Times, May 6, 2025, https://www.nytimes.com/2025/05/06/opinion
/college-technical-vocational-education.html.

120 **"have contradicted the":** Mark Lieberman and Brooke Schultz, "How the Trump
Administration's 'Indiscriminate Cutting' Will Affect Students," *Education Week*,
February 27, 2025, https://www.edweek.org/policy-politics/how-the-trump-admin
istrations-indiscriminate-cutting-will-affect-students/2025/02.

120 **"run counter to":** "Advance CTE, ACTE on U.S. Department of Education Funding &
Staffing Impacts on Career Technical Education," ACTE, March 12, 2025, https://
www.acteonline.org/blog/press/advance-cte-acte-on-u-s-department-of-education
-funding-staffing-impacts-on-career-technical-education.

121 **receive a significant share:** "Public School Revenue Sources," National Center for
Education Statistics, May 2024, https://nces.ed.gov/programs/coe/indicator/cma
/public-school-revenue.

121 **spends $10,313 per pupil:** Adam McCann, "Most & Least Equitable School Districts
in Pennsylvania," Wallet Hub, September 7, 2023, https://wallethub.com/edu/e
/most-least-equitable-school-districts-in-pennsylvania/77124.

121 **Black students are three and a half times more likely:** "New Report Finds Most
States Have Deprived Schools of Hundreds of Billions of Dollars Since 2016," AFT,
January 17, 2024, https://www.aft.org/press-release/new-report-finds-most-states
-have-deprived-schools-hundreds-billions-dollars-2016.

121 **Rural schools are also often underfunded:** Libby Stanford, "Report Outlines the
Distinct Challenges Facing Rural Schools," *Education Week*, November 16, 2023,
https://www.edweek.org/leadership/report-outlines-the-distinct-challenges
-facing-rural-schools/2023/11.

122 **writer Jonathan Kozol:** Rachel Lebeaux, "An Author's Rage over the Inequities in
American Education," *Wellesley Townsman*, October 13, 2005, https://www.wicked
local.com/story/wellesley-townsman/2005/10/13/an-author-s-rage-over
/40667191007.

122 **when a district increases:** Kira Barrett, "The Evidence is Clear: More Money for
Schools Means Better Student Outcomes," NEA Today, NEA, August 1, 2018, https://
www.nea.org/nea-today/all-news-articles/evidence-clear-more-money-schools
-means-better-student-outcomes.

122 **a study of ten thousand school districts:** Todd Butterworth, "Does Higher Teacher
Pay Result in Better Student Performance?," *Nevada Independent*, February 9, 2023,
https://thenevadaindependent.com/article/fact-brief-does-higher-teacher-pay
-result-in-better-student-performance.

122 **economist Eric Hanushek:** Matt Barnum, "An Economist Spent Decades Saying
Money Wouldn't Help Schools. Now His Research Suggests Otherwise," *Chalkbeat*,

May 16, 2023, https://www.chalkbeat.org/2023/5/16/23724474/school-funding -research-studies-hanushek-does-money-matter.

122 **average starting salary:** "Starting Teacher Salaries," NEA, accessed March 5, 2025, https://www.nea.org/resource-library/educator-pay-and-student-spending-how -does-your-state-rank/starting-teacher.

123 **the annual mean wage:** Kamaron McNair, "The Income Everyday Americans Earn in Every U.S. State—See How Your Salary Measures Up," CNBC, April 14, 2024, https:// www.cnbc.com/2024/04/14/median-annual-income-in-every-us-state.html.

123 **the Center for Economic and Policy Research:** "Teacher Pay Fell Further Behind in 2022," Economic Policy Institute, September 29, 2023, https://www.epi.org/press /teacher-pay-fell-further-behind-in-2022-teachers-made-26-4-less-than-other -similarly-educated-professionals.

123 **75 percent of parents said they would:** James Paterson, "Poll: Without Better Pay, Teaching Isn't Viable Career," NEA Today, NEA, September 1, 2022, https://www .nea.org/nea-today/all-news-articles/poll-without-better-pay-teaching-isnt -viable-career.

123 **enrollment in teacher training programs:** Madeline Will, "Some Positive Signs for the Teacher Pipeline, but It's Not All Good. What 3 Studies Say," *Education Week*, March 22, 2024, https://www.edweek.org/leadership/some-positive-signs-for-the -teacher-pipeline-but-its-not-all-good-what-3-studies-say/2024/03.

123 **districts are hiring more:** Astrid Galván, "Hiring Uncertified Teachers Is a Band-Aid Response to Shortages, Experts Say," *Axios*, August 22, 2023, https://www.ax ios.com/2023/08/22/teacher-shortages-uncertified-consequences-students -houston.

123 **An AFT task force:** "Teacher Shortage Task Force Report," AFT, accessed March 5, 2025, https://www.aft.org/teacher-shortage-task-force-report.

123 **an estimated 270,000 underqualified teachers:** Madeline Will, "What Will Teacher Shortages Look Like in 2024 and Beyond? A Researcher Weighs In," *Education Week*, December 21, 2023, https://www.edweek.org/leadership/what-will-teacher -shortages-look-like-in-2024-and-beyond-a-researcher-weighs-in/2023/12.

124 **My friend Lily Eskelsen García:** Madeline Will, "NEA's Lily Eskelsen García Talks Racial Justice, COVID Layoffs, and Leaving Office," *Education Week*, July 1, 2020, https://www.edweek.org/teaching-learning/neas-lily-eskelsen-garcia-talks -racial-justice-covid-layoffs-and-leaving-office/2020/07; "Remarks as Prepared of Lily Eskelsen Garcia, President for the National Press Club," NEA, September 8, 2017, https://www.nea.org/about-nea/media-center/press-releases/remarks-prepared -lily-eskelsen-garcia-president-national-press-club.

124 **"Public education is not broken":** Diane Ravitch, *Reign of Error: The Hoax of the Privatization Movement and the Danger to America's Public Schools* (Knopf, 2013), 4.

124 **"Over the past decade, there":** "NEWS: New Report on the Coordinated Effort by Billionaires to Dismantle the American Public School System," Bernie Sanders, U.S. Senator for Vermont, June 25, 2024, https://www.sanders.senate.gov/press-releases /news-new-report-on-the-coordinated-effort-by-billionaires-to-dismantle-the -american-public-school-system.

124 **"I favor school choice":** Troy Matthews, "Vivek: I Want School Choice on Steroids; Take Away School Budgets," Meidas News, August 30, 2023, https://meidasnews .com/news/vivek-i-want-school-choice-on-steroids-take-away-school-budgets.

125 **"What good is it to Walmart or Amazon":** Jack Schneider and Jennifer Berkshire, *A Wolf at the Schoolhouse Door: The Dismantling of Public Education and the Future of School* (New Press, 2020), 39.

126 **argues the free market is better:** Dave Powell, "Neoliberalism and the New Politics of Education," *Education Week*, June 28, 2016, https://www.edweek.org/leadership /opinion-neoliberalism-and-the-new-politics-of-education/2016/06.

126 **charter schools are free to pick:** Valerie Strauss, "Yes, Some Charter Schools Do Pick their Students. It's Not a Myth," *Washington Post*, January 17, 2021, https:// www.washingtonpost.com/education/2021/01/17/yes-some-charter-schools-do -pick-their-students-its-not-myth.

126 **Research shows that charter schools:** Bill Hangley, "Pa. Charters Deny 'Cherry-Picking' Students, but Data Show Special Ed Disparities," WHYY, July 1, 2020, https://whyy.org/articles/pa-charters-deny-cherry-picking-students-but-data -show-special-ed-disparities.

127 **I cofounded a charter school:** "Welcome to University Prep Public Schools," University Prep Public Schools, accessed March 5, 2025, https://www.uppublicschools.org/about.

127 **private schools aren't any better:** Jessica Campisi, "Study: Private Schools Offer Virtually No Special Advantages Compared with Public Counterparts," K-12 Dive, September 6, 2018, https://www.k12dive.com/news/study-private-schools-offer-vir tually-no-special-advantages-compared-with/531633.

127 **"risk of waste, fraud, and abuse":** Valerie Strauss, "Education Department Slammed for Charter School Oversight—by Its Own Watchdog Office," *Washington Post*, October 5, 2016, https://www.washingtonpost.com/news/answer-sheet/wp /2016/10/05/education-department-slammed-for-charter-school-oversight-by -its-own-watchdog-office.

127 **"cyber charter schools" have taken:** Sean Kitchen, "PA's Unregulated Cyber Charter Schools Spent $21 Million on Advertising Fees and Gift Cards," *Keystone Newsroom*, May 17, 2024, https://keystonenewsroom.com/2024/05/17/pas-unregulated-cyber -charter-schools-spent-21-million-on-advertising-fees-and-gift-cards.

127 **severely underfunded by $6.2 billion:** "New Analysis Funds Pennsylvania Schools Are Underfunded by $6.2 Billion, Including Basic and Special Education, with Shortfalls Concentrated in Poorest Districts," Public Interest Law Center, September 12, 2023, https://pubintlaw.org/cases-and-projects/new-analysis-finds-pennsylvania -schools-are-underfunded-by-6-2-billion-including-basic-and-special-education- with-shortfalls-concentrated-in-poorest-districts.

127 **according to one investigative report:** Kitchen, "PA's Unregulated Cyber Charter Schools."

128 **accumulated $88 million in real estate:** Peter Green, "In Pennsylvania, a Cyber Charter School Builds a Real Estate Empire," *Forbes*, May 20, 2024, https://www .forbes.com/sites/petergreene/2024/05/20/in-pennsylvania—a-cyber-charter -school-builds-a-real-estate-empire.

128 **At one of these schools, PA Cyber:** Andy Sheehan, "How Does the Performance at PA Cyber Compare to Traditional Schools?," CBS News, April 30, 2024, https://www .cbsnews.com/pittsburgh/news/pa-cyber-performance-compared-to-traditional -schools.

128 **In the wake of Hurricane Katrina:** Marta Jewson, "Five Years After Settlement in Sitywide Special Education Suit, Some New Orleans Families Still Struggle for Ser-

vices," The Lens, December 10, 2019, https://thelensnola.org/2019/12/10/five-years
-after-settlement-in-citywide-special-education-suit-some-new-orleans-families
-still-struggle-for-services.

128 54 percent of New Orleans schools earned: "How Many More Years of a Failed Reform Must Orleans Parish Endure?," *New Orleans Tribune*, November 18, 2022,
https://theneworleanstribune.com/2022/11/18/how-many-more-years-of-a
-failed-reform-must-orleans-parish-endure.

128 were routinely closed: Ariel Gilreath, "All-Charter No More: New Orleans Opens Its
First Traditional School in Nearly Two Decades," *Hechinger Report*, September 9,
2024, https://hechingerreport.org/all-charter-no-more-new-orleans-opens-its-first
-traditional-school-in-nearly-two-decades.

129 brand-new pre-K-through-eighth-grade: Gilreath, "All-Charter No More."

129 live in "food deserts": "Communities with Limited Food Access in the United
States," Annie E. Casey Foundation, August 4, 2024, https://www.aecf.org/blog
/communities-with-limited-food-access-in-the-united-states.

129 but also staggering poverty: Dylan Sullivan and Jason Hickel, "Capitalism and Extreme Poverty: A Global Analysis of Real Wages, Human Height, and Mortality
Since the Long 16th Century," *World Development* 161 (January 2023), https://www
.sciencedirect.com/science/article/pii/S0305750X22002169.

129 According to U.S. Census data: Jeremy Ney, "The Surprising Poverty Levels Across
the U.S.," *Time*, October 4, 2023, https://time.com/6320076/american-poverty
-levels-state-by-state.

129 More than one in ten Americans currently lives: Ney, "The Surprising Poverty Levels Across the U.S."

129 And the share of Americans: William Cooper, "We Have Extreme Inequality in
America, and It's getting Worse," Fulcrum, October 7, 2024, https://thefulcrum.us
/business-democracy/wealth-inequality-in-america.

130 An overwhelming majority of American parents: Matt Barnum, "The public is sour-
ing on American education, but parents still give own child's school high marks,"
Chalkbeat, September 5, 2023, https://www.chalkbeat.org/2023/9/5/23859890
/parents-polling-surveys-schools-american-education-pandemic.

130 And in states like Ohio: Ravitch, "The Dark History of School Choice."

130 "the very evil that *Brown I* was aimed at": Elissa Nadworny and Cory Turner,
"This Supreme Court Case Made School District Lines a Tool for Segregation," NPR,
July 25, 2019, https://www.npr.org/2019/07/25/739493839/this-supreme-court-case
-made-school-district-lines-a-tool-for-segregation.

131 "Our nation, I fear": Robyn Vincent, "Still Segregated and Unequal: The Reverbera-
tions of *Milliken v. Bradley* in Detroit 50 Years Later," *Chalkbeat*, July 29, 2024,
https://www.chalkbeat.org/detroit/2024/07/29/milliken-v-bradley-affects
-segregation-inequity-in-education-50-years-later.

131 In the summer of 1963: Christopher Bonastia, "Black Leadership and Outside Allies
in Virginia Freedom Schools," *History of Education Quarterly* 56, no. 4 (November
2016): 532–59, https://www.jstor.org/stable/26356284.

131 one of the inspirations for the freedom schools: Leo Casey, "When Privatization Means Segregation: Setting the Record Straight on School Vouchers," *Dissent*,
August 9, 2017, https://www.dissentmagazine.org/online_articles/private-school
-vouchers-racist-history-milton-friedman-betsy-devos.

131 **AFT members went on to teach:** "News," United Federation of Teachers, July 30, 1964, https://www.crmvet.org/docs/640710_fskools_uft_pr.pdf.

131 **never got to study at an integrated school:** Joe Bubar, "The 16-Year-Old Who Fought Segregation," *Scholastic/New York Times Upfront*, April 22, 2019, https://upfront.scholastic.com/issues/2018-19/042219/the-16-year-old-who-fought-segregation.html?language=english#1120L.

132 **She became a teacher:** "Biography: Barbara Rose Johns Powell, 1935–1991," Robert Russa Moton Museum, accessed March 5, 2025, https://motonmuseum.org/learn/biography-barbara-rose-johns-powell.

4: TEACHERS BUILD STRONG UNIONS

133 **Karen Lewis was born:** Julie Bosman, "Karen Lewis, Who Fought for Chicago's Teachers, Dies at 67," *New York Times*, February 8, 2021, https://www.nytimes.com/2021/02/08/us/karen-lewis-dead.html.

133 **finally admitted women:** Bosman, "Karen Lewis."

133 **was the only Black woman:** Lisa Furlong, "Karen (Jennings) Lewis '74," *Dartmouth Alumni Magazine*, May–June 2011, https://dartmouthalumnimagazine.com/articles/karen-jennings-lewis-%E2%80%9974.

133 **"hated medical school":** Furlong, "Karen (Jennings) Lewis '74."

133 **"That got me involved":** Furlong, "Karen (Jennings) Lewis '74."

133 **In 2010, Karen was elected:** Bosman, "Karen Lewis."

134 **In the 1960s:** "History of Chicago Public Schools," *Chicago Reporter*, accessed March 5, 2025, https://www.chicagoreporter.com/cps-history.

134 **In 1979, mismanagement:** Nathaniel Sheppard, "Chicago Schools Nearing Shutdown in Fiscal Crisis," *New York Times*, December 30, 1979, https://www.nytimes.com/1979/12/30/archives/chicago-schools-nearing-shutdown-in-fiscal-crisis-hopes-for.html.

134 **In 1995, the Republican:** "Reform Before the Storm: A Timeline of the Chicago Public Schools," *Chicago Magazine*, October 2, 2012, https://www.chicagomag.com/chicago-magazine/november-2012/reform-before-the-storm-chicago-public-schools-timeline.

134 **"an era of school reform":** "Building Bridges and Growing the Soul of Chicago: A Blueprint for Creating a More Just and Vibrant City for All," Transition Team Report to Mayor Brandon Johnson, Chicago for the People, July 2023, https://www.chicago.gov/content/dam/city/depts/mayor/TransitionReport/TransitionReport.07.2023.pdf.

134 **The act also:** Don Terry, "Chicago's Mayor Gains School Control That New York's Mayor Would Envy," *New York Times*, June 29, 1995, https://www.nytimes.com/1995/06/29/us/chicago-s-mayor-gains-school-control-that-new-york-s-mayor-would-envy.html.

134 **"like a stock portfolio":** Jan Resseger, "What Is the Legacy of Renaissance 2010 School Choice in Chicago?," National Education Policy Center, August 13, 2018, https://nepc.colorado.edu/blog/what-legacy.

134 **fifty "under-enrolled" schools:** Resseger, "What Is the Legacy."

135 **In 2015, twelve parents:** Manny Ramos, "5 Years Later, Dyett High School Hunger Strikers Recall Their Fight," *Chicago Sun-Times*, August 17, 2020, https://chicago

.suntimes.com/education/2020/8/17/21372534/dyett-high-school-hunger-strikers
-five-year-anniversary.

135 **They won and the city agreed:** Matt Masterson, "Dyett High School Reopening 1
     Year After Activist Hunger Strike," WTTW, September 1, 2016, https://news.wttw
     .com/2016/09/01/dyett-high-school-reopening-1-year-after-activist-hunger-strike.

135 **"We're tired of our children":** Sean McCollum, "Closed for Business," *Learning for
     Justice* 52 (Spring 2016), https://www.learningforjustice.org/magazine/spring-2016
     /closed-for-business.

135 **merely forced teachers:** Brian A. Jacob, "Accountability, Incentives and Behavior:
     The Impact of High-Stakes Testing in the Chicago Public Schools," *Journal of Public
     Economics* 89, no. 5–6 (June 2005): 761–96, https://www.sciencedirect.com/sci
     ence/article/abs/pii/S0047272704001549.

135 **That year, the graduation rate:** Mauricio Peña and Mila Koumpilova, "Chicago's
     Four-Year High School Graduation Rate Hits Record High," *Chalkbeat*, October
     24, 2022, https://www.chalkbeat.org/chicago/2022/10/24/23421421/chicago-public
     -schools-graduation-rates-freshman-on-track-nations-report-card.

135 **"Bargaining for the Common Good":** Jackson Potter, "The Strike That Started the
     Red Wave," *In These Times*, September 22, 2022, https://inthesetimes.com/article
     /chicago-teacher-strike-2012-anniversary-labor-union-education.

136 **86 percent of Chicago public school students:** "Appendix A: District and Commu-
     nity Demographics," Chicago Public Schools, 2013, https://sis-production.cps.edu
     /globalassets/cps-pages/about-cps/finance/budget/budget-2013/appendixa_dis
     trictcommunity.pdf.

136 **Over ten thousand of the district's students:** "Number of Homeless Students Surges,
     Putting Strain on Schools," *eSchoolNews*, January 11, 2012, https://www.eschool
     news.com/district-management/2012/01/11/number-of-homeless-students-surges
     -putting-strain-on-schools.

136 **in their negotiation with the city:** Sarah Jaffe, "The Chicago Teachers Strike Was a
     Lesson in 21st-Century Organizing," *The Nation*, November 16, 2019, https://www
     .thenation.com/article/archive/chicago-ctu-strike-win.

136 **would "cheapen" the district:** "Chicago Teachers Strike After Contract Talks Break
     Down," *The Guardian*, September 10, 2012, https://www.theguardian.com/world
     /2012/sep/10/chicago-teachers-strike-talks-fail.

136 **The right of private-sector workers:** Charles B. Craver, "The Right to Strike and Its
     Possible Conflict with Other Fundamental Rights of the People in the United
     States," George Washington University Law School, 2012, https://scholarship.law
     .gwu.edu/faculty_publications/472.

136 **there is currently no:** Margaret Poydock, Joe Fast, and Daniel Perez, "271,500
     Workers Went on Strike in 2024," Economic Policy Institute, February 20, 2025,
     https://www.epi.org/publication/271500-workers-went-on-strike-in-2024
     -current-labor-law-doesnt-adequately-protect-workers-fundamental-right-to
     -strike.

137 **a patchwork of state laws:** David R. Osborne and Andrew Holman, "The Battle for
     Worker Freedom: Grading State Public Sector Labor Laws (4th Edition)," Common-
     wealth Foundation, September 2024, https://www.commonwealthfoundation.org
     /wp-content/uploads/2024/08/50-State-Public-Sector-Labor-Laws-paper.pdf.

137 **Utah banned collective:** Hannah Schoenbaum, "Utah Governor Signs Collective Bargaining Ban for Teachers, Firefighters and Police Unions," Associated Press, February 14, 2025, https://apnews.com/article/utah-governor-unions-collective -bargaining-76b1fe205aae7b4097c1d0b4a1a13cc6.

137 **including South Dakota:** Makenzie Huber, "Legislation Restricting Labor Union Activity Passes SD Committee," *South Dakota Searchlight*, February 10, 2025, https://southdakotasearchlight.com/briefs/legislation-restricting-labor-union -activity-passes-sd-committee.

137 **and Kentucky have:** Liam Niemeyer, "Legislation Further Limiting State Labor Protections Passes House," *Kentucky Lantern*, February 26, 2025, https://ken tuckylantern.com/2025/02/26/legislation-further-limiting-state-labor-protections -passes-house.

137 **And in March 2025:** "Executive Order 14251 of March 27, 2025, Exclusions from Federal Labor-Management Relations Programs," 90 FR 14553 (2025), https:// www.govinfo.gov/app/details/FR-2025-04-03/2025-05836.

137 **2009 saw just five major strikes:** "Annual Work Stoppages Involving 1,000 or More Workers, 1947–Present," U.S. Bureau of Labor Statistics, accessed March 5, 2025, https://www.bls.gov/web/wkstp/annual-listing.htm.

137 **Chicago hadn't seen a labor strike:** Brandis Friedman, "How 2012 Chicago Teachers Strike Changed Fight over Public Education," WTTW, January 5, 2017, https:// news.wttw.com/2017/01/05/how-2012-chicago-teachers-strike-changed-fight -over-public-education.

137 **got a new anti-union law passed:** Ben Goldberger, "Karen Lewis, Street Fighter," *Chicago Magazine*, October 2, 2012, https://www.chicagomag.com/Chicago-Magazine /November-2012/Karen-Lewis-Street-Fighter.

137 **"Brothers and sisters, if we":** Jody Sokolower, "Karen Lewis Explains Why Teachers Unions Are Essential," *Progressive Magazine*, February 15, 2021, https://progres sive.org/public-schools-advocate/karen-lewis-why-teachers-unions-essential -soklower-210215.

138 **90 percent of CTU members voted:** Ben Goldberger, "Karen Lewis, Street Fighter," *Chicago Magazine*, October 2, 2012, https://www.chicagomag.com/Chicago-Magazine /November-2012/Karen-Lewis-Street-Fighter.

138 **For nine months:** Theresa Moran, "Behind the Chicago Teachers Strike," Labor Notes, September 10, 2012, https://labornotes.org/2012/09/behind-chicago-teachers-strike.

138 **because of the overemphasis:** Moran, "Behind the Chicago Teachers Strike."

138 **his mom an educator:** Kade Heather, "Susan Duncan Dies at 89; South Side Educator and Mother of Former U.S. Education Secretary Arne Duncan," *Chicago Sun-Times*, July 11, 2024, https://chicago.suntimes.com/obituaries/2024/07/11/susan-duncan -obituary-education-south-side-reading-sue-duncans-childrens-center-chicago -civil-rights.

138 **Duncan worked at early in his career:** Alia Wong, "Arne Duncan: 'Everyone Says They Value Education, but Their Actions Don't Follow,'" *The Atlantic*, August 7, 2018, https://www.theatlantic.com/education/archive/2018/08/arne-duncan-how -schools-work/566987.

138 **if they were run like corporations:** Zoë Carpenter, "The Legacy of Arne Duncan, 'A Hero in the Education Business,'" *The Nation*, October 12, 2015, https://www.the nation.com/article/archive/the-legacy-of-arne-duncan.

138 **"the central messenger"**: Jitu Brown, Eric Gutstein, and Pauline Lipman, "Arne Duncan and the Chicago Success Story: Myth or Reality?," *Rethinking Schools* 23, no. 3 (Spring 2009), https://rethinkingschools.org/articles/arne-duncan-and-the-chicago-success-story-myth-or-reality.

139 **"the incubator, test case and model"**: Pauline Lipman, *The New Political Economy of Urban Education: Neoliberalism, Race, and the Right to the City* (Taylor & Francis, 2013), 19.

139 **"not only marked a pivotal moment"**: William O'Keefe, "Chicago Teachers Union Sets a Racial Example for Nation's Teachers Unions," Illinois Policy, April 19, 2024, https://www.illinoispolicy.org/chicago-teachers-union-sets-a-radical-example-for-nations-teachers-unions.

139 **"The strike was the first"**: Kurt Hilgendorf, "Striking Back Against Corporate Education Reform: The 2012 Chicago Teachers Union Strike," *The Councilor* 74, no. 2 (2013), https://thekeep.eiu.edu/cgi/viewcontent.cgi?article=1071&context=the_councilor.

139 **"After facing 30 years"**: Potter, "The Strike That Started the Red Wave."

139 **closed for seven days**: Friedman, "How 2012 Chicago Teachers Strike Changed Fight over Public Education."

139 **the Chicago community supported**: "As Chicago Teachers Strike Enters Fourth Day, a New Poll Proves Majority of Parents and Taxpayers Approve of Fair Contract Fight," Chicago Teachers Union, September 13, 2012, https://www.ctulocal1.org/posts/as-chicago-teachers-strike-enters-fourth-day-a-new-poll-proves-majority-of-parents-and-taxpayers-approve-of-fair-contract-fight.

139 **Parents joined teachers**: Don Babwin, "Chicago Strike: Parents Support Teachers, but for How Long?," *Christian Science Monitor*, September 11, 2012, https://www.csmonitor.com/USA/Latest-News-Wires/2012/0911/Chicago-strike-Parents-support-teachers-but-for-how-long.

139 **"I'm going to stay strong"**: Babwin, "Chicago Strike."

139 **"I am protesting because"**: Dana Liebelson, "What Happened with the Chicago Teacher Strike, Explained," *Mother Jones*, September 11, 2012, https://www.motherjones.com/politics/2012/09/teachers-strike-chicago-explained.

139 **"Together we bargain"**: Liebelson, "What Happened with the Chicago Teacher Strike."

139 **"the strike and the resulting"**: Hilgendorf, "Striking Back Against Corporate Education Reform."

139 **secured important pay raises**: Moran, "Behind the Chicago Teachers Strike."

140 **limited the impact**: Hilgendorf, "Striking Back Against Corporate Education Reform."

140 **Strikes and protests erupted**: Valerie Strauss, "The Historic Strikes and Protests by Teachers Across the Country Aren't Over," *Washington Post*, April 10, 2019, https://www.washingtonpost.com/education/2019/04/10/historic-strikes-protests-by-teachers-around-country-arent-over.

141 **protected under a mix of federal**: "National Labor Relations Act (29 U.S.C. §§ 151–169)," National Labor Relations Board, accessed March 6, 2025, https://www.nlrb.gov/guidance/key-reference-materials/national-labor-relations-act.

141 **and state laws**: "Building Worker Power in Cities & States: State Constitutions and Public Sector Collective Bargaining Rights," Center for Labor and a Just Economy,

Harvard Law School, September 1, 2024, https://clje.law.harvard.edu/publication /building-worker-power-in-cities-states/state-constitutions-and-public-sector -collective-bargaining-rights.

141 **in the AFT, we have chapters:** "About Us," AFT, accessed March 6, 2025, https:// www.aft.org/about.

141 **more than three thousand locals:** "About Us," AFT.

142 **All the employees represented:** "Agreement Between the UAW and General Motors LLC," UAW, October 16, 2019, https://uaw.org/wp-content/uploads/2023/11/UAW -GM-National-Agreement.pdf.

142 **just like the machinists at Boeing:** "2024 Contract Proposal," International Association of Machinists and Aerospace Workers District 157, accessed March 6, 2025, https://www.iam751.org/2024StrikeProposal.

142 **and the Teamsters at UPS:** "UPS Agreements 2023–2028," International Brotherhood of Teamsters, accessed March 6, 2025, https://teamster.org/ups-ta-2023-2028.

142 **bargains with the New York City:** "Contract 2023," United Federation of Teachers, accessed March 6, 2025, https://www.uft.org/your-rights/contracts/contract-2023.

142 **the White Plains Teachers Association:** "Agreement Between the City School District of the City of White Plains, New York, and the White Plains Teachers Association, July 1, 2022–June 30, 2026," accessed March 6, 2025, https://resources .finalsite.net/images/v1682538735/whiteplainspublicschoolsorg/zm94sgbasvvm 7hi4dvnw/WPTA2022-2026CBA_.pdf.

142 **Unions raise wages:** "Labor Unions and the Middle Class," U.S. Department of the Treasury, August 2023, https://home.treasury.gov/system/files/136/Labor-Unions -And-The-Middle-Class.pdf.

142 **Over nine out of ten union members:** Asha Banerjee et al., "Unions Are Not Only Good for Workers, They're Good for Communities and for Democracy," Economic Policy Institute, December 15, 2021, https://www.epi.org/publication/unions-and -well-being.

143 **union workers are more likely to have:** "Union Workers More Likely Than Nonunion Workers to Have Retirement Benefits in 2019," U.S. Bureau of Labor Statistics, October 25, 2019, https://www.bls.gov/opub/ted/2019/union-workers-more-likely-than -nonunion-workers-to-have-retirement-benefits-in-2019.htm.

143 **average wages are higher:** Banerjee et al., "Unions Are Not Only Good for Workers."

143 **non-union workers go up 0.3 percent:** Treasury Department, "Labor Unions and the Middle Class."

143 **Jean Hardisty called "mobilizing resentment":** Jean V. Hardisty, *Mobilizing Resentment: Conservative Resurgence from the John Birch Society to the Promise Keepers* (Beacon, 1999), https://archive.org/details/mobilizingresent0000hard.

143 **remember, the wealthiest person in the world:** "Musk's Millions for Trump Make Him Biggest US Political Donor," *Barron's*, December 6, 2024, https://www.barrons .com/news/musk-s-millions-for-trump-make-him-biggest-us-political-donor -134ebd08.

143 **Musk reportedly gloated:** Steve Greenhouse, "Elon Musk Says Letting Workers Unionize Creates 'Lords and Peasants.' What?," *The Guardian,* December 20, 2023, https:// www.theguardian.com/commentisfree/2023/dec/20/elon-musk-unions-tesla.

143 **ruled that Musk illegally threatened:** "Elon Musk Broke Law with Threat to Tesla Workers' Stock Options, Court Rules," *The Guardian*, March 31, 2023, https://www

.theguardian.com/technology/2023/apr/01/elon-musk-broke-law-with-threat-to
-tesla-workers-stock-options-court-rules.

143 **disagrees with "the idea of unions":** "Elon Musk: I Disagree with the Idea of Unions,"
posted by CNBC Television, YouTube, at 02:50, https://www.youtube.com/watch
?v=sctgA2qa-rA.

143 **"That the world's richest human":** Greenhouse, "Elon Musk Says Letting Workers
Unionize Creates 'Lords and Peasants.'"

144 **as much as 40 percent less:** Nora Naughton and Grace Kay, "Tesla Workers Still
Make Less Than Those at Ford and GM, Even After Raises," *Business Insider*, February
9, 2024, https://www.businessinsider.com/tesla-pay-vs-ford-gm-uaw-union-factory
-workers-2024-2?op=1.

144 **Musk filed an audacious suit:** Space Exploration Technologies Corp. v. National Labor Relations Board et al, No. 6:2024cv00203—Document 43 (W.D. Tex. 2024),
https://law.justia.com/cases/federal/district-courts/texas/txwdce/6:2024cv0
0203/1172784245/43.

144 **dozens of lawsuits:** Andrea Hsu, "Accused of Violating Worker Rights, SpaceX and
Amazon Go After Labor Board," NPR, November 18, 2024, https://www.npr.org
/2024/11/18/nx-s1-5192918/spacex-amazon-nlrb-labor-board-elon-musk.

144 **bailed out and propped up:** Paul Kiel, "The Bailout Was 11 Years Ago. We're Still
Tracking Every Penny," *ProPublica*, October 3, 2019, https://www.propublica.org
/article/the-bailout-was-11-years-ago-were-still-tracking-every-penny.

144 **most unionized profession in the United States:** "Union Members—2024," U.S.
Bureau of Labor Statistics, January 20, 2025, https://www.bls.gov/news.release/pdf
/union2.pdf.

145 **"It is one of the characteristics":** Franklin D. Roosevelt, "A Proof of Democracy:
Ours Is a Great Heritage," Delivered before the International Teamsters Union,
Washington, D.C., September 11, 1940, https://www.ibiblio.org/pha/policy/1940
/1940-09-11a.html.

145 **In ancient Egypt:** Joshua J. Mark, "The First Labor Strike in History," *World History
Encyclopedia*, July 4, 2017, https://www.worldhistory.org/article/1089/the-first
-labor-strike-in-history.

145 **In the Middle Ages:** *Britannica*, "guild," March 4, 2025, https://www.britannica
.com/topic/guild-trade-association.

145 **were enslaved Blacks:** "Slavery in America," History.com, April 25, 2024, updated
January 14, 2025, https://www.history.com/topics/black-history/slavery.

145 **and enslaved Native Americans:** "Colonial Enslavement of Native Americans Included Those Who Surrendered, Too," Brown University, February 15, 2017, https://
www.brown.edu/news/2017-02-15/enslavement.

145 **the first known union in the United States:** "History of the National Education Association and the U.S. Labor Movement," NEA, accessed March 6, 2025, https://www
.nea.org/advocating-for-change/new-from-nea/history-national-education
-association-and-us-labor-movement.

145 **Mill workers in Lowell:** "Lowell Mill Women Create the First Union of Working
Women," AFL-CIO, accessed March 6, 2025, https://aflcio.org/about/history/la
bor-history-events/lowell-mill-women-form-union.

145 **In 1867, around three thousand:** "Stanford Project Gives Voice to Chinese Workers
Who Helped Build the Transcontinental Railroad," Stanford Report, Stanford,

April 9, 2019, https://news.stanford.edu/stories/2019/04/giving-voice-to-chinese -railroad-workers.

145 **at the time the largest strike:** Chris Fuchs, "150 Years Ago, Chinese Railroad Workers Risked Their Lives in Pursuit of the American Dream," NBC News, April 24, 2019, https://www.nbcnews.com/news/asian-america/150-years-ago-chinese-rail road-workers-risked-their-lives-pursuit-n992751.

145 **National Teachers Association was founded:** "History of the National Education Association and the U.S. Labor Movement," NEA, accessed March 6, 2025, https:// www.nea.org/advocating-for-change/new-from-nea/history-national-education -association-and-us-labor-movement.

145 **Later, my union:** "History of the AFT," AFT-New Hampshire, accessed March 6, 2025, https://nh.aft.org/about-us/history-aft.

146 **regularly worked twelve hours a day:** Jeanne Sahadi, "Why Do We Work 9 to 5? The History of the Eight-Hour Workday," CNN, September 9, 2023, https://www.cnn .com/2023/09/09/success/work-culture-9-to-5-curious-consumer/index.html.

146 **Between 1890 and 1910:** "History of Child Labor in the United States—Part 1: Little Children Working," *Monthly Labor Review*, U.S. Bureau of Labor Statistics, January 2017, https://www.bls.gov/opub/mlr/2017/article/history-of-child-labor-in-the -united-states-part-1.htm.

146 **the Triangle Shirtwaist Factory:** Dr. Howard Markel, "How the Triangle Shirtwaist Factory Fire Transformed Labor Laws and Protected Workers' Health," PBS, March 31, 2021, https://www.pbs.org/newshour/nation/how-the-triangle-shirtwaist-fac tory-fire-transformed-labor-laws-and-protected-workers-health.

146 **passed the Fair Labor Standards Act:** "The Fair Labor Standards Act (FLSA): An Overview," Congressional Research Service, March 8, 2023, https://crsreports.con gress.gov/product/pdf/R/R42713.

146 **Occupational Safety and Health Act:** Judson MacLaury, "The Job Safety Law of 1970: Its Passage Was Perilous," *Monthly Labor Review*, U.S. Department of Labor, March 1981, https://www.dol.gov/general/aboutdol/history/osha.

147 **"to spy on, interrogate, discipline":** "National Labor Relations Act (1935)," National Archives, accessed March 6, 2025, https://www.archives.gov/milestone-documents /national-labor-relations-act.

147 **Enacted in 1935:** "National Labor Relations Act 29 U.S.C. §§ 151–169," National Labor Relations Board, accessed March 6, 2025, https://www.nlrb.gov/guidance/key -reference-materials/national-labor-relations-act.

147 **"The middle class built America":** Chris Megerian, "At Mich. Chip Plant, Biden Says Unions 'Built Middle Class,'" Associated Press, November 29, 2022, https://apnews .com/article/gretchen-whitmer-biden-technology-government-and-politics -michigan-4d5ac5a4bec5a2e61b4567639240d97c.

147 **Unionization peaked in 1954:** Drew Desilver, "Job Categories Where Union Membership Has Fallen Off Most," Pew Research Center, April 27, 2015, https://www .pewresearch.org/short-reads/2015/04/27/union-membership.

147 **In 1962, Dolores Huerta:** "United Farm Workers of America," National Farm Worker Ministry, accessed March 6, 2025, https://nfwm.org/farm-workers/farm worker-partners/united-farm-workers-of-america.

147 **"Once you see the outcomes":** "Interview: Dolores Huerta Discusses Grassroots Activism and Weaving Movements," San Diego Foundation, August 12, 2016, https://

www.sdfoundation.org/news-events/sdf-news/interview-dolores-huerta
-discusses-grassroots-activism-and-weaving-movements.

147 **Because as unionization goes up:** Aurelia Glass, David Madland, and Christian E. Weller, "Unions Build Wealth for the American Working Class," Center for American Progress, May 3, 2023, https://www.americanprogress.org/article/unions-build -wealth-for-the-american-working-class.

147 **historic charts of union membership:** Laura Feiveson, "Labor Unions and the U.S. Economy," U.S. Department of the Treasury, August 28, 2023, https://home.trea sury.gov/news/featured-stories/labor-unions-and-the-us-economy.

148 **"Antipathy to labor unions":** Jason Stanley, *How Fascism Works: The Politics of Us and Them* (Random House, 2018), 171.

148 **"Fascism is most effective":** Spencer Bokat-Lindell, "Fascism: A Concern," *New York Times*, July 30, 2020, https://www.nytimes.com/2020/07/30/opinion/fascism -us.html.

148 **Arendt called being "atomized":** Hannah Arendt, *Essays in Understanding, 1930–1954* (Knopf Doubleday, 2011).

148 **"promote solidarity across differences":** Bokat-Lindell, "Fascism: A Concern."

148 **In December 1922:** Antonio Sonnessa, "The 1922 Turin Massacre (*Strage di Torino*): Working Class Resistance and Conflicts Within Fascism," *Modern Italy* 10, no. 2 (2005): 187–205, https://www.cambridge.org/core/journals/modern-italy/article /abs/1922-turin-massacre-strage-di-torino-working-class-resistance-and -conflicts-within-fascism/23C63F8A72DEC858B66851BEE04D2AE5.

148 **In May 1933:** "2 May 1933: Dissolution of German Trade Unions," Holocaust Memorial Day Trust, accessed March 6, 2025, https://hmd.org.uk/resource/2-may-1933 -dissolution-of-german-trade-unions.

149 **From Franco in Spain:** "Spain Accused in U.N.; Charged with Suppressing Free Union and Torturing Leaders," *New York Times*, April 27, 1954, https://www.ny times.com/1954/04/27/archives/spain-accused-in-u-n-charged-with-suppressing -free-union-and.html.

149 **to Pinochet in Chile:** Edward Schumacher, "Chile Rights Abuses Persist, Monitors in Country Report," December 6, 1982, https://www.nytimes.com/1982/12/06 /world/chile-rights-abuses-persist-monitors-in-country-report.html.

149 **to Perón in Argentina:** "Argentina Declassification Project: History," Intel.gov, accessed March 6, 2025, https://www.intel.gov/argentina/history.

149 **In the United States, in 1947:** "1947 Taft-Hartley Passage and NLRB Structural Changes," National Labor Relations Board, accessed March 6, 2025, https://www .nlrb.gov/about-nlrb/who-we-are/our-history/1947-taft-hartley-passage-and-nlrb -structural-changes.

149 **opened the door for states to pass:** Amy Canvercort-Clark, "Taft-Hartley Act Overview," *FindLaw*, April 22, 2024, https://www.findlaw.com/employment/wages-and -benefits/taft-hartley-act-overview.html.

149 **started by the United Mine Workers:** "CIO Unions History and Geography," Mapping American Social Movements Project, Civil Rights and Labor History Consortium, University of Washington, accessed March 6, 2025, https://depts.washington .edu/moves/CIO_intro.shtml.

149 **launched a major effort:** Chandra Childers, Dave Kamper, and Jennifer Sherer, "Operation Dixie Failed 78 Years Ago. Are Today's Southern Workers About to Change

All That?," Economic Policy Institute, May 14, 2024, https://www.epi.org/blog/op eration-dixie-failed-78-years-ago-are-todays-southern-workers-about-to-change -all-that.

149 **The CIO was racially integrated:** "C.I.O. Organizing Committee. Operation Dixie [microform]: The C.I.O. Organizing Committee Papers, 1946–1953," C.I.O. Organizing Committee, ArchiveGrid, accessed March 6, 2025, https://researchworks.oclc .org/archivegrid/collection/data/122515695.

149 **a Texas man named Vance Muse:** Michael Pierce, "Vance Muse and the Racist Origins of Right-to-Work," American Constitution Society, February 22, 2018, https:// www.acslaw.org/expertforum/vance-muse-and-the-racist-origins-of-right-to -work.

149 **Christian American Association:** William Canak and Berkeley Miller, "Gumbo Politics: Unions, Business, and Louisiana Right-to-Work Legislation," *Industrial and Labor Relations Review* 43, No. 2 (January 1990): 258–71, http://www.jstor.org/sta ble/2523703?origin=JSTOR-pdf.

149 **first floated by William Ruggles:** Michael Pierce, "Vance Muse and the Racist Origins of Right-to-Work," American Constitution Society, February 22, 2018, https:// www.acslaw.org/expertforum/vance-muse-and-the-racist-origins-of-right-to -work.

150 **"the American economic system":** Lewis F. Powell Jr., "The Memo," Washington & Lee University School of Law Scholarly Commons, August 23, 1971, https://www .reuters.com/investigates/special-report/assets/usa-courts-secrecy-lobbyist /powell-memo.pdf.

150 **was sent confidentially:** Timothy Noah, "The Blueprint for Corporate Power Turns 50," *Washington Monthly*, August 24, 2021, https://washingtonmonthly.com/2021 /08/24/the-blueprint-for-corporate-power-turns-50.

150 **"blueprint for corporate power":** Noah, "The Blueprint for Corporate Power Turns 50."

150 **Less than two months later:** "Powell Memorandum: Attack on American Free Enterprise System," Washington & Lee University School of Law Scholarly Commons, accessed March 6, 2025, https://scholarlycommons.law.wlu.edu/powellmemo.

150 **seminal moment came in 1981:** "The 1981 PATCO Strike," UTA Libraries, September 2, 2021, https://libraries.uta.edu/news/1981-patco-strike.

150 **over twelve thousand members:** "1981—Ronald Reagan Fires 11,359 Air-Traffic Controllers," History.com, accessed March 6, 2025, https://www.history.com/this -day-in-history/reagan-fires-11359-air-traffic-controllers.

150 **Historian Joseph McCartin has pointed out:** "The 1981 PATCO Strike," UTA Libraries, September 2, 2021, https://libraries.uta.edu/news/1981-patco-strike.

151 **unleash a generation of:** "When Reagan Broke the Unions," Planet Money, *NPR*, December 18, 2019, https://www.npr.org/transcripts/788002965.

151 **Corporate spending on anti-union:** Lawrence Mishel, Lynn Rhinehart, and Lane Windham, "Explaining the Erosion of Private-Sector Unions," Economic Policy Institute, November 18, 2020, https://www.epi.org/unequalpower/publications/pri vate-sector-unions-corporate-legal-erosion.

151 **Today, American companies spend:** Celine McNicholas et al., "Employers Spend More Than $400 Million Per Year on 'Union-Avoidance' Consultants to Bolster Their Union-Busting Efforts," Economic Policy Institute, March 29, 2023, https:// www.epi.org/publication/union-avoidance.

151 **just 10 percent of the American workforce:** Andrea Hsu, "Union Membership Grew Last Year, but Only 10% of U.S. Workers Belong to a Union," NPR, January 23, 2024, https://www.npr.org/2024/01/23/1226034366/labor-union-membership-uaw -hollywood-workers-strike-gallup.

151 **spread across the South and Midwest:** "Right-to-work laws," Ballotpedia, accessed March 6, 2025, https://ballotpedia.org/Right-to-work_laws.

151 **elected governor of Wisconsin:** "Scott Walker (Wisconsin governor)," Ballotpedia, accessed March 6, 2025, https://ballotpedia.org/Scott_Walker_(Wisconsin_gov ernor).

151 **"a product of a loose network":** Patrick Healy and Monica Davey, "Behind Scott Walker, a Longstanding Conservative Alliance Against Unions," *New York Times*, June 8, 2015, https://www.nytimes.com/2015/06/08/us/politics/behind-scott-walker -a-longstanding-conservative-alliance-against-unions.html.

151 **enact legislation that severely restricted:** Valerie Strauss, "Wisconsin Gov. Scott Walker's Assault on Public Education Could Be Coming Back to Bite Him," *Washington Post*, October 16, 2018, https://www.washingtonpost.com/education/2018/10 /16/wisconsin-gov-scott-walkers-assault-public-education-could-be-coming-back -bite-him.

151 **"radical Islamic terrorists":** Valerie Strauss, "Yes, Scott Walker Really Did Link Terrorists with Protesting Teachers and Other Unionists," *Washington Post*, February 27, 2015, https://www.washingtonpost.com/news/answer-sheet/wp/2015/02 /27/yes-scott-walker-really-did-link-terrorists-with-protesting-teachers-and-other -unionists.

151 **Shortly thereafter, Walker slashed:** Strauss, "Wisconsin Gov. Scott Walker's Assault on Public Education Could Be Coming Back to Bite Him."

151 **by $800 million:** Henry Grabar, "Scott Walker's War on the Public Sector Came Back to Bite Him," *Slate*, November 8, 2018, https://slate.com/business/2018/11 /scott-walker-lost-wisconsin-education-unions.html.

152 **"He castigated faculty":** Karin Fischer, "A Playbook for Knocking Down Higher Ed," *Chronicle of Higher Education*, October 18, 2022, https://www.chronicle.com /article/a-playbook-for-knocking-down-higher-ed.

152 **cut $250 million:** Danielle Douglas-Gabriel, "Scott Walker's Real Record on Higher Education in Wisconsin," *Washington Post*, August 13, 2015, https://www.washing tonpost.com/news/wonk/wp/2015/08/13/scott-walkers-real-record-on-higher -education-in-wisconsin.

152 **secretly tried to change the very mission:** Strauss, "Wisconsin Gov. Scott Walker's Assault on Public Education Could Be Coming Back to Bite Him."

152 **"The Wisconsin Idea has always held":** John Nichols, "Scott Walker Objects to 'the Search for Truth,'" *The Nation*, February 4, 2015, https://www.thenation.com/arti cle/archive/scott-walker-objects-search-truth.

153 **did public education in Wisconsin:** David Madland and Alex Rowell, "Attacks on Public-Sector Unions Harm States: How Act 10 Has Affected Education in Wisconsin," Center for American Progress Action, November 15, 2017, https://www.americanpro gressaction.org/article/attacks-public-sector-unions-harm-states-act-10-affected -education-wisconsin.

153 **"I am proud to be the pro-education":** Caitlin Emma and Daniel Strauss, "Scott Walker Broke the Unions. Now He Says He's the 'Education Governor,'" *Politico*,

July 31, 2018, https://www.politico.com/story/2018/07/31/walker-wisconsin-edu cation-unions-751243.

153 **"inconsistent performance among":** Michelle Ye Hee Lee, "Scott Walker's Exaggerated Education Claims," *Washington Post*, March 3, 2015, https://www.washingtonpost .com/news/fact-checker/wp/2015/03/03/scott-walkers-exaggerated-education -claims.

153 **faced an "extreme shortage":** Madland and Rowell, "Attacks on Public-Sector Unions Harm States."

153 **In 2010, 14.2 percent of Wisconsin workers:** Shawn Johnson, "A Decade After Act 10, It's a Different World for Wisconsin Unions," Wisconsin Public Radio, February 11, 2021, https://www.wpr.org/economy/labor/decade-after-act-10-its-different-world -wisconsin-unions.

153 **Wisconsin Education Association Council:** Johnson, "A Decade After Act 10."

153 **During the time Walker was governor:** David Cooper, "As Wisconsin's and Minnesota's Lawmakers Took Divergent Paths, So Did Their Economies," Economic Policy Institute, May 8, 2018, https://www.epi.org/publication/as-wisconsins-and-minnesotas -lawmakers-took-divergent-paths-so-did-their-economies-since-2010-minnesotas -economy-has-performed-far-better-for-working-families-than-wisconsin.

154 **Walker survived a recall election:** Monica Davey and Jeff Zeleny, "Walker Survives Wisconsin Recall Vote," *New York Times*, June 5, 2021, https://www.nytimes.com /2012/06/06/us/politics/walker-survives-wisconsin-recall-effort.html.

154 **Walker bizarrely tried to boast:** Grabar, "Scott Walker's War on the Public Sector Came Back to Bite Him."

154 **the Wisconsin state Supreme Court:** Hope Karnopp, "Act 10, Abortion Laws, Gerrymandering: Status of Issues Before Wisconsin Supreme Court," *Milwaukee Journal Sentinel*, April 2, 2025, https://www.jsonline.com/story/news/politics/elections /2025/04/02/will-susan-crawford-be-part-of-supreme-court-act-10-abortion -cases/82779092007.

154 **A lower court judge:** Rich Kremer, "Dane County Judge Strikes Down Act 10, Restoring Public Employee Union Bargaining Rights," Wisconsin Public Radio, published December 2, 2024, updated December 3, 2024, https://www.wpr.org/news/dane -county-judge-strikes-down-act-10-restoring-public-employee-union-bargaining -rights.

154 **In 2023, Florida's Republican Governor:** McKenna Schueler, "Florida's Brazen Assault on Public Sector Workers Puts Unions in Survival Mode," *In These Times*, June 5, 2024, https://inthesetimes.com/article/florida-target-public-sector-workers-anti -union-senate-bill-256-decertification-teachers-desantis.

154 **fifty-four public-sector unions:** Daniel Rivero, "More Than 63,000 Florida Workers Have Lost Union Representation Due to New Law," WLRN Public Media, September 3, 2024, https://www.cfpublic.org/economy/2024-09-03/more-than-63-000-flor ida-workers-have-lost-union-representation-due-to-new-law.

154 **largest school district in the state:** "Largest school districts in the United States by enrollment," Ballotpedia, updated May 13, 2024, https://ballotpedia.org/Largest _school_districts_in_the_United_States_by_enrollment#Florida.

154 **tried to lure teachers:** Aaron Withe, "Miami-Dade's Teacher Union Has Failed in Its Mission. Here's How We Want to Replace It," *Miami Herald*, February 13, 2024, https://archive.ph/CiMg5#selection-1493.19-1493.106.

154 **sham union it created:** Clara-Sophia Daly, "Miami-Dade Teachers Vote to Keep Their Union. This Right-Wing Group Vows to Bust It," *Miami Herald*, October 24, 2024, https://www.miamiherald.com/news/local/education/article294430484.html.

154 **"spend whatever it takes":** Francisco Alvarado, "Trojan Hearse? A Right-Wing Think Tank Aims to Abolish the Miami-Dade Teachers' Union," *Miami New Times*, September 19, 2024, https://www.miaminewtimes.com/news/miami-teachers-union -faces-challenge-funded-by-right-wing-think-tank-21313035.

155 **United Teachers of Dade won:** Daly, "Miami-Dade Teachers Vote to Keep Their Union."

155 **Between 1985 and 2011:** Ed Robinson, "Do Unions Boost the Middle Class?" *Chicago Booth Review*, December 9, 2015, https://www.chicagobooth.edu/review/do-unions -boost-the-middle-class.

155 **data show that anywhere:** Bruce Western and Jake Rosenfeld, "Unions, Norms, and the Rise in U.S. Wage Inequality," *American Sociological Review* 76, no. 4 (2011): 513– 37, https://www.asanet.org/wp-content/uploads/savvy/images/journals/docs/pdf /asr/WesternandRosenfeld.pdf.

155 **In 2024, seven out of ten Americans:** "New Gallup Poll: 70% of Americans Approve of Labor Unions," AFGE, September 3, 2024, https://www.afge.org/article/new -gallup-poll-70-of-americans-approve-of-labor-unions.

155 **trust in unions has increased:** Michael Podhorzer, "As Go Unions, So Goes America," Weekend Reading, September 3, 2024, https://www.weekendreading.net/p /as-go-unions-so-goes-america.

155 **"regular people having agency":** "AFT Book Club: Heather Cox Richardson on the Future of Democracy," AFT, October 22, 2024, https://www.aft.org/news/aft-book -club-heather-cox-richardson-future-democracy.

156 **an estimated one in five voters:** Andrea Hsu, "Labor Unions Make a Final Push Canvassing Door to Door in Swing States," NPR, October 28, 2024, https://www.npr .org/2024/10/28/nx-s1-5159947/labor-unions-make-a-final-push-canvassing -door-to-door-in-swing-states.

156 **research shows that union members:** Tova Wang, "Union Impact on Voter Participation—and How to Expand It," Ash Center for Democratic Governance and Innovation, Harvard Kennedy School, June 2020, https://ash.harvard.edu/wp -content/uploads/2024/02/300871_hvd_ash_union_impact_v2.pdf.

156 **Patrick Flavin and Benjamin Radcliff:** Wang, "Union Impact on Voter Participation."

156 **Even non-union members:** Wang, "Union Impact on Voter Participation."

157 **when teachers are unionized:** Eunice S. Han and Thomas N. Maloney, "Teacher Unionization and Student Academic Performance: Looking Beyond Collective Bargaining," *Labor Studies Journal* 46, no. 1 (2019), https://journals.sagepub.com/doi /abs/10.1177/0160449X19883373.

157 **spend more money on public education:** Eric Brunner, Joshua Hyman, and Andrew Ju, "School Finance Reforms, Teachers' Unions, and the Allocation of School Resources," *The Review of Economics and Statistics* 102, no. 3 (July 2020): 473–89, https://direct.mit.edu/rest/article-abstract/102/3/473/96775/School-Finance -Reforms-Teachers-Unions-and-the.

157 **Lucie Aubrac was a brilliant:** Sarah Pruitt, "The History Teacher Who Outwitted the Gestapo," History.com, August 23, 2016, updated August 29, 2018, https://www .history.com/news/lucie-aubrac-the-history-teacher-who-outwitted-the-gestapo.

157 **competitive and prestigious higher degree:** Julian Jackson, "Lucie Aubrac," *The Guardian*, March 16, 2007, https://www.theguardian.com/news/2007/mar/16/guardia nobituaries.france.

158 **in her memoir:** Lucie Aubrac, *Outwitting the Gestapo* (Thorndike, 1993), https://ar chive.org/details/outwittinggestap00aubr/page/n3/mode/2up.

158 **He named Lucie a member:** Jackson, "Lucie Aubrac."

159 **"Voting is like going":** Podhorzer, "As Go Unions, So Goes America."

159 **In 2021, there were 1,638:** "Election Petitions Up 53%, Board Continues to Reduce Case Processing Time in FY22," National Labor Relations Board, October 6, 2022, https://www.nlrb.gov/news-outreach/news-story/election-petitions-up-53-board -continues-to-reduce-case-processing-time-in.

159 **the AFT organized 185 new:** "In Address to Union, AFT's Weingarten Champions Real Solutions for a Better Life, Celebrates Historic 1.8 Million-Member Milestone," AFT, July 22, 2024, https://www.aft.org/press-release/address-union-afts-weingarten -champions-real-solutions-better-life-celebrates.

160 **"Many forces have conspired":** Randi Weingarten, "Bargaining for the Common Good: How Unions and Labor Contracts Create a Better Life for All (David E. Feller Memorial Labor Law Lecture—April 15, 2021)," *Berkeley Journal of Employment & Labor Law* 43, no. 1 (2022), https://lawcat.berkeley.edu/record/1229064?ln=en&v =pdf.

160 **cut spending on childhood cancer research:** Michael Daly, "The Awkward Truth About Trump, Musk, and Kids with Cancer," *Daily Beast*, March 6, 2025, https:// www.thedailybeast.com/the-awkward-truth-about-trump-musk-and-kids-with -cancer.

161 **"Today, an oligarchy is taking shape":** "Full Transcript of President Biden's Fare-well Address," *New York Times*, January 15, 2025, https://www.nytimes.com/2025 /01/15/us/politics/full-transcript-of-president-bidens-farewell-address.html.

161 **"No one is asking for a handout":** Senator Elizabeth Warren, "Elizabeth Warren's 'A Fighting Chance': An Exclusive Excerpt on the Foreclosure Crisis," *Boston Globe*, April 27, 2014, https://www.bostonglobe.com/magazine/2014/04/26/elizabeth-warren -new-memoir-exclusive-excerpt-foreclosure-crisis/c02alOTRWXiYCMLx bakSiO/story.html.

161 **was diagnosed with an aggressive:** Matt Masterson, "CTU President Karen Lewis to Retire," WTTW, June 22, 2018, https://news.wttw.com/2018/06/22/ctu-president -karen-lewis-retire.

162 **"Karen built a movement":** Randi Weingarten, "Remarks of AFT President Randi Weingarten at the Funeral of Karen Lewis," Medium, February 12, 2021, https:// rweingarten.medium.com/remarks-of-aft-president-randi-weingarten-at-the -funeral-of-karen-lewis-c7d935813d04.

162 **"knew that transformation":** "Chicago Teachers Union President: 'You Strike Be-cause You Have to Take Power,'" United Electrical, Radio & Machine Workers of America, November 15, 2023, https://www.ueunion.org/ue-news/2023/chicago -teachers-union-president-you-strike-because-you-have-to-take-power.

162 **And as this book:** "Highlights of the Proposed Tentative Agreement," Chicago Teachers Union, accessed April 6, 2025, https://www.ctulocal1.org/wp-content /uploads/2025/03/Highlights-Proposed-TA-2025-03-31.pdf.

CONCLUSION: THE WAY FORWARD—FOR ALL

165 **shuttering the Department of Education:** "Executive Order 14242 of March 20, 2025, Improving Education Outcomes by Empowering Parents, States, and Communities," 90 F.R 13679 (2025), https://www.federalregister.gov/documents/2025/03/25/2025-05213/improving-education-outcomes-by-empowering-parents-states-and-communities.

165 **Department of Education provides about:** "What Percentage of Public School Funding in the US Comes from the Federal Government?," USA Facts, accessed April 6, 2025, https://usafacts.org/answers/what-percentage-of-public-school-funding-comes-from-the-federal-government/country/united-states.

165 **funding overwhelmingly goes to help:** Nora Gordon and Sarah Reber, "Funding High-Poverty School Districts: Federal Policy Tools and the Limits of Incentives," *Education Finance and Policy* 19, no. 1 (2024): 169–81, https://direct.mit.edu/edfp/article/19/1/169/116642/Funding-High-poverty-School-Districts-Federal.

165 **According to AFT's research:** "Protecting Our Kids: The Consequences of Gutting Federal Education Funding," AFT, accessed March 7, 2025, https://www.aft.org/sites/default/files/media/documents/2025/ed_factsheet_0213.pdf.

166 **Title 1 is the federal program:** "Title 1," Commonwealth of Pennsylvania, accessed March 6, 2025, https://www.pa.gov/agencies/education/programs-and-services/federal-programs/title-i.html.

166 **class sizes will soar:** Beth Treffeisen, "As Details Emerge, Here's What Trump's Plan to Abolish DOE Could Mean for Mass. Schools," Boston.com, March 7, 2025, https://www.boston.com/news/education/2025/03/07/as-details-emerge-heres-what-trumps-plan-to-abolish-doe-could-mean-for-mass-schools; Colin Seeberger, "Project 2025's Plan to Gut Checks and Balances Harms the American People," Center for American Progress, August 8, 2024, https://www.americanprogress.org/article/project-2025s-plan-to-gut-checks-and-balances-harms-the-american-people.

166 **gets over 20 percent:** "What Percentage of Public School Funding in Mississippi Comes from the Federal Government?," USA Facts, accessed April 6, 2025, https://usafacts.org/answers/what-percentage-of-public-school-funding-comes-from-the-federal-government/state/mississippi.

166 **heralded as a model:** Harry Anthony Patrinos, "Mississippi's Education Miracle: a Model for Global Literacy Reform," The Conversation, March 26, 2025, https://theconversation.com/mississippis-education-miracle-a-model-for-global-literacy-reform-251895.

166 **increase in white supremacist organizations:** Ashley Murray, "White Nationalist, Anti-LGBTQ Activity on the Rise, Annual Hate Report Shows," *Missouri Independent*, June 5, 2024, https://missouriindependent.com/2024/06/05/white-nationalist-anti-lgbtq-activity-on-the-rise-annual-hate-report-shows.

166 **organizations and propaganda:** "White Supremacist Propaganda Incidents Soar to Record High in 2023," Anti-Defamation League, March 26, 2024, https://www.adl.org/resources/report/white-supremacist-propaganda-incidents-soar-record-high-2023.

166 **Anti-LGBTQ hate:** Delphine Luneau, "New FBI Data: Anti-LGBTQ+ Hate Crimes Continue to Spike, Even as Overall Crime Rate Declines," Human Rights Campaign, September 23, 2024, https://www.hrc.org/press-releases/new-fbi-data-anti-lgbtq-hate-crimes-continue-to-spike-even-as-overall-crime-rate-declines.

166 **and anti-Semitism:** Holly Honderich, "Antisemitic Incidents in US Surge to Record High—Report," BBC, October 6, 2024, https://www.bbc.com/news/articles/c9wkx v9d99vo.

166 **Office for Civil Rights was established:** "Funding Federal Civil Rights Enforcement: 2000 and Beyond—Chapter 1: Office for Civil Rights, U.S. Department of Education," U.S. Commission on Civil Rights, accessed March 6, 2025, https://www.usccr .gov/files/pubs/archives/crfund01/ch1.htm.

166 **echoed racist conspiracy theories:** Jude Joffe-Block and Odette Yousef, "How Trump Is Relying on a Racist Conspiracy Theory to Question Election Results," NPR, September 13, 2024, https://www.npr.org/2024/09/13/g-s1-22583/trump -great-replacement-conspiracy-theory; Claire Wang, "'A Very Old Political Trope': The Racist US History Behind Trump's Haitian Pet Eater Claim," *The Guardian*, September 14, 2024, https://www.theguardian.com/us-news/2024/sep/14/racist -history-trump-pet-eating-immigrant; Tamara Keith, "Trump's Racist 'Birther' Attacks on Harris Are a Return to Familiar Territory," NPR, August 15, 2020, https:// www.npr.org/2020/08/15/902756963/trumps-attacks-on-harris-are-a-return -to-familiar-territory.

166 **using the Office for Civil rights to punish:** Brooke Schultz, "Trump Admin. Warns Schools: End Race-Based Programs or Risk Losing Funds," *Education Week*, February 18, 2025, https://docs.google.com/document/d/1l54cVK7NpiKNxURz5womY sCS1AVuDiKzO-fzsdIqsT8/edit?tab=t.0.

166 **polling published on March 3, 2025:** Domenico Montanaro, "Poll: Majorities Say State of the Union Is Not Strong, and Trump Is Rushing Change," NPR, March 3, 2025, https://www.npr.org/2025/03/03/nx-s1-5312033/trump-poll-doge-economy -favorability.

167 **farm assistance, and:** "Lawmakers Worry House Budget Plan Could Tank New Farm Bill," *Farm Policy News*, February 26, 2025, https://farmpolicynews.illinois .edu/2025/02/lawmakers-worry-house-budget-plan-could-tank-new-farm-bill.

167 **address rampant poverty:** "Historical Background and Development of Social Security," Social Security Administration, accessed March 7, 2025, https://www.ssa.gov /history/briefhistory3.html.

167 **relied on by 97 percent of older Americans:** "Policy Basics: Top Ten Facts About Social Security," Center on Budget and Policy Priorities, May 31, 2024, https://www .cbpp.org/research/social-security/top-ten-facts-about-social-security.

167 **"the biggest Ponzi scheme of all time":** "Musk Calls Social Security a 'Ponzi Scheme,'" posted by MSNBC, YouTube, https://www.youtube.com/watch?v=GgH SislSWpk.

167 **"a brazen willingness":** Peter Baker, "In Trump's Alternate Reality, Lies and Distortions Drive Change," *New York Times*, February 23, 2025, https://www.nytimes .com/2025/02/23/us/politics/trump-alternative-reality.html.

167 **"The impact of our universities":** Michael I. Kotlikoff, "Universities Like the One I Run Aren't Afraid to Let People Argue," *New York Times*, March 31, 2025, https:// www.nytimes.com/2025/03/31/opinion/ideas-universities-controversy-protest .html.

167 **"If any of us want":** "J.D. Vance | The Universities are the Enemy | National Conservatism Conference II," posted by National Conservatism, YouTube, https://www .youtube.com/watch?v=0FR65Cifnhw.

168 **repeated his famous quote:** Dan Glaister, "Tricky Dicky: Nixon Recordings Confirm Popular View," *The Guardian*, December 3, 2008, https://www.theguardian.com /world/2008/dec/04/richard-nixon-recordings.

168 **"obsessed with indoctrinating":** Katherine Knott, "Trump's 'Secret Weapon'? College Accreditation," *Inside Higher Ed*, May 4, 2023, https://www.insidehighered .com/news/government/politics-elections/2023/05/04/trump-pledges-fire -radical-left-college-accreditors.

168 **"It's a bedrock principle":** Knott, "Trump's 'Secret Weapon'?"

168 **"due to the school's":** Alexandra Marquez, "Trump Administration Cancels $400 Million in Grants for Columbia University," NBC News, March 7, 2025, https:// www.nbcnews.com/politics/politics-news/trump-administration-cancels-400 -million-grants-columbia-university-rcna195373.

168 **pressured the university:** Troy Closson, "Columbia Agrees to Trump's Demands After Federal Funds Are Stripped," *New York Times*, March 21, 2025, https://www .nytimes.com/2025/03/21/nyregion/columbia-response-trump-demands.html.

168 **Elon Musk retweeted:** Kate Conger, "Elon Musk Shared, Then Removed a Post Absolving Dictators for Genocide," *New York Times*, March 14, 2025, https://www.ny times.com/2025/03/14/technology/elon-musk-x-post-hitler-stalin-mao.html.

168 **interpreted as a Nazi salute:** Jill Colvin and Adriana Gomez Licon, "Steve Bannon Is Accused of Doing a Straight-Arm Nazi Salute at CPAC but Says It Was Just 'a Wave,'" Associated Press, February 21, 2025, https://apnews.com/article/steve -bannon-cpac-nazi-salute-gesture-wave-43a06de6184fe58940c8ae3d743bc6ba.

168 **"We should be holding":** Jonathan Greenblatt, "We Must Fight for Jewish Students— And Our Values," *eJewish Philanthropy*, April 3, 2025, https://ejewishphilanthropy .com/we-must-fight-for-jewish-students-and-our-values.

169 **"beacon of conservatism":** Patricia Mazzei, "DeSantis's Latest Target: A Small College of 'Free Thinkers,'" *New York Times*, February 14, 2023, https://www.nytimes .com/2023/02/14/us/ron-desantis-new-college-florida.html.

169 **none other than Chris Rufo:** Michelle Goldberg, "Trump's Plan to Crush the Academic Left," *New York Times*, January 24, 2025, https://www.nytimes.com/2025 /01/24/opinion/trump-dei-education-harvard.html.

169 **faculty report the new administration:** Josh Moody, "A Clash over Core Curriculum at New College of Florida," *Inside Higher Ed*, October 29, 2024, https://www.inside highered.com/news/faculty-issues/curriculum/2024/10/29/clash-over-core -curriculum-new-college-florida.

169 **statewide, DeSantis has weakened:** Mazzei, "DeSantis's Latest Target."

169 **noting reporting that shows:** Zach Montague, "On X, Conservative Activists Find a Direct Pipeline to Musk's Team," *New York Times*, February 26, 2025, https://www .nytimes.com/2025/02/26/us/politics/elon-musk-doge-x-accounts-activists.html.

169 **In his first administration:** Max Zahn, "What Trump's Reelection Means for Union Workers, According to Experts," ABC News, November 12, 2024, https://abcnews .go.com/Business/trumps-reelection-means-union-workers-experts/story?id =115731176.

169 **abandoned a broad expansion:** Heidi Shierholz, "The Trump Administration's Overtime Rule Leaves Millions of Workers Behind," Economic Policy Institute, September 24, 2019, https://www.epi.org/press/the-trump-administrations-overtime -rule-leaves-millions-of-workers-behind.

169 **tried to gut:** Heidi Shierholz et al., "Employers Would Pocket $5.8 Billion of Workers' Tips Under Trump Administration's Proposed 'Tip Stealing' Rule," Economic Policy Institute, December 12, 2017, https://www.epi.org/publication/employers -would-pocket-workers-tips-under-trump-administrations-proposed-tip-stealing -rule.

170 **Trump weakened the Occupational Safety:** Deborah Berkowitz, "OSHA Enforcement Activity Declines Under the Trump Administration," National Employment Law Project, June 11, 2018, https://www.nelp.org/insights-research/osha-enforcement -activity-declines-trump-administration.

170 **He repeatedly assaulted the union:** "Donald Trump's Catastrophic and Devastating Anti-Labor Track Record," AFL-CIO, September 27, 2023, https://aflcio.org/press /releases/donald-trumps-catastrophic-and-devastating-anti-labor-track-record.

170 **in the Department of Labor:** Kenneth Quinnell, "9 Reasons Why Trump's Secretary of Labor Pick Andy Puzder Is No Friend of Working People," AFL-CIO, December 19, 2016, https://aflcio.org/2016/12/19/9-reasons-why-trumps-secretary-labor-pick -andy-puzder-no-friend-working-people.

170 **and the National Labor Relations Board:** Celine McNicholas, Margaret Poydock, and Lynn Rhinehart, "Unprecedented: The Trump NLRB's Attack on Workers' Rights," Economic Policy Institute, October 16, 2019, https://www.epi.org/publica tion/unprecedented-the-trump-nlrbs-attack-on-workers-rights.

170 **undermine child labor law protections:** Deborah Berkowitz, "The Trump Administration Moves to Roll Back Child Labor Rules and Expose Teen Workers to Hazardous Jobs," National Employment Law Project, October 26, 2018, https://www.nelp .org/insights-research/trump-administration-moves-roll-back-child-labor-rules -expose-teen-workers-hazardous-jobs.

170 **have weakened their child labor laws:** Jennifer Sherer and Nina Mast, "Child Labor Laws Are Under Attack in States Across the Country," Economic Policy Institute, March 14, 2023, https://www.epi.org/publication/child-labor-laws-under-attack.

170 **praised his billionaire backer:** Tom Krisher, "Trump and Musk Discussed Firing Striking Workers. The UAW Is Now Seeking an NLRB Investigation," PBS, August 13, 2024, https://www.pbs.org/newshour/politics/trump-and-musk-discussed-firing -striking-workers-the-uaw-is-now-seeking-an-nlrb-investigation.

170 **fired thousands of federal workers:** Will Peischel, "How Many Federal Workers Have Lost Their Jobs?," *New York*, February 26, 2025, https://nymag.com/intelli gencer/article/how-many-federal-employees-fired-jobs-cut-trump-doge.html.

170 **overseen mass layoffs:** Nandita Bose and Akash Sriram, "Musk Will Stay Until He Completes DOGE Mission, White House Says," Reuters, April 2, 2025, https://www .reuters.com/business/retail-consumer/trump-tells-cabinet-others-that-musk -will-leave-soon-politico-reports-2025-04-02.

170 **one-third of federal workers are veterans:** Michael A. Cohen, "DOGE's Mass Firings Will Only Make Government Less Efficient," MSNBC, February 26, 2025, https:// www.msnbc.com/opinion/msnbc-opinion/elon-musk-doge-mass-firings-govern ment-rcna193563.

170 **one out of every four federal workers:** "Union Membership in Federal Sector Went Up in 2023," AFGE, January 29, 2024, https://www.afge.org/article/union-member ship-in-federal-sector-went-up-in-2023.

170 **especially targeted agencies like:** Eric Lipton and Kirsten Grind, "Elon Musk's Business Empire Scores Benefits Under Trump Shake-Up," *New York Times*, February 11, 2025, https://www.nytimes.com/2025/02/11/us/politics/elon-musk-companies -conflicts.html.

170 **stopping credit card companies:** "CFPB Bans Excessive Credit Card Late Fees, Lowers Typical Fee from $32 to $8," Consumer Financial Protection Bureau, March 5, 2024, https://www.consumerfinance.gov/about-us/newsroom/cfpb-bans-excessive -credit-card-late-fees-lowers-typical-fee-from-32-to-8/.

170 **the Project 2025 blueprint contains:** Paul Dans and Steven Groves, eds., "2025— Mandate for Leadership: The Conservative Promise," Project 2025 Presidential Transition Project, Heritage Foundation, 2023, https://static.project2025.org/2025 _MandateForLeadership_FULL.pdf.

171 **proposes repealing wage protections:** Dans and Groves, "2025—Mandate for Leadership."

171 **to "rein in" OSHA:** Edwin J. Feulner, "Onward! (2025—Mandate for Leadership Afterword)," Project 2025 Presidential Transition Project, Heritage Foundation, 2023, https://static.project2025.org/2025_MandateForLeadership_AFTERWORD .pdf.

171 **about one million:** Rebecca Davis O'Brien, "Federal Worker Unions Sue to Block Trump from Stripping Bargaining Rights," *New York Times*, April 4, 2025, https:// www.nytimes.com/2025/04/04/us/politics/trump-unions-lawsuit.html.

171 **carried out mass deportations:** Laura Barrón-López, Doug Adams, and Ian Couzens, "Migrants in U.S. Legally and with No Criminal History Caught up in Trump Crackdown," *PBS News Hour*, March 28, 2025, https://www.pbs.org/newshour/show /migrants-in-u-s-legally-and-with-no-criminal-history-caught-up-in-trump -crackdown.

171 **ignored orders from:** Katherine Faulders, "Trump Administration Ignores Judge's Order to Turn Deportation Planes Around: Sources," ABC News, March 16, 2025, https://abcnews.go.com/US/trump-admin-ignores-judges-order-bring-deportation -planes/story?id=119857181.

171 **pursued retribution against:** Melissa Quinn, "Trump's Crusade Against Big Law Firms Sparks Fears of Long-Lasting Damage," CBS News, April 2, 2025, https:// www.cbsnews.com/news/trumps-big-law-firms-retribution.

171 **banned from the White House:** David Bauder, "The Associated Press, Banned from White House Press Pool, Renews Request to Court for Reinstatement," Associated Press, March 27, 2025, https://apnews.com/article/trump-ap-white-house-press -pool-ban-cdf091900ae5371329234ddfafef3a91.

171 **food safety inspections:** Christina Jewett, "Food Safety Jeopardized by Onslaught of Funding and Staff Cuts," *New York Times*, March 19, 2025, https://www.nytimes .com/2025/03/19/health/food-safety-trump-fda-cutbacks-deadly-outbreaks.html.

171 **to cancer research:** Lauran Neergaard and Michael Casey, "Federal Judge Blocks Drastic Funding Cuts to Medical Research," Associated Press, March 5, 2025, https://apnews.com/article/trump-nih-medical-research-funding-cut-indirect -costs-e7629d0d45d141b2ac47c5455041laff.

171 **announced he was cutting:** Cheyenne Haslett, Will McDuffie, and Dr. Mark Abdelmalek, "Mass Layoffs Begin at HHS, Some Employees Turned Away After Showing

up to Work," ABC News, April 1, 2025, https://abcnews.go.com/Politics/mass-layoffs -begin-hhs-reaching-impacts-public-health/story?id=120374327.

171 **"Mass layoffs," noted one:** Elizabeth Cooney, "50 Canceled Measles Clinics, and Other Local Impact from HHS Cuts," *STAT News*, April 1, 2025, https://www.stat news.com/2025/04/01/hhs-layoffs-local-officials-react-rif-impacts-public-health.

171 **rampant economic uncertainty:** Nik Popli, "'He's Going to Tank Our Economy': Trump's Tariffs Draw Strong Reactions in Congress," *Time*, April 3, 2025, https:// time.com/7274573/trump-tariffs-congress.

171 **Trump mused about a third term:** Hansi Lo Wang, "Presidents Can Be Elected Twice. Trump Could Try End Runs Around That, Experts Say," NPR, March 31, 2025, https://www.npr.org/2025/03/31/nx-s1-5191889/is-trump-running-for-a-third -term.

173 **"Public service is a noble calling":** Brochure, Bush School of Government & Public Service, Texas A&M University, accessed March 7, 2025, https://bush.tamu.edu /wp-content/uploads/2020/08/Bush_PBMG_Gatefold2017.pdf.

174 **Teachers like Damiano Mastrandrea:** "CTE Pathways," Brooklyn STEAM Center, accessed March 7, 2025, https://brooklynsteamcenter.org/cte-pathways.

174 **Karen Reyes, a formerly undocumented:** "Don't Panic, Organize: Karen Reyes on the Fight for Immigrant Rights," AFT Voices, AFT, February 6, 2025, https://aft voices.org/dont-panic-organize-karen-reyes-on-the-fight-for-immigrant-rights -929919170dfa.

174 **vocational agriculture teacher John Lindsey:** "Career and Technical Education Builds Real-World Skills and Then Some," AFT, September 11, 2023, https://www .aft.org/news/career-and-technical-education-builds-real-world-skills-and-then -some.

174 **in Rio Rancho, New Mexico:** "Unions Give Out 30,000 Books in Rio Rancho, NM," posted by AFT, YouTube, https://www.youtube.com/watch?v=Gz4s-5EvI68.

175 **"The role of a teacher":** Tamika Edwards, "Weingarten: Path Forward for Public Education," posted January 9, 2017, posted by AFT, Facebook, https://www.face book.com/AFTunion/videos/weingarten-path-forward-for-public-education /10154506389894160.

176 **"I want our young":** Katie Reilly, "Read What Michelle Obama Said in Her Final Remarks as First Lady," *Time*, January 6, 2017, https://time.com/4626283/michelle -obama-final-remarks-transcript.